LEADERSHIP UNDER FIRE

Leadership under Fire

The Challenging Role of the Canadian University President

ROSS H. PAUL

McGill-Queen's University Press
Montreal & Kingston • London • Ithaca

© McGill-Queen's University Press 2011

ISBN 978-0-7735-3887-0

Legal deposit fourth quarter 2011
Bibliothèque nationale du Québec

Printed in Canada on acid-free paper that is 100% ancient forest free
(100% post-consumer recycled), processed chlorine free

This book has been published with the help of a grant from the
Association of Universities and Colleges of Canada.

McGill-Queen's University Press acknowledges the support of the
Canada Council for the Arts for our publishing program. We also
acknowledge the financial support of the Government of Canada
through the Canada Book Fund for our publishing activities.

Library and Archives Canada Cataloguing in Publication

Paul, Ross H., 1943–
    Leadership under fire : the challenging role of the Canadian
university president / Ross Paul.

Includes bibliographical references and index.
ISBN 978-0-7735-3887-0

    1. College presidents – Canada. 2. Universities and colleges –
Canada – Administration. 3. Educational leadership – Canada.
I. Title.

LB2341.8.C3P38 2011   378.1'110971   C2011-902170-6

Typeset by Jay Tee Graphics Ltd. in 10.5/13 Sabon

Contents

Preface

Being president of a university is no way for an adult to make a living.
Which is why so few adults actually attempt to do it. It is to hold a
mid-nineteenth-century ecclesiastical position on top of a late-twentieth-
century corporation.

A. Bartlett Giamatti, former president of Yale[1]

This is a book about leadership in general and university leadership
in particular. More uniquely, it is about Canadian university leadership. It argues that there was never a more important time for strong
leadership from Canadian university presidents and that the stakes
go well beyond the future of our universities to issues of the whole
economic, social, and political future of this country. "Coordinated
and sustained leadership, which is not higher education's strength,
will be the key issue in postsecondary institutions in the next five
years. The specific quality of this leadership will literally determine
which institutions survive and thrive in the context of the external
and internal forces now bombarding universities."[2]

There are many apparent contradictions surrounding the role of a
university president, a role that over the past few decades has evolved
in most Western jurisdictions from moral leader presiding over a
relatively small, somewhat isolated institution to chief executive
officer (CEO) of a major, public and complex enterprise. The range
of the president's responsibilities has grown tremendously in recent
years, and much more is expected of the holder of the position. No
one has summarized this better than Montreal native Harold Shapiro, former president of two of the United States' most prestigious
universities – Michigan and Princeton:

> I manage to survive; I manage to plan, organize, staff, coordin-
> ate, budget, report, and make decisions regarding the future of

this organization; I manage to serve this organization as part
figurehead, part pastor of interpersonal relations, part spokesperson, part disburser of institutional propaganda and positive
reinforcement to students, faculty, alumni and trustees; I manage to be an unprincipled (at times) promoter and principled
(at other times) huckster of the institution and its objectives; I
manage to bring forward the historical traditions of the institution and give some of them new life and meaning in a different
world; I manage to articulate a set of goals for the institution
that, despite all odds, actually covers all the activities of what
increasingly has become a general-service-public utility; I manage an organization of bewildering scope with at least a little
dignity, respectability, some authority, and (occasionally) wis-
dom. I manage to preserve some sense of community in a sea
of independent and fiercely self-regulating disciplines; I manage
to blur the contradictory obligations the modern university too
eagerly assumes; I manage to convince others that our elitism is
not of the unjustified sort; I manage to persuade our patrons that
no single university can address all the needs of modern life.[3]

With the CEO moniker come expectations of power and authority, and yet a university's primary professional group, the faculty,
has tremendous autonomy in all matters of the core business of the
institution. The president's actual powers are much more limited
than those of the leaders of any other institution in our society, public or private. No less an authority than Peter Drucker, one of the
best-known organizational theorists of the twentieth century, cited a
university presidency as the hardest job in modern society because it
was answerable to so many stakeholders in one of the most decentralized of institutions.[4]

Notwithstanding these limitations on a president's authority, he or
she is increasingly hired as a change agent while also being expected
to preserve and protect traditional academic structures, academic
freedom, and collegial modes of decision making. It's as if the message is – you're being hired to change those other people but you
had better not interfere with my academic freedom: "The whole
notion of faculty working as a team driving toward attainment of
the president's agenda runs counter to the academic culture in which
faculty prize academic freedom, autonomy and choice."[5]

What emerges from all this is a confusing picture of the executive head's job in a university: "The role appears to be constructed

around a series of bipolar descriptions, making the job simultaneously powerful and powerless, ordered and chaotic, crushingly mundane and challengingly creative."[6]

While most references so far have emanated from American and British writers, the context and limitations on the president's role and authority would be very familiar to a Canadian reader. At the same time, the issues in this country have a distinctly Canadian flavour. To cite one example, the very notion of a "president" in the American context carries with it an authority and respect that is less prominent in Canada. Such an elusive and yet important difference in national character suggests the need for further consideration of the cross-national differences, and yet there is a relative dearth of Canadian writing on the subject.

This is the first volume to look exclusively at the role of the Canadian university president and how it both parallels and differs from that of other Western jurisdictions. It uniquely combines theoretical perspectives on leadership with the experiences of some of Canada's best practitioners of the past three decades and examines some of the most pressing issues facing post-secondary education in Canada, always from the perspective of the president's office. The primary source materials are the interviews with practitioners, books and journal articles on university leadership, some original research into the background of recent Canadian university presidents, and the author's own experience in leadership positions in four institutions of higher learning in three provinces over thirty-five years.

At the book's heart is a passionate belief in the central responsibility of the university in Canadian society – to produce graduates who are curiosity-driven independent learners, critical and creative thinkers, and open-minded citizens well prepared for a fast-changing global society. The central theme is the role of the president in this endeavour, achieved through open management, the concept that institutions should be managed according to the core values they espouse. The book is divided into four sections.

PART ONE
(CANADIAN UNIVERSITIES AND THEIR LEADERSHIP)
The first two chapters examine the ways in which Canadian higher education is distinguished from other national jurisdictions and the implications of these differences for university leadership in the country. With particular reference to the eleven presidents interviewed for this book, the section looks at the people who serve in

the role of president, considering the advantages and disadvantages
of the uniquely Canadian process of selecting university leaders.

PART TWO
(ACADEMIC LEADERSHIP AND ORGANIZATIONAL CULTURE)
The three chapters in the second section focus on leadership theory
and its practical applications to universities. The section starts with
an analysis of organizational culture in the academic setting, underlining the importance of understanding not only the generic academic culture but its particular manifestations in Canada and in a
given institution. Within this context, it focuses on two key presidential roles – setting the institutional direction and ensuring effective
academic leadership.

PART THREE
(KEY ISSUES FOR TODAY'S PRESIDENTS)
This section is comprised of seven chapters, each of which considers
a major challenge for today's university presidents. The respective
subjects are: student access and success (and the increasing concern
about the quality of undergraduate education); international outreach; financial challenges; day-to-day administration; the president's external roles; institutional governance and presidential
accountability; and institutional autonomy and system diversity

PART FOUR
(THE WAY FORWARD)
The final two chapters respectively consider how much difference
a president can really make to an institution and the particular
demands facing current Canadian university presidents.

Acknowledgments

This project has been a labour of love. After almost forty years of senior academic administration, where almost every day was filled with multiple activities and competing and conflicting priorities, it was very special to have the luxury of working on a single academic project for most of the past year and a half.

I am indebted to many people and several institutions for their support of this endeavour. All eleven presidents interviewed for the book readily agreed to give me some of their precious time and were open and forthcoming in their comments and observations. Each was given an opportunity to review the quotes attributed to them, and many made valuable recommendations that I have incorporated into the text. I also acknowledge and appreciate the commentary of Janet Wright, president of JWA and Associates, on the contents of chapter 2, on presidential selection.

The University of Windsor made the whole endeavour possible through its generous administrative leave at the conclusion of my presidency. I completed my second term at the end of June 2008, and my wife, Jane, and I moved to Vancouver at the end of August.

Publication was facilitated by a grant from the Association of Universities and Colleges of Canada (AUCC), and I will always appreciate the encouragement and support for this book that I received from Paul Davidson and Christine Tausig-Ford, respectively the president and vice-president of that organization. I especially appreciate their interest in using the book as part of AUCC's seminar for new presidents. The year 2011 is a special one for AUCC – its hundredth anniversary of helping to coordinate, advance, and promote Canadian universities.

I am especially grateful to professors Don Fisher and Kjell Rubenson at the University of British Columbia (UBC), who warmly welcomed me and facilitated my appointment as adjunct professor at very short notice. The resulting office space on their beautiful campus allowed me to write in relative calm, given the chaos of moving our residence four times in two years; storing, moving, selling, and giving away furniture, clothes, and all the "stuff" that one accumulates; and living through interminable major renovations to our current residence while trying to live there.

I also appreciate the efficiency of the UBC libraries, which greatly facilitated my catching up on the relevant literature on university leadership and gave me the opportunity to participate in the intellectual life at the university through seminars and social events. The experience has reinforced my love of university life and my gratitude that I have been able to be part of it for so many years.

McGill-Queen's University Press has been supportive from the beginning thanks to legendary director Philip Cercone, and I have been extremely lucky to work with editor Mark Abley, whose criticisms and suggestions have always been helpful, constructive, and effective, and copy editor Judith Turnbull, who helped clarify and sharpen the manuscript.

Finally, none of this would have happened without the encouragement, support, patience, and love of my wife, Dr Jane Brindley. Notwithstanding her own very busy academic life, teaching online for Oldenburg University and the University of Maryland, she assumed overall responsibility for the renovations project, as she has done many times in the past, thus ensuring that I had the free time to devote to this book. We have frequently talked over the issues addressed herein and I owe her a huge debt not only for her personal support but for her professional and academic expertise as well.

Abbreviations

AUCC	Association of Universities and Colleges of Canada
CAATS	colleges of applied arts and technology
CAUBO	Canadian Association of University Business Officers
CAUT	Canadian Association of University Teachers
CCL	Canadian Council on Learning
CEGEP	Collège d'enseignement générale et professionel
CEO	chief executive officer
CFI	Canada Foundation for Innovation
CIDA	Canadian International Development Agency
COU	Council of Ontario Universities
CREPUQ	Conférence des recteurs et des principaux des universités du Québec
GTA	Greater Toronto Area
HEQCO	Higher Education Quality Council of Ontario
ICRPS	income-contingency repayment plans
KPI	key performance indicator
NSSE	National Survey of Student Engagement
OCAD	Ontario College of Art and Design
ODL	open and distance learning
OERS	open educational resources
OISE	Ontario Institute for Studies in Education
SUAC	Senior University Administrators Course
SWAAC	Senior Women Academic Administrators of Canada
UBC	University of British Columbia
UNB	University of New Brunswick
UNBC	University of Northern British Columbia
U of T	University of Toronto
UOIT	University of Ontario Institute of Technology

UPEI	University of Prince Edward Island
VPA	vice-president, academic
VPR	vice-president, research

PART ONE

Canadian Universities and Their Leadership

Distinguishing Characteristics of Canadian Universities with Implications for Their Leadership

At first glance, Canadian universities are much like their counterparts in the United States, the United Kingdom, and many of the Commonwealth nations. As is the case with so many other Canadian institutions, however, there are significant differences, and these are critical to an understanding of the challenges faced by Canadian universities as well as to their governance and management. Any discussion of the role of the president of a Canadian university must begin by taking into account the distinguishing characteristics of the higher education system and the national culture within which it functions.

A good place to start is the British North America Act (BNA), which founded the Dominion of Canada in 1867.[1] Section 93 of the act gave, among other powers, exclusive jurisdiction over education to the provinces as part of a series of checks and balances between the federal and provincial governments. The result has been a significantly decentralized educational system, with many important and historical differences among schools and universities among and within all provinces.

One important manifestation of the delegation of responsibility for education to the provinces has been a relative lack of central federal authority over universities. In fact, Canada is the only federated country without a national office or minister of education.[2] This is in contrast to countries like Australia where, although the separate states have considerable jurisdiction over their universities, Canberra wields much more direct power and authority than does Ottawa.[3]

The decentralization of Canadian higher education has both advantages and disadvantages for its universities. On the one hand, it protects universities from the sort of national intervention in their mandate, organization, and governance that so characterized Britain under Margaret Thatcher[4] and Australia in the late 1980s under John Dawkins, the minister of employment, education and training.[5] Similar reforms in Canada would have required the collaboration of thirteen ministers of education and their respective provincial cabinets!

On the other hand, the lack of coordination can be a disadvantage, especially in its impact on the international profile and promotion of Canadian universities. For example, Canada is one of the very few countries without a national accreditation system. Notwithstanding that Canada's academic standards match the best in the world, as evidenced by the performance of Canadian graduates in top international schools and Canada's fifth-place standing in the Times Higher Education World University Rankings,[6] there is no formal national mechanism to document this quality. This leaves Canadian universities at a disadvantage when they attempt to recruit the best students and faculty from abroad.

In a country like India, for instance, where degree-granting institutions cover the gamut from top technical institutes to bogus, for-profit operations, formal accreditation is the only way that an uninformed observer can separate the credible institutions from the degree mills. Our lack of a formal accreditation agency may discourage top Indian students from applying because they are unsure which of our universities are credible. While there have been efforts to address the accreditation issue in Canada, notably by the Association of Universities and Colleges of Canada (AUCC), provincial governments are very protective of their jurisdiction over education. The subject of national accreditation has been discussed in meetings of the Council of Ministers of Education, Canada, but without follow-through to date.

Canada stands out in international comparisons for its lack of a coordinated approach to post-secondary education. For example, it is the only one of eight jurisdictions surveyed by the Canadian Council on Learning (CCL), including the United Kingdom, the United States, Australia, and New Zealand, that has not conducted a recent major national review of post-secondary education and that lacks national goals and objectives and a central quality-assurance agency for the sector.[7]

This lack of any central coordination of higher education in Canada has other significant disadvantages. In its 2007 report, *Post-secondary Education in Canada: Strategies for Success*, the CCL identified the difficulties of gathering comparable data from provincial jurisdictions and called for the development of a "comprehensive pan-Canadian data strategy" to provide the information needed to strengthen the country's post-secondary education sector. It also recommended a national accreditation strategy, more student mobility across the provinces, and an ongoing pan-Canadian forum on post-secondary education.[8]

The main impetus behind the CCL report was the concern that Canada is losing its international leadership position in higher education and that this trend will continue if Canada does not develop such a national strategy.[9] While a number of prominent educators and others have endorsed the report, it is difficult to envision immediate action on its main recommendations. With provinces jealously guarding their authority in education, none more so than Quebec, for which education is a lynchpin in the preservation and advancement of its distinct language and cultural policies, there is little evidence of any political will at the federal level to intervene, especially during the current prolonged period of minority governments. Furthermore, at the electoral level, there is not widespread recognition of or interest in the issue, especially in comparison to interest in that other top federal/provincial football, health care.

The unlikelihood of federal action along the lines recommended by the CCL was underscored in January of 2010 when the Canadian government announced that it would eliminate its grants to the agency effective 31 March 2010, thus putting the CCL's very existence in serious jeopardy.[10] These were hardly the actions of a government seeking to play a stronger national role in the coordination of post-secondary education in Canada.

The primary funding agent for a Canadian public university is its provincial government, which provides about half of its operating funds and much of its capital investment as well. While public universities are independent to a considerable degree,[11] almost all of their operating revenues come from two primary sources – provincial grants and tuition fees, the latter usually fairly strictly regulated by politicians. This has a significant impact on the role of the president, whose primary lobbying target for most operational matters, other than research funding, is the provincial government. The eternal quest is to get a bigger share from the provincial coffers, first for the post-secondary education sector, in competition with health care, elementary and secondary education, and municipalities, and then for the specific institution.

While less directly involved in university funding than governments in most countries, the central government of Canada nevertheless has significant authority over the institutions in related areas not delegated to the provinces by the British North America Act. The most notable area is research, where the federal government plays the predominant role, but other important jurisdictions include technology, agriculture, environmental issues, and Aboriginal affairs. So, for instance, the major research granting councils are national and the great majority of research funds come from Ottawa, with the provinces offering, for the most part, matching funds. These matching funds are intended to attract and keep the best researchers in the given province, with the hope, in turn, that their academic performance attracts back at least the province's share of centrally collected tax revenues in the form of competitive research awards.

Not surprisingly, as products of British and French colonialism, Canada's academic institutions have English and French roots, notably those emanating from religious institutions. Of the twenty-eight major current Canadian universities established before 1960, for example, no fewer than eighteen have Christian origins – Roman Catholic (eight), Church of England (four), Baptist (three), Presbyterian (two) and United Church (Methodist) (one).[12] Moreover, this does not include the many other colleges and universities that are either constituents of the major universities or private, most of the latter being faith based.

Today, almost all public Canadian universities are secular institutions, having exchanged their confessional status for government grants in the 1960s (the time frame varies slightly for each province), that being a condition of public funding in each case. Canada has become one of the most multicultural countries in the world in recent decades, and the separation of church and state in education is very well established.

The great majority of Canadian universities are "public" institutions governed by relatively independent boards of governors and senates. The few private universities are small and niche based. Most are confessional, although there have been a few recent efforts to establish small private secular universities focusing on teaching and innovation. Many of these newer institutions are struggling financially and in no way resemble the major private and well-endowed universities that are the hallmarks of the best of American higher education.

There is another important difference between the American and Canadian systems of higher education. While the former is characterized by great diversity, its institutions ranging from the very best to fly-by-night operations and from prestigious graduate schools to two-year colleges, Canada's system is much more homogeneous. First of all, in Canada there are far fewer institutions for a given population. Other than in the largest centres, there is usually only one university for a significant geographic region, and hence there is more uniformity of academic offering across institutions, as each tries to provide a full range of arts, sciences, and professional programs for its catchment area. Even Canada's largest metropolitan region, the Greater Toronto Area (GTA), has only three main universities (Toronto, York, Ryerson), which contrasts starkly with the similarly sized Philadelphia metropolitan area with its twenty-eight universities, including seventeen four-year institutions.

Having far fewer institutions, yet institutions that tend to be similar to each other, has also meant that there is greater uniformity of quality in Canada than there is in America. An undergraduate degree from any Canadian public university will match the best standards anywhere, as evidenced by the performance of its graduates in international graduate schools. This is pertinent to the recruitment of presidents for Canadian institutions, as the similarities across institutions encourage considerable mobility across the country.

Notwithstanding their French and British origins, Canadian universities have grown to be far more like their American counterparts in recent decades, evolving from institutions primarily devoted to teaching to those where research and scholarship are predominant. This process was probably accelerated by the recruitment of so many American professors during the Vietnam War era and, increasingly, by the number of Canadian scholars with at least one graduate degree from a major American university.

As part of a world trend, Canadian universities are much more accessible than they were a few short decades ago, with 25 per cent or more of the age cohort at the turn of the twenty-first century going to university compared to 3–5 per cent in 1960.[13] Expansion was particularly strong as the baby boomers hit university age in the 1960s; it was during this period that the number of universities in Ontario grew from six in five cities in 1956 to fifteen in twelve centres less than ten years later. One in twenty eighteen-year-olds went to university in 1956, one in ten by the mid-1960s and one in six by the early 1970s.[14] In the past fifteen years, university participation has increased by 57 per cent, with some 900,000 students attending in 2010.[15]

The dramatically greater participation rate, together with increased immigration and the demographic increases emanating from the "echo boom,"[16] has put great pressure on the institutions to develop a broader range of programs and to accept more and more students. The response has varied in the different provinces, but one clear manifestation has been an increase in the size of Canadian universities. Not only was there a proliferation of new universities during the 1960s and 1970s, but the existing ones grew dramatically. For example, Queen's and Western were small by today's standards in 1960 (3,500 and 3,800 full-time students respectively), but Queen's is six times as large today and Western eight times bigger.[17] Such dramatic increases in student, faculty, and staff numbers have brought additional complexities, challenging both university leadership and management.

Furthermore, operating budgets have not kept pace with growth and inflation, contributing to an ever-increasing student/faculty ratio. For example, the CCL found that the national ratio of students to full-time faculty in Canada's universities went up 26 per cent, from 15.6 students per faculty member in 1993–94 to 19.6 in 2004–05.[18] The response has been both larger classes and the increasing use of sessional instructors and teaching assistants in the classroom.

There has also been a wave of "new" institutions in recent years, mainly in the evolution to university status of community and affiliated or federated colleges. British Columbia and Alberta have been particularly active in granting university status to former community colleges; the transformation has been easier in those provinces because, unlike in Ontario, many of British Columbia's and Alberta's colleges offer the first two years of university as part of their mandate. Ontario has added a few institutions in recent years. Ryerson University was transformed from a polytechnic; Nipissing and, most recently, Algoma were formerly degree-granting affiliates of Laurentian University; and the University of Ontario Institute of Technology was created as an addendum to Durham College. As well, there is active discussion of transforming one or more of the large community colleges in the GTA to university status in response to the huge demographic pressures there. This combination of decentralization and yet relative homogeneity, then, characterizes university education in Canada. These unique national characteristics, together with the rapid expansion and increasing complexity of the past few decades, have significant implications for the role of Canadian university presidents.

Canadian universities have evolved in another very important way, one that both leads and mirrors changes in the country as a whole. Whereas up until the mid-1960s most Canadian universities were not only small but also parochial in both their clientele and outlook, today's institutions are much more international in both.

A critical but less easily documented difference between American and Canadian universities is the style of leadership in each, directly reflecting the differences in their respective national characters. While "national character" is never an absolute, there is plenty of anecdotal evidence of significant differences across nations, even those as indistinguishable to outsiders as Canada and the United States. The differences are represented in the countries' national slogans – America's more individualistic "life, liberty and the pursuit of happiness" versus Canada's more conservative and communal "peace, order and good government."[19] The counterpart to "as American as apple pie" is the more convoluted and ironic "As Canadian as possible under the circumstances."[20]

Although their academic cultures have many similarities, it can be argued that Canadians and Americans differ in their willingness to give authority to a "president." In the United States, the country's president is not only the political leader but also the head of state, whereas Canada separates the two roles between the prime minister (the political leader) and the governor-general (the representative of the queen, who is the country's official head of state). This division makes a significant difference to the way that the president and the prime minister are perceived in the respective countries. For example, Americans are often amazed by the partisan attacks on the Canadian prime minister in the House of Commons, something that would never be seen in the US Congress, where even an unpopular president is treated with great respect. There is considerable evidence that this deference to the authority of a president permeates

American society, including at the university level with its history of "great" leaders, including two American presidents, Woodrow Wilson at Princeton and Dwight D. Eisenhower at Columbia. An excellent example of the belief in the "hero" leader in the American academic culture is Arthur Padilla's book *Portraits in Leadership: Six Extraordinary University Presidents*, which offers a series of tributes to leaders of the national stature of Clark Kerr at the University of California and Ted Hesburgh at Notre Dame.[21]

As usual, Canadian perspectives on presidency fall somewhere between European and American views. The traditional European university head is seen as an academic leader, often with a certain disdain for "management," in contrast to the more heroically oriented American perception.[22] While expecting their presidents to lead and to manage, Canadians are less likely to put them on pedestals, and this is reflected in the lower-key style of leadership they exhibit.

Throughout the book, it is argued that the styles of leadership that are most effective on Canadian campuses reflect these cross-national differences, that it is no accident that few Canadian university presidents have come from outside the country, and that few of those who have assumed a presidency without significant prior experience as academic administrators in Canada have fared very well.

EVOLUTION OF THE ROLE OF PRESIDENT SINCE 1960

Given the dramatic increases in the number, size, and complexity of Canadian universities since 1960, it is not surprising that the role of president[23] has changed both substantially and substantively. As already noted, there were far fewer universities in the fifteen years following the Second World War, they were much smaller institutions, and teaching was paramount. Most students were full-time and lived on or very near the campus. No more than 3–5 per cent of the age cohort attended university. Most students saw university as the best route to social connections and a good job. In contrast to today's university students, an individual's identity in that era was usually exclusively that of "student," and far fewer individuals worked at a job during the school year than is the case today. Most undergraduates were seventeen to twenty-two years of age, and their university experience involved more than just classes. Living in residence, participating in extracurricular activities and athletics, and enjoying a vibrant social life were central to the university experience for the majority. Today's students tend to be older, and many fit being a student around full- or part-time employment.

In the largest universities of the 1960s (Toronto, McGill, Montréal, British Columbia), the undergraduate experience was probably a more personal one than it is today in most Canadian urban universities. At that time, even these universities were smaller than the so-called mid-sized universities of today.[24] Before the student radicalism of the late 1960s raised their profile, universities were not prominently in the public eye. They catered to a much smaller segment of the general population, in many cases serving as finishing schools for the social elites. They certainly were not places for everyone.

In such an environment, the role of president was simpler than it is today. In fact, he (and it was almost always a "he") was more apt to "preside over" than to lead or manage the institution. Not only were students on campus around the clock, but faculty often lived there as well (in faculty housing or as deans of residence). With the expansion boom of the 1960s, many young professors were hired and it was expected that they would stay with the institution for many years, if not for life. Indeed, many faculty members grew up with their institution, and in the early days at least, their partners and children were also part of the campus milieu (for example, through attendance at sporting events and participation in faculty clubs and family activities).

A university president circa 1960 was more apt to have moral than ascribed line authority, and many of today's prevailing challenges scarcely existed then. Among the key changes of the past forty years have been the following:

1 A significant lessening of the personal touch with rapid expansion in student numbers and an increase in organizational complexity
2 The rise of faculty and staff unions and their implications for academic governance (especially for senates) and internal human relations
3 Increased competition among universities for scarce resources and the resulting expectations for presidential lobbying, government relations, fundraising, alumni development, marketing, and promotion
4 Research gradually displacing teaching at the centre of the institution's mission, with all of its implications for organization,

infrastructure, lobbying, private-public partnerships, and other expectations for the leadership role of the president

5 Increased financial pressures as expansion and increases in costs, notably salaries, outpaced revenues from government grants and tuition fees

6 Initially, dramatic changes in student activism in the late 1960s and early 1970s, which seriously challenged the authority of boards of governors and administrations, and, more recently, an increased sense of entitlement from students who are paying comparatively higher tuition fees than did those in earlier eras

A president of a university of 3,500 students (the size of Queen's in 1960) would know almost all of the faculty and staff members and many of the students. He or she would set the tone for the institution, teaching one or two courses, hosting teas and dinners, eating lunch with faculty and students, participating actively in campus debates and seminars, attending athletic events, and spending most of the time on campus. The president would also represent the institution in the immediate community and make the occasional foray to the provincial legislature to ensure good relations and fair funding, but such expeditions would be fairly low key, as universities were not generally in the public eye.

Contrast this with the same university in 2010. Its student population, faculty, and staff numbers are many times larger, and the external components of the president's role dominant. The operating budget might exceed $500 million, and key issues of academic leadership, collective bargaining, government and community relations, public affairs, and communications involve individuals working in departments that hadn't existed forty or fifty years earlier.[25]

Following from Harold Shapiro's words cited in the preface to this book, the modern president is answerable at one and the same time to a diverse range of stakeholders and communities:

- The faculty want an academic leader who will bring profile, reputation, and prestige to the institution, someone who strongly defends academic freedom while finding as much money as possible for teaching and research.
- The board wants a strong leader with excellent management, communication, and human relations skills, a good fundraiser and

promoter, and a leader of unquestioned integrity and strength who ensures the financial stability of the institution.

- Students want an informal role model who is actively engaged on campus, highly accessible, and particularly sensitive to such concerns as support services, teaching and learning, and affordable tuition fees.
- Alumni want a highly visible and personable representative of the institution who actively supports their activities and intercollegiate sports and who is both knowledgeable about and appreciative of the institution's history and culture.
- The local community wants a high-profile promoter of the institution and its environs who is highly visible and approachable.
- The governments want change agents who know how to work within the academic culture, understand the fiscal challenges, are openly accountable for the use of public monies, and help realize public policy priorities through leadership of their respective institutions.

Given the stark contrast between the 1960 and 2010 versions of the job, one might expect a significant change in the kind of person recruited to the presidency today. The earlier time would suit a personable and articulate academic with a strong set of values and the ability to inspire others to forge a first-rate institution, while, in addition to these qualities, today's challenges call for a chief executive officer, someone with strong leadership and management skills who is a good delegator, planner, and advocate, and has high energy and the ability to function in many different venues as the moment requires. Surprisingly, the background and preparation of today's Canadian university presidents are not much different from what they were in 1960. Although there is certainly no mould for a university president today, almost all come to the position with previous experience as a vice-president, dean, or president in a Canadian university, usually a different institution than the one to which they are being appointed.

ELEVEN PRESIDENTS WHO HAVE MADE A DIFFERENCE

The latent absurdity of being the executive leader of an organization that does not know what it is doing haunts the presidential role.

Michael D. Cohen and James G. March, 1986[26]

Central to this book is an attempt to learn from the experience and viewpoints of some of Canada's most successful university presidents of the past few decades. That immediately raises the question as to how one measures success in the context of a university.

As the above quote from Cohen and March suggests, much of the discussion around the position of university president concerns all of the limits on his or her power and how difficult it is to assess a leader's performance in such a complex and decentralized institution. Nevertheless, the individuals selected for interview represent a strong cross-section of Canada's most effective university presidents over the past thirty years, men and women who have not only achieved significant change and improvements for their own institutions but have also had a positive impact on the whole higher-education environment as well. The emphasis in selection has been on experience. Most served at least two full terms in the position and would be on any knowledgeable observer's list of our best presidents. At the time of the interviews, five of the presidents had already left the post, four have since done so, one other will have retired by the date of publication of this book, and only one, Roseann Runte, is expected to continue as a president past 2011.

As one who has served in the presidential or vice-presidential role in four institutions in three provinces, my own orientation is doubtlessly skewed favourably towards presidential colleagues. That made the selection more difficult in that at least as many more with exemplary records in the position could have been chosen. The key factors in selection included their serving more than one term, having a significant national or international profile, being president of more than one institution, having had a demonstrable impact on institutional performance as president, and my own familiarity with his or her work.

That each is well known to and admired by the author may be seen as both an advantage and a limitation on the validity of the representation. On balance, I believe that the personal relationship and common experience added considerable informality to the interviews and permitted exploration of issues in more depth than might otherwise have been the case. Nevertheless, the colleague-to-colleague relationship must be acknowledged, and especially because I chose subjects whom I already admired, there can be no pretence to true objectivity in the depictions of each one's career. The following chart identifies the individuals and institutions represented.

Presidential Interviewees

Name	Institution(s)	Location(s)	Dates
Paul Davenport	Alberta	Edmonton	1989–94
	Western	London	1994–2009
Jim Downey	Carleton	Ottawa	1978–79
	New Brunswick	Fredericton	1980–90
	Waterloo	Waterloo	1993–99
Peter George	McMaster	Hamilton	1995–2010
Myer Horowitz	Alberta	Edmonton	1979–89
David Johnston	McGill	Montreal	1979–94
	Waterloo	Waterloo	1999–2010
Bill Leggett	Queen's	Kingston	1994–2004
Dave Marshall	Nipissing	North Bay	1990–2003
	Mount Royal	Calgary	2003–11
Bonnie Patterson	Trent	Peterborough	1998–2009
Martha Piper	University of British Columbia	Vancouver	1997–2006
Rob Prichard	Toronto	Toronto	1990–2000
Roseann Runte	Ste Anne	Pte-de-l'église, NS	1983–88
	Victoria	Toronto	1994–2001
	Old Dominion	Norfolk, VA	2001–08
	Carleton	Ottawa	2008 to present

While these eight men and three women represent a broad cross-section of Canadian university presidents, there is no claim to proportional representation of institutions across the country. Only six of the ten provinces are represented, and the sample is strongly skewed towards Ontario, where I spent almost all of my years as a university president. Eight of the Canadian institutions represented are in the medical/doctoral category, three are comprehensive universities, and only two are in the smaller, primarily undergraduate category.[27] The only francophone university represented is tiny Sainte-Anne in Nova Scotia. Notwithstanding the predominance in the book of representatives of the larger and more research-intensive universities and of Ontario, it is argued that the responsibilities and challenges of their post will be familiar to the president of almost any Canadian university. At the same time, the implications of some provincial, regional, and mission-related differences for the roles and responsibilities of the president may not be as evident in most of the universities represented in this book. While there are far more similarities than differences in the job of president in universities of various sizes and mandates, certain important provincial, regional, and/or mission-related differences can have a significant impact on institutional leadership.

FRANCOPHONE UNIVERSITIES IN QUEBEC

The most obvious case is Quebec, where the rapid evolution of today's "distinct society" is intertwined with the recent history of higher education in the province. Education, language, and politics are central to the province's unique identity, adding an extra dimension to the role of recteur of any of Quebec's francophone universities.

The "Quiet Revolution" ushered in with the election of the Jean Lesage government in 1960 transformed education in the province. A teaching brother, later identified as Jean-Paul Desbiens, wrote *Les insolences de Frère Untel* in that same year (subsequently published in English as *The Impertinences of Brother Anonymous*),[28] which attacked the quality of language in Quebec and the province's system of public education. The subsequent (1963–66) eloquently written five-volume *Rapport de la Commission Royale d'enquete sur l'enseignement dans la province de Québec* (referred to as "The Parent Report" after its principal author, Laval University vice-rector Msgr Alphonse-Marie Parent) spurred major reforms that "fundamentally altered the character and pattern of education, changing it from a decentralized, church dominated system serving an elite to a centralized, state controlled one catering to a mass population."[29]

The ensuing creation of the CEGEP (Collège d'enseignement générale et professionel) system in 1967, combining the *collèges classiques* and technical institutes into single institutions, and the unique Université de Québec system in 1968 (now a network of nine quasi-independent universities) brought higher education to communities throughout the province. While the CEGEP integrated existing institutions on the francophone side, it was a brand new concept for anglophone students. Instead of going to four years of university after grade 11, from 1969 forward with the creation of Montreal's

Dawson College, they had to attend two years of CEGEP and three years of university for a baccalaureate degree, adding a full year (sixteen instead of fifteen) of formal education, thus bringing Quebec's English system into line with most other provinces and with the rest of Quebec.

There are important, if subtle, differences in the respective presidential roles of Quebec's francophone and anglophone universities. In most of the francophone universities, the recteur is elected from within by an electoral college or assembly, and the presidents of the institutions in the Université de Québec system are appointed by the provincial government on the basis of university election results and board recommendations.[30] This is in contrast to the rest of Canada and the province's English universities (McGill, Concordia, and Bishop's), where the president is almost always from outside the institution and appointed, rather than elected, by the institution's board of governors. Quebec's francophone practice places the recteur closer to a European model of university leadership, which is more collegial and less managerial. Often leading to a shorter term of office (popularity with faculty in particular is increasingly difficult to sustain in complex times), this practice is increasingly under review, as Quebec institutions face the same challenges for accountability and fiscal juggling as those in the rest of Canada.

There is one other factor that, while different in degree rather than in kind, sets Quebec apart and challenges every rector/principal/president of a Quebec university, English or French. The provincial government has more strictly regulated tuition fees than have its counterparts in the rest of Canada, and thus the fees in Quebec are easily the lowest in the country. For 2010–11, for example, the average undergraduate tuition fees for Quebec were less than half the Canadian mean ($2,415 compared to $5,138).[31] While, as a result, state financial support for universities has sometimes been more generous than elsewhere in Canada, the overall revenues per student in Quebec universities are usually lower, with consequent implications for their financial leadership.[32]

PROVINCES IN WHICH A SINGLE UNIVERSITY DOMINATES

Newfoundland and Prince Edward Island each have only one university (Memorial and the University of Prince Edward Island [UPEI], respectively). This gives those institutions, and their leaders, a greater presence and a leadership role in the province. This can be a mixed blessing: while it may increase these universities' opportunities and resources, it also renders them more visible and potentially more vulnerable to political interference. The most startling recent example was the 2009 intervention by Newfoundland education minister Joan Burke in the search for a new president for Memorial University; this case is discussed in chapter 11 on university governance.

The presidency of either Memorial or UPEI has a dimension lacking in institutions in provinces where the presence of a university and its ties to government are less evident. Some of the elements of close government relationships can also be seen in presidential posts in other smaller provinces, especially in those where the largest university is located in the capital city, sometimes only steps from the legislature (as is the case for Dalhousie in Halifax, the University of New Brunswick (UNB) in Fredericton, the University of Manitoba in Winnipeg, and the University of Alberta in Edmonton).

Political prominence and visibility are also associated with being among the largest and longest-established institutions in the province, whose alumni play leadership roles in government (politicians and public servants), the business community, and other parts of the public sector. Examples include the Universities of British Columbia (UBC), Alberta, Saskatchewan, Manitoba, New Brunswick, and Dalhousie (Nova Scotia). While the case could also be made for the University of Toronto, its dominance is tempered by the existence of many other prominent universities in the province, as is the case for Montréal, McGill, and Laval in Quebec.

SMALLER, TEACHING-FOCUSED, AND RESIDENTIAL UNIVERSITIES

Notably, in the three Maritime provinces (Nova Scotia, New Brunswick, and Prince Edward Island), the predominant university model is of a primarily undergraduate teaching university with many of its students residing on or very near the campus. Only one of Nova Scotia's eleven university-level institutions (Dalhousie) has more than 10,000 students, with all of the rest, save for Saint Mary's, having fewer than 5,000, as is the case for Mount Allison and Saint Thomas, in New Brunswick, and the University of Prince Edward

Island. Some of the newly created and/or private universities in the rest of Canada are also small, and the other provinces have very few long-established teaching universities, except for Bishop's in Quebec and Brandon in Manitoba.

The presidents of these smaller institutions are expected to be more personally involved in the academic and social life of the campus, hearkening back to an earlier era when almost all Canadian universities were small and more self-contained. With many Canadian institutions growing larger, emphasizing research, and continuing to rely on sessional instructors and teaching assistants, these smaller, primarily undergraduate universities may increasingly be able to promote themselves successfully to students who seek a more personal and well-rounded experience on campus. As will be discussed further in chapter 6, most of these institutions score highly on the National Survey of Student Engagement (NSSE).

SPECIAL MISSION UNIVERSITIES

A number of institutions have specific missions that separate them somewhat from the rest in terms of the missions' implications for university leadership.

Bilingual Universities

Reflecting my own experience as president/recteur of Laurentian University/Université Laurentienne, the presidency of an officially bilingual university carries extra dimensions. Ottawa University is the largest and best known such university, while York University's Glendon College is another example. The biggest challenges are in recruiting faculty and staff and in dealing regularly with language issues, which are often volatile in Canada, and with communications, where the necessity of translating countless official missives and publications adds both cost and time to the process. Being head of a bilingual institution also means membership in a greater number of external groups, with the addition, for example, of Le regroupement des universités de la francophonie hors Québec (RUFHQ) and L'association des universités partiellement ou entièrement de la langue française (AUPELF) to the usual provincial and national associations in Canada.

Distance Teaching Institutions

Universities like Athabasca and TÉLUQ offer most of their courses through distance education. The consequent absence of students on campus and the unique roles played by faculty, tutors, and instructional and visual designers render their leadership challenges significantly different from those of campus-based institutions. Through my own experience during eleven years at Athabasca, I found the atmosphere more like a publishing house than a bustling university campus.

Almost all Canadian universities offer some courses and programs via distance education, but none of them comes close to the Australian notion of "dual mode" institutions, which offer the same degree programs to both on- and off-campus students.

Professional Institutes

Several former professional colleges and institutes now enjoy university status. Notable among the colleges are the Emily Carr University of Art and Design, the Nova Scotia College of Art and Design University (NSCAD U), and the Ontario College of Art and Design (OCAD). Again, this new status adds other professional bodies to the leader's affiliations and has an impact on the way others view the institution. Especially where conversion to university status is recent, as is the case for the visual arts institutions, for example, the president may face particular challenges in re-establishing the institution's identity, although the focus on clear areas of strength is a significant advantage to that task.

Federated and Affiliated Universities

Many Canadian universities have federated and affiliated universities within them, most of which are confessional in character. Many were originally independent institutions that federated to form the parent institution, suspending their own degree-granting authority except in divinity. The Association of Catholic Colleges and Universities of Canada (ACCUC) has nineteen such members; twenty-one post-secondary educational institutions are affiliated with the Anglican Church; six are associated with the United Church; and a few have with other religious linkages.

Judging by my own experience at Laurentian and Windsor, both of which were formed by the federation of institutions representing the Catholic, Anglican, and United Churches, an important role for the president of the parent institution is to liaise with the respective executive heads of the federated universities, seeking an appropriate balance of collaboration and independence.

Federated and affiliated institutions vary in size and independence, but most have considerable autonomy with respect to their parent institution. Prominent examples include HÉC, École polytechnique (Université de Montréal), and Victoria University (University of Toronto).

Private Universities

As already noted, Canada has relatively few private universities and the majority of these are small and confessional. Several fledgling universities in British Columbia (Quest, University Canada West) and New Brunswick (Yorkville, Landsbridge) promote themselves in specific subject areas in high demand and/or on the basis of their services to students (convenience, fast-tracking, personal attention, innovative curricula). Most of these newer, non-confessional institutions cater especially to international students. Private post-secondary education is relatively unknown in Canada, and institutional leaders have an uphill battle in finding an appropriate balance between affordable tuition fees and the quality of programs and services that would build their reputation.

Despite the differences among the universities, the roles and responsibilities of university presidents are fairly consistent across the institutions. Moreover, the backgrounds of those profiled in this book, in both their similarities and differences, are typical of university leaders across Canada. Five (George, Johnston, Leggett, Marshall, Patterson) grew up in Ontario; three (Davenport, Piper, Runte) are Americans who came to Canada for graduate work or employment; and the final three are from, respectively, Newfoundland (Downey), Quebec (Horowitz), and England (Prichard, although he came to Toronto at an early age). Several of the group had senior administrative experience in institutions in other provinces before assuming a presidency. They include Piper (McGill, Alberta); Davenport, Horowitz, and Leggett (McGill); and Johnston (Western). The disciplinary groups represented are Economics (Davenport, George), Education (Horowitz, Marshall), Law (Johnston, Prichard), Biological Sciences (Leggett), Physical Therapy (Piper), English (Downey), French Literature (Runte), and Business (Patterson).

The presidents came to their positions in very different ways. Some seemed born to the presidential role and even to the given institution. Rob Prichard came to Canada from England at a very early age when his father was appointed to the Hospital for Sick Children and the faculty of medicine at the University of Toronto. Prichard learned to swim at Hart House pool and to skate at Varsity Arena. He even met his wife, Ann, on their mutual first day of law school at the U of T, and before assuming the presidency, he had been a professor of law and then dean.

Paul Davenport, too, grew up in an environment very conducive to academia. Both of his parents were graduates of distinguished universities (his father went to Lehigh, his mother to Wellesley). His parents read Shakespeare and poetry to him as a child, and it wasn't long after he went to Stanford University that he aspired to an academic career as a professor of economics.

At the other extreme, in terms of academic roots, are Jim Downey, who grew up in a small Newfoundland outport and got all his schooling in a two-room schoolhouse; and Bill Leggett, whose first eight grades were in a one-room schoolhouse with the same teacher. Myer Horowitz's uncle was the only one in his family to have a university education, but his influence on his nephew was profound. Horowitz's father-in-law was always disappointed that he never reached what he believed to be the pinnacle position in education – a high school principal! Bonnie Patterson was the first person in her family to go to university, the primary influence being a high school teacher with whom she boarded after leaving home at fifteen.

Appendix A offers capsule profiles of each of the presidents interviewed for the book. Its purpose is to demonstrate the similarities and the many differences in the orientations and backgrounds of these university presidents. As well, it provides context for their views and experiences that are represented throughout the book in the discussions of the major issues facing universities today.

Canadian University Presidents:
Who They Are and How They Are Selected

Universities have become more central in the knowledge society. They no longer focus only on grooming the elite for future leadership but increasingly seek to provide equal opportunity for all, as society has recognized the importance of higher overall levels of educational attainment and the value of research and scholarship that will drive our future economic and social development.

One result of this change has been a greater interest in the position of university president, and a greater sense of the importance of this position, not just to our universities, but to Canada as a whole. This draws particular attention to the whole process of presidential recruitment – how it is done, who are chosen, how long they last, and how successful they are. While faculty, in particular, tend to minimize the importance of the position of president while the incumbent is in place, they inevitably show great interest in presidential selection, either to protect aspects of the institution in which they believe or to change those parts that they don't favour – or both.

Not very long ago, searches for presidents of Canadian universities were wide-open affairs involving highly politicized university committees that were dominated by faculty who conducted the search and recommended the final selection to the board of governors. Confidentiality was often a misnomer – not only did interested members of the academic community know the names of the candidates on the short lists (and the names of those who did not make it that far), but they often knew how each member of the committee had voted. Reference checking was haphazard, at best.

THE PROFESSIONALIZATION OF PRESIDENTIAL
SEARCHES

Practices and procedures have tightened up significantly in recent decades, notably since the late 1980s when the majority of Canadian universities started engaging professional executive search companies to assist in presidential recruitment and selection. High-profile searches for the presidents of Toronto, Western, and UBC between 1982 and 1986 demonstrated the value and importance of such assistance, and by the 1990s, the great majority of universities were using search consultants for presidencies and, increasingly, for vice-president positions and deanships.

This professionalization of the presidential search process has had a number of significant impacts, dramatically increasing the cost of such exercises (up to a third of the annual salary of the recruited position) but going a long way to ensuring confidentiality and thorough reference checking before any names are put forward. Unlike many American states, Canadian provinces do not have "sunshine laws" that require public divulgence of candidate lists throughout the search process.[1]

The use of consultants has a number of major benefits, especially in the very competitive environment inhabited by top academic administrators.

Search Potential

Only very occasionally does a strong candidate emerge through the direct application process in response to advertising. The great majority of qualified candidates are identified by the search firm through its own networks and from suggestions and nominations from presidents and other contacts across the Canadian university system. Every search firm with experience with universities keeps a roster of potential leaders, some of whom are open to being a candidate for quite a wide range of institutions and communities, while others are very particular about what universities they would consider. An important role for the search consultant is to persuade a reluctant candidate who seems particularly well qualified for a position at a given institution to at least participate in the process, even if his or her initial inclination is not to consider it.

Building the Profile of the Ideal Candidate

The consultant brings experience and an unbiased external perspective to the task of helping the university and its search committee define the kind of leadership it needs and thereby develop a position profile that will guide both the search and selection process. As a professional and experienced outside observer, the consultant can be especially helpful to the chair of the search committee (who is usually the chair of the board or the chancellor) in finding consensus among the rather disparate members of most such committees (experienced board members, senior faculty, a student leader, a community or alumni representative).

Traditionally, the incumbent president in most Canadian universities is not involved in the search for the successor, other than being provided an opportunity at the outset to give the search committee his or her perspectives on the state of the university and its forthcoming challenges and opportunities. The outgoing president's views become input to the process along with representation from many other stakeholder groups, including faculty, students, alumni, and community members. These practices stand in stark contrast to those followed in most private and some public sector institutions, where effective succession planning is a major responsibility of the incumbent leader.

Protecting Confidentiality

The consultant strongly emphasizes to the search committee the importance of confidentiality in the whole process. A more open process might discourage some of the best-qualified people because they are not willing to have their candidacy known, especially to their current employer and colleagues. Confidentiality is particularly important if the candidate is already a university president – nothing undermines an incumbent's authority more quickly than the knowledge that he or she is looking elsewhere.

However, not all institutions permit candidates total confidentiality throughout the process, until the moment of decision. Some require the finalist (or, more rarely, finalists) to appear publicly on the prospective campus to give a wider cross-section of the university an opportunity to assess the candidate's qualifications and provide feedback to the search committee or board before the process is completed. However, this happens less frequently than it used to and is far less common for presidents than it is for deans, provosts, or vice-presidents, research (VPRS) – positions for which finalists may be asked to give an academic paper at an open forum as part of the selection process. I understand that even this practice has become increasingly rare at this level, as universities recognize the importance of confidentiality to strong candidates already in senior positions elsewhere.

Compared to the process described above, the processes for the selection (or, more commonly, election) of "le recteur" in most francophone universities in Canada are much more open and closer to practices in many European universities than to those in the rest of North America. The selection processes are lengthy and very public, usually with several levels of committee and regular reporting on who the top candidates are and how they rank. Appointments at francophone institutions are more frequently internal than is the case for most Canadian universities, and an incumbent interested in a renewed term is apt to be put through a full competition, while the practice elsewhere is to offer renewal to an interested incumbent who has successfully passed a thorough review process.

Vetting and Pre-screening

The presidency of a Canadian university is a high-profile position that usually attracts a broad range of candidates. Inevitably, a number of names can be fairly easily eliminated once the position profile has been clearly outlined because they lack the formal qualifications or experience. Working closely with the search committee and, in some cases, meeting with promising candidates to gather further information on its behalf, the consultant performs a vetting service, but no candidate is ever eliminated without the approval of the search committee. Especially given the relatively large size of most university search committees and the challenges of finding mutually agreeable times to meet, the vetting process can save the committee a lot of meeting time and ensure that it focuses its attention on the best-qualified candidates.

Selling the Institution

Presidential recruitment involves much more than merely identifying the candidate best suited to the particular post. A given candidate may have significant concerns about the institution or even about serving in the role of a university president, or he or she may be entertaining more than one possibility. It is thus very important for the committee to work with the consultant and to be as persuasive as possible in order to land the right candidate, once identified.

The natural chauvinism of so many amateur participants in a search process may obscure the critical importance of selling the institution to the best potential candidates. It is no accident that the term "search" (or sometimes "nominating") is much more common than "selection" in the name of the committee; its members cannot assume that the candidates will automatically accept an offer. A huge part of the process involves taking the candidates on campus tours, entertaining them and their partner, and doing everything possible to convince a potential president that theirs is a first-rate institution and that their community is a good place to live. All this is important, not only in seducing the leading candidates but also in leaving a good impression with those who are not chosen or who decide not to pursue their candidacy. If a good candidate leaves the interview process with a very positive sense of the institution, this can pay dividends in many other ways in the future even if he or she never sets foot on the campus again. Of such things are institutional reputations and reference networks made.

This issue has another side. There are some illuminating stories of rejected candidates "badmouthing" the institution in local drinking establishments, at least one of which involved a candidate who would otherwise have been offered the position because the first choice had declined the offer. Each candidate and the institution are better served if both complete the process with high mutual respect, regardless of the actual selection decision.

Reference Checking

It is remarkable how little reference checking was done in earlier years for the top position in a university, frequently to the institution's regret. Professional search firms have helped to change that with both formal and informal reference checking behind the scenes. Especially since almost all Canadian university presidents come from senior academic administrative positions in Canada, assessments of a candidate's performance in his or her current or recent positions are usually augmented by information picked up more informally by search committee members, especially the faculty. A candidate's previous performance in leadership positions is still the best predictor of ability to perform a new job and one that is considerably more reliable than the average interview.

Nevertheless, the interview still plays the major role in the presidential selection process, and it is critical that the external search consultant help the search committee recognize its limitations. Janet Wright, the dean of Canadian university search consultants, notes that even candidates with superb credentials and references rarely recover from a poor interview. Bonnie Patterson believes that interviews help reinforce the strong tendency of committee members to be attracted to candidates from outside the institution: "The issue of being willing to take a risk on someone whom you know less about is a human characteristic. For presidents, people are always looking for vision and charisma and demonstrated leadership – you may not know about these in five minutes but you know within the first forty minutes of an interview whether someone has them or not."[2]

Ensuring a Fair and Equitable Process

By its very nature, a university search has a number of checks and balances to ensure an objective and fair process. The search committee is made up of diverse representatives of the community, and notwithstanding the tight security of modern search processes, its deliberations are monitored carefully by all stakeholders, notably faculty and students. As noted above, interviews are notoriously unreliable, and it is critical that committees use as many additional means as possible to assess potential candidates – how well they "fit" the position profile, their performance in their current and past leadership positions, and, of course, their references.

One of the trends of recent years has been to do as much as possible to encourage candidates from under-represented groups, emphasizing the importance not only of human rights but of diversity in institutional leadership. While there have been some advances, notably in the number of women who have been appointed, progress has been much slower than most advocates would have envisioned when the equity provisions were established. At the time of writing, only nine of the more than fifty long-established Canadian universities were led by women, and in eight of these nine, the incumbent was the first female president in the institution's history. It may be slightly more encouraging to note that a number of Canada's largest and best-known universities have had a woman president for the first time in recent years, including UBC, Alberta, Manitoba, McMaster, York, Queen's, Carleton, McGill, Concordia, UNB, and, most recently, Calgary. However, in seven of the first ten cases, the female incumbent was replaced by a male, and the number of women who lead top universities in Canada is lower than it was just a few years ago.

Given that the same pattern is in evidence at the vice-presidential level as well, it is all too apparent that we are not doing enough to groom women leaders through the ranks. By extension, Canada would also benefit immeasurably from a broader range of ethnic representation in its university leadership positions, and a slew of recent hires is most encouraging from this perspective.[3]

Contractual Advice

Once the board has approved an appointment, it is usually the board chair who negotiates its terms with the candidate. These go well beyond direct compensation, including such benefits as an additional pension, university housing, and the offerings of the particular community (schooling, economic issues, attractions of the particular city or region). Recent media victories establishing the right to make these terms public have raised the profile of presidential contracts, an issue addressed below in the section on compensation practices.

The Limited Pool: An Increasing Challenge

This section on the recruitment of university presidents would be incomplete without some commentary on the shrinking size of the pool of potential candidates. Everyone knows superb academics and even academic administrators who would make great university presidents but decline all overtures to that effect. Many people prefer the relative freedom to do what they love as members of the academy and want more control over their own lives than the position affords. The evolution of the role away from campus to more external responsibilities further contributes to the reluctance of academics to get involved at any level of administration, let alone a presidency. This concerns Bill Leggett, who worries that as interpersonal relations on campuses become more strained, the role of president, and even that of chair, dean, and vice-president, becomes less attractive to potential candidates: "I have also noticed that there has been a tremendous increase in the recycling of presidents who go from one institution to another. That's not bad in itself but I think that the frequency of it is a worrying sign that there aren't as many people enthusiastically stepping forward to fill this role. I know many people with terrific careers and great potential who, for one reason or another, are asking themselves why they should get involved in the hassle when they can prosper in their teaching and research, and perhaps consult."

Usher et al. cite natural hiring cycles as another factor limiting the internal pool of potential academic leaders at this time: "Due to a decade-long period in the 1990s when hiring and advancement within universities were limited, fewer academics today are experienced in administration, and there are fewer tenured individuals in mid-career who can be brought forward as potential candidates for senior administrator roles."[4] Their recent study, based on interviews with thirty-one senior administrators in twenty-four universities in eight provinces, underlines the critical importance of senior search processes in Canada and offers a useful list of practices more likely to lead to successful hires.[5]

WHO GETS SELECTED: INTERNAL VERSUS EXTERNAL APPOINTMENTS

While the above processes might be familiar to academics in other countries, there are some distinctly national tendencies that have a vital impact on who becomes president of a Canadian university. The following information is derived from a careful analysis of the most recent (as of November 2010) presidential searches in forty-seven established Canadian universities and, for some issues, in eighteen Ontario institutions.[6] For comparison purposes going back a few years, the data do not include some of Canada's newest universities or those that are subsets of a larger institution. The universities included are listed in Appendix B.

It is interesting to note that forty-one, or almost 90 per cent, of the most recent presidential selections in each of the forty-seven universities have been external to the institution. In fact, only about one-third of the universities surveyed selected an internal candidate in their last three searches, and only a couple from the sample (Toronto, Ottawa) have selected more than one internal candidate in the past twenty years.[7] However, while the overwhelming majority of

recently appointed Canadian university presidents come from outside the institution, the process is not nearly as far-reaching as that
might suggest. In fact, the searches have been startlingly parochial!
Of the forty-one Canadian universities that did select an external
candidate in the most recent round, no fewer than thirty-five (85 per
cent) chose a candidate who held a senior academic administrative
position in a sister Canadian university. The majority of these were
vice-presidents (twenty-six), the rest being deans (six) or presidents
from another institution (three).

There have been only two non-Canadian appointments in recent
memory where the candidate came to the position without previous Canadian university experience and only two where a Canadian
came from such a position after academic administrative experience exclusively in the United States. There have been several cases
where an American assumed the presidency of a Canadian university
only after significant Canadian experience in a vice-presidential or
dean position (as was the case with two of those interviewed for this
book – Martha Piper and Paul Davenport). Finally, there is Roseann
Runte, now a dual citizen, who came to Canada from America to
work as a departmental chair and then assistant dean at Dalhousie
before assuming the presidency of Université Ste-Anne and who then
headed Glendon College and Toronto's Victoria University before
returning to the United States as president of Old Dominion University and finally coming back to Canada as Carleton's executive head.

Underlining the parochialism of Canadian presidential appointments, a number of Canada's most prominent universities, including Toronto and Western, prohibit the hiring of a president who is
not a Canadian citizen. This contrasts dramatically with the practice of universities in many other countries of going outside national
boundaries for their presidents. At least a few of the reasons for Canada's relatively inward-looking approach are fairly evident. For all
the historical concerns about Canada's autonomy beside the American elephant, there seems to be a very strong prevailing Canadian
culture in our institutions of higher learning. While this may breed
resistance to American candidates in particular, it has also meant
that those who have come to Canada without previous administrative experience in our university system (whether they are American
or Canadian) have not always fared as well as those who have. The
differences, while subtle, can be very important to a position as reli-
ant on the ability to read the in-house culture as is the presidency.

More ironically, faculty members on presidential search committees tend to favour external appointment. Professors, even when in the minority, often dominate the committee because they know the institution, its history, and its culture in ways that public board members, no matter how powerful in their own milieu, cannot match. A university is still a strange place to many external appointees, and they will usually bow to faculty opinion when it comes to determining which candidates are most suitable. Bonnie Patterson suggests that student assessments are also pivotal: "Yes, faculty members have a powerful role on a search committee, but if the student feedback is that someone would be terrible with students, they won't get hired. So, how someone appeals to both faculty and student agendas, quite different factors, plays a significant role in presidential selection. This also leads us to be willing to place more risk on someone we don't know as well but appears to meet these two characteristics."

Notwithstanding that faculty are interested in candidates who share their views of and comfort with the prevailing academic culture, they tend resist the appointment of internal candidates. This applies especially to aspirants who have served as vice-president, academic (VPA), a post that involved making difficult personnel decisions, bargaining with the faculty and other staff associations, and overseeing the financial management of the academic sector. Even though the position remains the primary route to a presidency, only three current Canadian university presidents served as VPA in their own institution (Alastair Summerlee at Guelph, Colin Dodds at Saint Mary's, and Feridun Hamdullahpur at Waterloo, although the latter's tenure in the VPA position was a relatively short thirteen months) and only a handful have managed this in recent decades (including Myer Horowitz). Paul Davenport has an intriguing explanation for this, dubbing it the immaculate conception of the president:

It is my experience that when a new president is being recruited, what most faculty believe they want is a full-time faculty member who has devoted his/her life to teaching and research and suddenly, one day, is transformed into a president. What that says is that it is difficult to groom people for the job because faculty are suspicious of those who want the job. If you are seen to campaign for the presidency, you are probably the wrong person.

It is equally difficult, I think, to rise up through the ranks of your own university by showing administrative competence and administrative leadership and then going on to be president in the same place because, again, you look like a careerist administrator. Over the last decade, most presidents at major universities in Canada have come from the outside.

So, I think the reason that the outgoing president is not at all involved in the selection of the successor, which is the case at every major university I know, is so the new president can have this immaculate conception aura around him or her. It's an odd system, isn't it? In the rest of the world, in large organizations like this one, one of the primary duties of the president is to groom his or her successor.

We don't do that and I believe, in the long run, our system works very well by ensuring that, on a regular basis, there are new ideas and new approaches at the top of the university administration.

Indeed, at least two of those interviewed for this book spoke directly about enhancing their own candidacy for president by resisting opportunities to be VPA in their own institution. For example, Rob Prichard, in part on the advice of his predecessor, turned down the opportunity to be a candidate for provost at Toronto – even though he agreed completely with the priorities set out and being implemented by the incumbent president and had the latter's support for the job – on the premise that association with the previous administration would be a liability in the presidential selection process.[8] The regularity of presidential appointments from other Canadian universities means incumbent presidents are usually, if not intentionally, developing successors, not for themselves, but for their colleagues in sister institutions across the country.

The prevailing practice of hiring from within Canada may have been strengthened (or exacerbated, depending upon one's viewpoint) by the influence of the executive search firms. One of the most important strengths of a search firm is the network of contacts it has built up across the country, not only for reference checking but for the identification and promotion of strong candidates. While these networks are immensely valuable to search committees and a primary basis for hiring search firms in the first place, they may somewhat ironically reinforce parochial tendencies in academia. A search firm has a vested interest in recruiting an appointee who will perform well in the new post, but it also stands to benefit if it can win the contract to search for the replacement of the successful candidate, and the opportunity for this is much stronger when the prevailing practice is to hire Canadians exclusively.

There are, of course, exceptions. A few vice-presidents and deans have been appointed in their own institutions (six of the current forty-seven): David Naylor at Toronto from dean of medicine, Peter MacKinnon at Saskatchewan from dean of law, and Elizabeth Cannon at Calgary from dean of engineering, in addition to the aforementioned VPAS, Alastair Summerlee at Guelph, Colin Dodds at Saint Mary's, and, very recently, Feridun Hamdullahpur at Waterloo.[9]

There have also been recent appointments from outside the academy – two politicians (former Liberal cabinet ministers Lloyd Axworthy at Winnipeg and Allan Rock at Ottawa), two public servants (Dominic Giroux at Laurentian, John Harker at Cape Breton), a business leader (Sean Riley at St Francis Xavier, who also had a public service background), and a media executive (Michael Goldbloom at Bishop's, although he had served as vice-principal, public affairs, at McGill for a short period of time immediately prior to his appointment). It is not clear, however, that such appointments are a trend or even a new phenomenon. Jim Downey cites a number of successful presidents recruited from outside academia during an earlier era – Gerald Hagey at Waterloo (an advertising executive), Roger Guindon at Ottawa (a priest), John Deutsch at Queen's (primarily a civil servant with some teaching experience), Davidson Dunton at Carleton (a journalist), Colin Mackay at UNB (a lawyer), and Henry Hicks at Dalhousie (also a lawyers).

In such cases, there is a natural tendency to look to the vice-president, academic, or provost for strong leadership on the academic side and to see the president as more oriented to the external environment. People like Myer Horowitz and Bill Leggett, however, disagree with the increasingly common notion that a president is much like a chief executive officer, believing instead that he or she must be the senior academic officer in a university. Others, like Bonnie Patterson, are more philosophical: "When you bring in someone from outside the academy, it may result in a very different emphasis on the VPA position, so the internal/external mix will be very different in those institutions. Given all the challenges of the position and concerns about the supply of strong candidates, I would expect boards to take more risk on someone whose background is quite different but he or she would have to have quite a strong appreciation of the institution. It will be interesting to watch."

While the VPA post was previously the primary route to a presidency, more and more vice-presidents, research, are being appointed. Most recently, in Ontario for example, there have been almost as many recent promotions of VPRs (four) as VPAs (five). This should not be surprising. Vice-presidents, academic, deal with much more of the nitty-gritty administrative work, while the vice-president, research, is attuned more to the external domain – government relations, private and public sector partnerships, fundraising, and institutional promotion. More pointedly, the VPR's relationships with faculty are more frequently positive (celebrating success, attaining grants), without the sort of conflict inherent in the VPA's more direct involvement in personnel decisions, budget management (which usually means budget cutting these days), and collective bargaining.

Finally, some very successful role models have come in the form of three women who have been highly visible leaders at some of Canada's strongest research universities – Martha Piper at UBC, Indira Samereskera at Alberta, and Heather Munroe-Blum at McGill, respectively the past VPRs at Alberta, UBC, and Toronto.

There appears to have been some change in the academic backgrounds of Canadian university presidents. While an earlier study found an under-representation of the arts in the background of presidents in Canada compared to the United States,[10] Canadian presidents thirty years later come from a broad range of disciplines. For example, the distribution of disciplines across the forty-seven universities surveyed indicates a fairly even distribution over the three main categories – sciences (sixteen), humanities and social sciences (fifteen), and professional schools (sixteen). It is interesting to note that professional schools play a stronger role in the background of the presidents of the larger universities, where research is more prominent. For example, no fewer than ten of the current presidents of the G13 (Group of Thirteen) institutions come from professional schools (four from engineering, three from medicine, two from law, and one from forestry).

In many ways, the prevailing tendency to hire a president from another Canadian university can be portrayed as representing the best of both worlds. The institution gets a new leader who is thoroughly familiar with the prevailing academic culture in Canada, its governance, government relations, the federal granting agencies for research, the economic and social priorities of the country, and, less tangibly, Canada's national character. The external appointee may also bring valuable networks of key contacts across the country. He or she has none of the baggage associated with the previous administration, and whatever problems and challenges he or she might have faced in the previous institution have been left behind.[11] Hence, the institution gets someone with a clean slate, fresh ideas and new approaches within a familiar and common milieu.

Yet there is also much to criticize in this practice. Each institution has its own particular history and politics, and an external appointee might have difficulty discovering which aspects of the local culture are most crucial and figuring out quickly enough whose advice to heed the most. Hiring the candidate who best compensates for the outgoing president's weaknesses is understandable but not always fortunate. It can set up a time-consuming and even damaging pendulum swing whereby each new president spends too much time and energy undoing aspects of the predecessor's work, even if the latter was quite successful.

Continuity of leadership is important to an institution. This argues for the value of second terms for successful leaders and for hiring someone who will strive to build upon the best work of the immediate predecessor. Two of Canada's most successful recent presidents, both interviewed for this book, recognize the lead provided in somewhat different ways by their predecessors. Martha Piper built on the expansionist and international plans for UBC established by David Strangway, and Rob Prichard went a long way to making the aspirations contained in the visionary planning of George Connell a reality.

In conclusion, notwithstanding my belief that many of our institutions would be better served by the appointment of an internal candidate well familiar with the local history, culture, opportunities, and challenges, I recognize that the current system of appointing an academic administrator from another Canadian university has generally worked quite well. Given that the job is becoming more challenging and complex each year, however, universities should be much more aggressive, innovative, and even bold in their search; they should seek out new kinds of leaders, people who will bring new leadership talents and new perspectives to academic management. Once again, we can turn to David Johnston, who strongly endorses this suggestion: "We're not systematically developing the leaders in the first place and, secondly, we're not being broad enough in the kind of people we are bringing in." Nevertheless, and most importantly, Johnston goes on to note that it is highly unlikely that the system will change. It is just far too entrenched in the Canadian academic culture.

READINESS FOR THE POSITION

One of the great ironies about universities around the world is that even though they represent the highest levels of education and training in society, their professional staffs are very seldom trained in any formal way for the core activities they perform. For example, few faculty members have educational training, and so they tend to teach the way they were taught during their own student days (which was often not very well). Similarly, very few university presidents have any education or training in management, administration, and leadership, let alone such detailed aspects of their role as strategic planning, financial management, collective bargaining, or fundraising. The overwhelming majority of Canadian university presidents have developed these skills on the job, only sometimes enhanced by professional development courses or seminars in specific areas.

Readiness for the position is not only a question of having the requisite skills, but also a question of knowing what the job is in the first place. Without exception, the eleven presidents interviewed for this book had extensive previous experience as departmental chairs, deans, and/or vice-presidents, and so they came into their first presidency with good general knowledge of academic culture and management. A few had some experience within a president's office and/or were mentored by an effective colleague, but for the most part the majority learned on the job what needed to be done and how to allocate their time. Those who went on to assume another presidency (Davenport, Downey, Johnston, Marshall, Runte) all noted how much better prepared they felt the second time around. Paul Davenport is a case in point: "There's no substitute for being in the job. Even though I had watched David Johnston, a master of the trade, in action in the McGill Principals Advisory Group and had listened to a great many of his speeches, you don't really know what it's like day-to-day until you're in the job."

There was general consensus among all interviewed that, whatever their earlier experience in academic administration, they found the role of president very challenging and had to learn much of it once on the firing line. It was just a matter of getting better at it as they went along. Dave Marshall went so far as to say that the presidency of Mount Royal, which followed his time at Nipissing, was the first job in his life for which he felt properly qualified and prepared.

At the same time, many had learned a good deal beforehand by working closely with their predecessor, even when they were not always in agreement with the individual's approach. This was especially the case in the few instances where the successful candidate was hired in his own institution – Myer Horowitz following Harry Gunning at Alberta, Rob Prichard after George Connell at Toronto, and Dave Marshall after Tony Blackburn at Nipissing.

Some presidents have participated, usually at an earlier stage in their administrative career, in the one-week Senior University Administrators Course (SUAC), run out of the University of Manitoba, or, upon appointment, in the shorter Seminar for New Presidents, initiated by Jim Downey on behalf of AUCC. Some have taken various executive programs at Queen's, Western, Harvard, or elsewhere, and some women presidents have had the experience of the Senior Women Academic Administrators of Canada (SWAAC) conferences. Until very recently, Judith Gibson ran the Quality Network through the Conference Board of Canada, a regular seminar for incumbent presidents augmented by international tours to exemplary institutions. I participated both in the seminar series and in a whirlwind tour of top American universities and found both experiences extremely helpful. I also took the Queen's Executive Program one summer. As the only "academic" at the latter, I found it particularly useful in that it helped me better understand the challenges of management in the corporate sector. Such programs provide useful exposure to case studies in leadership as well as interaction with experienced practitioners, but are perhaps most useful for the networks of contacts they establish for subsequent referral when problems and opportunities arise.

There is not much evidence of forthcoming changes in the way university presidents are trained in Canada. The strength of the prevailing academic culture will almost certainly ensure that, for many years to come, they will do most of their learning on the job, as deans or vice-presidents and in incumbency. Nevertheless, the professional development groups and programs referred to above will continue to provide valuable advice, experience, and networking opportunities to participants, and they are to be strongly encouraged and further developed.

HOW LONG DO THEY SERVE?

Presidents are hired for fixed terms, usually five and sometimes six years in length. This is a departure from earlier eras when most presidencies were open-ended, and some incumbents stayed in office for years, even decades.[12] Now, incumbents may be renewed following a successful evaluation of the first term, and even a second, but many institutions require a more open and competitive search before a third consecutive term of office.

One obvious way to ensure more consistency in institutional direction is to hire successful presidents to a second term of office. Even with internal appointments, an institution may not be well served by too many consecutive one-term presidents. For example, Rob Prichard attributes his ability to bring about a focused and clearer identity for the University of Toronto during his tenure to the fact that he was the first two-term president since the university introduced specific terms for its presidents in the 1960s.

On the other hand, an individual can stay too long in such a post. I have long believed that a person should not serve as president of a given institution for more than ten years. Whatever someone is good at will presumably have had its impact by about year seven, while an individual's weaknesses will become increasingly glaring after that. My own experience reinforces this. I received strong endorsement in being renewed for a second term of office in each of my last four positions – at Dawson College, Athabasca University, Laurentian University, and the University of Windsor. I left Dawson and Laurentian relatively early in my second term for other appointments but served full terms at Athabasca and Windsor. In the latter cases, faculty, board members, and others questioned my leadership much more at the end of my second term that they had earlier. This ties in with my observations of others' experiences elsewhere in Canada and with an American faculty survey by Birnbaum, who found that presidents were supported by 75 per cent of faculty members in the first three years of their term of office but by only 25 per cent when they were more than five years into the job.[13]

There is a rhythm to a presidential term of office that can affect perceptions of an individual's performance. A new appointment brings a significant boost in energy to the campus, not only during the honeymoon period but throughout the first term if the incumbent delivers on the promise that he or she has shown from the outset. This helps explain the relatively high re-engagement rate.[14] Not long after a renewal, however, the incumbent's weaknesses become more apparent, and at about the eight- or nine-year mark, when the question of renewal is again raised, the campus perception is usually that it is time for new leadership. Myer Horowitz took this into account in his own case. Many people thought that because he had had quadruple bypass surgery three years into his second term in 1987, he had decided not to seek a third term for health reasons. The truth was that he had made that decision when he accepted the second term, on the premise that "if I don't accomplish something in ten years, I'm not going to accomplish it in fifteen."

As with any rule of thumb, there are notable exceptions, including three of the interviewees for this book – Paul Davenport (1994–2009 at Western), Peter George (1995–2010 at McMaster), and David Johnston (1998–2010 at Waterloo). Tom Traves was appointed early in 2009 to his fourth term as president of Dalhousie, and more recently, David Turpin's presidency was extended for a third term at the University of Victoria. Nonetheless, the majority of presidents serve less than two terms. For example, for those Ontario presidents who completed their first term in the past 20 years, the average length of service was 8.4 years.[15] The situation would be similar in most universities in other provinces, although there are one or two institutions with a history of high turnover among presidents at certain periods in their history, the most recent examples being the University of Regina, which has recently appointed its third president in four years after the original four covered its first thirty-one years, and Concordia, which, at the time of writing, was seeking its third president in five years.

In the past few years, a number of Canadian university presidents have left their posts before the completion of their first term. While the reason for an early departure is not always known publicly, it commonly lies in incompatibility between the new president and his or her board (especially the board chair) or in the incumbent's decision not to continue in a stressful situation. Excluding situations where an incumbent left before serving five years because of an appointment elsewhere, there have been about ten such cases in the past decade. This is a higher rate than previously and perhaps underlines the growing demand for accountability in these more complex and pressurized times.

In a similar number of cases, a president completed a first term but was not re-engaged for a second, either because the office-holder chose to step down for reasons other than retirement or a better opportunity or because the board decided not to rehire the incumbent. Overall, however, there is less such turnover in Canada than in many other jurisdictions. Even in Ontario, the most competitive university market, no fewer than nineteen (or almost half of the past forty-three presidents who have completed their terms since 1990) served in the role for ten years or more, with one other serving two three-year terms. Of the nine who did not complete a second term of office, seven went on to new presidencies elsewhere. Eleven completed one term but did not seek a second, in only one case because of the opportunity to lead a larger institution. Three left before completing a first term.

In a few of the presidential appointments in recent years, a strong internal candidate lost out and went on almost immediately to lead a rival Canadian university. While both the sending and the receiving institutions may have benefited in some cases, in others the institution lost one of its strongest people and yet the appointee had to struggled to adjust to the culture in the new place, sometimes to the latter university's detriment. Moreover, recently there have been several cases where a president who had been successful in one institution, in two cases even completing two full terms, was not well received in the new institution and resigned well before the completion of his or her first term. Such cases underline the differences in institutional culture across institutions and the importance of a president's internal relationships, notably those with faculty and with the chair and other key members of the board of governors. This issue is discussed further in chapter 11, on institutional governance.

PRESIDENTIAL COMPENSATION

In 1996, at the same time as a similar initiative was undertaken in British Columbia, Ontario premier Mike Harris introduced a bill requiring mandatory public disclosure of all public sector salaries over $100,000.[16] This information was to be published at the beginning of April each year, based on the taxable income awarded in the preceding calendar year. The ostensible purpose was to put pressure on institutions to limit their payrolls during difficult economic times, but the move seems to have had exactly the opposite impact.

In Ontario, when the official salaries of university presidents first became known in 1996, the top wage earner was Lorna Marsden at Wilfrid Laurier University, one of the smallest institutions in the province. For the first time, official presidential compensation data were publicly available for all to see. The reaction of the province's independent university boards was swift. Presidential salaries and other benefits escalated quickly, partly as a result of representation from incumbent presidents, but also as a result of board compensation committees viewing the comparative level of presidential compensation as a reflection on their institution's status and its ability to attract the best candidates.

More recently, in response to stakeholder and media pressures for accountability, there has been public disclosure of presidential contracts, including such details as travel allowances, additional pension provisions, post-presidential leaves, and other benefits. Such disclosure has further raised the profile of the issue, especially in relation to similar actions in the private sector. There is a fine line between offering a competitive compensation package to ensure that one's institution attracts the best possible candidates and offering salaries and benefits that are seen as excessive to the extent that they undermine the integrity of the incumbent, whose position is so dependent upon moral authority.

One often controversial aspect common to most presidential contracts is the post-presidency administrative leave. This arrangement mirrors the standard practice of awarding deans and academic vice-presidents a sabbatical leave after their administrative term to give them the opportunity to catch up on their discipline and research before returning to the faculty ranks. While these leaves are almost always negotiated as part of presidential compensation at the original time of hiring and are well understood throughout academia, the practice has generated strong interest in the popular press, given the recent combination of much higher salaries and full disclosure of such payouts on an annual basis. Most post-presidency administrative leaves are based on two months leave at full pay for every year of service. If they are paid out as a lump sum at the end of a presidential term, the amount usually ensures that the departing president is the highest-paid public servant in his or her community that year. On the other hand, if the leave is paid out on a monthly basis for up to two years, the public may well wonder why a long-departed president is still receiving such a high level of compensation so long after the job is finished.

On balance, however, with executive compensation now in the public domain, new presidents have a much stronger bargaining position than their predecessors. A related issue, familiar to those in human resources, is that an incumbent, previously happy with his or her compensation, can suddenly feel underappreciated when it becomes public that others in comparable or lesser positions are earning more money. While it is probably true that most candidates are not attracted to the job for financial reasons (as compared to such factors as the prestige of the institution or the opportunity to make a real difference), compensation can be an important factor in a final decision or in a choice between competing institutions.

That there has been a significant change in presidential compensation since public disclosure first came into effect in most provinces is indisputable. In an article in the *Calgary Herald* about the latest salary figures for 2007, Janice Tibbetts notes that the presidents of the largest universities were making well over $400,000 a year, "more than double the pay that would have been considered generous a decade ago."[17] There has been a similar, if lesser, impact on salaries for vice-presidents, deans, campus principals, research chairs, and other competitive positions, although insufficient to prevent a growing gap between, say, presidential and vice-presidential salaries, which can be a serious issue on some campuses.

University presidents are paid considerably more than most others in the public sector, with the exception of the heads of a few crown corporations and the larger hospitals. There is a sizable gap between the salaries of university presidents and deputy ministers, the latter making at least a third less in most cases.[18] While politicians are naturally concerned about escalating salaries in difficult financial times, they have more direct control over public service salaries than they do over universities, which are governed by autonomous boards.[19]

In general, there has been widespread board support for the substantial presidential salary increases of recent years. It has been recognized, for example, that university presidents were probably underpaid when the British Columbia and Ontario legislation came in. There is some evidence, however, of a backlash against the rapid escalation, especially at a time of national fiscal crisis when cuts are made to other parts of the university budget while tuition fees continue to escalate. Faculty and student groups are increasingly vocal in their criticism of the compensation levels of the senior executive team, and boards are paying a lot more attention to the details. While on a completely different scale, the prevailing mood may also be affected by public reaction to the most publicized private sector cases of chief executive officers receiving millions in compensation even where their company has performed very poorly.

The very nature of a university presidency, especially in the Canadian context, makes the incumbent more dependent upon public, especially faculty, opinion than is the case in the private sector or even in other institutions in the public sector. At a time of shrinking resources, it is difficult for a president or a board to justify large salary increases, and it is sometimes the president who takes the lead in recognizing this. For example, in response to major challenges in overcoming operational deficits, Heather Munroe-Blum at McGill introduced voluntary 3 per cent cuts for members of the senior administration, including deans, in March of 2009, and Alastair Summerlee and his colleagues at Guelph took a salary freeze for 2009/10. While these actions may or may not have an impact on faculty and staff attitudes, they do lend moral authority to the senior team that otherwise might be undermined by executive increases at such sensitive times.

There are those who strongly defend current salaries and even believe that they should be significantly higher. David Johnston, an outstanding leader of both McGill and Waterloo, has a particularly interesting take on this. He contrasts his work as a member of compensation committees in the corporate sector with his review of the performance of his own vice-presidents and deans:

My view is that we still under-invest in our public education at all levels ... Look at the scandal on Wall Street with the excessive compensation, not simply with the folks doing derivatives. I sit on three compensation committees on boards, and I always have to add one or two zeros in comparison with what happens on campus.

When I meet with our Senior Officers Evaluation Committee, it's a question of whether we pay a dean $160,000 or $170,000. And the next day, at the corporate level, the discussion is whether it is $5.5 or $7 million in the package for the number four or five person in the corporation when the reality is that the people I'm dealing with at the corporate board are often less talented and less effective than the professors we employ.

Johnston does not advocate paying faculty ten times their salaries but believes that we still under-invest in public education and should pay more for meritorious performance at all levels, from elementary to university. On balance, it is difficult to disagree, especially at a time when public education in general and universities in particular are seen as so critical to economic and social success in the knowledge economy. It follows that boards will continue to compete for the best presidential candidates and that salaries will continue to escalate in the long term, even if they are more responsive to the politics of the most recent fiscal difficulties than has been the case for some time.

Peter George, who led all Canadian university presidents with a salary of more than $500,000 in 2009, believes that the tide may be turning on executive compensation: "I think the pendulum is swinging back on presidential salaries. But it is very hard to change it – when they hire a president to replace me, my salary will be the standard and it will be very hard to ratchet it back. They might say they want to hire someone who loves the academy and that the market doesn't matter, but they have to hire on the basis of a market of competing lovers of the academy. I don't know how we get to a happy medium on this."

In conclusion, while the search processes have been sharpened considerably in recent years and no one hires at the presidential level without careful reference checking, there is no guarantee that a new appointee will perform at expected levels. Some individuals, like those interviewed for this book, stand out as excellent performers, but others fall short of even their own expectations. Most are in between – they do a credible job, are tireless promoters of their institution, and make the tough decisions that only the president can.

I have had the privilege of knowing almost all of the two hundred individuals who have served as a president of a Canadian university over the past three decades. There is no mould, no prototype, no stereotypical university president. Some are superb academics who have been unable to resist the pressure of their peers to take on increasingly demanding administrative jobs. Others are born leaders or excellent administrators, people who take great pleasure in the success of others. Whatever their differences, they are almost universally people who care deeply about higher education, about their country, and about its future.

PART TWO
Academic Leadership and Organizational Culture

3

Organizational Culture and the University

While none of the rich and growing literature, primarily American, around organizational leadership is yet definitive or conclusive, the most elusive studies of all concern the leadership of colleges and universities. Leadership studies are central to the management of a private sector organization, but efforts to apply them to universities have had to wrestle first with such prior questions as, What are the goals of a university and who should be responsible for their realization? However optimistic or cynical the approach, the results are inevitably the same – universities are among the most difficult of all organizations to lead.

Leadership is about change, and any change strategy must take full account of the culture of the organization. As Schein has shown, an organization's culture is deeply embedded in the shared tacit assumptions that underlie the way the organization functions, and the effective change agent must go beyond the artifacts and espoused values to understand these underlying (and often hidden) assumptions that so influence the way its members behave.[1]

According to Bergquist, an organizational culture exists, not for its own sake, but to provide a context conducive to the achievement of the goals of the organization and its players. It influences how individuals and groups interpret issues and events and is usually invisible. It is perhaps most evident when an institution is struggling with a particularly complicated or intractable problem.[2]

Perhaps the biggest single challenge in managing a university finding a way is to work through a very strong academic culture to initiate change while respecting and supporting the traditional autonomy and independence of individual faculty members. Notwithstanding the significant changes in Western universities over the decades since the student protest movements of the late 1960s and early 1970s, the university remains one of the longest-running and least-changed institutions in our society. Ironically, while it is often at the forefront of societal change, the institution is also often associated with slowness and resistance to change. This contradiction emanates from the heart of the collegial academic culture. A university is defined first by academic freedom, the concept fundamental to the search for truth, unfettered by political, religious, or other non-rational interference in the free pursuit of knowledge. The university thus seeks not only to protect freedom of speech but to permit faculty members to teach and develop new knowledge in their own ways.[3]

Like their American counterparts, Canadian universities are products of both British and German models of higher education, the former emphasizing interdependence, collaboration, and mentorship, the latter based more on the independent researcher model.[4] However, British influences have been stronger for a longer time in Canada, and the evolution to more research intensive institutions has occurred much more recently here than in the United States.

There is a high tolerance for autonomous activity and even eccentricity in the collegial culture. With academic freedom the dominant norm, faculty design their own courses, choose their own areas of research, and pursue their interests individually or with colleagues with the same interests. For faculty to work effectively in the culture, they generally engage in the complex give-and-take of campus politics, with leadership usually emanating from the politically skilled and longer-serving faculty members.[5]

As a result of American/German influence, Canadian universities have been moving away from their British roots, which emphasized teaching and campus life, towards a stronger research culture, and this movement has had profound implications for their management. Applying Alvin Gouldner's classic definitions,[6] one might say that today's university faculty members are much more apt to be "cosmopolitans" than "locals," meaning that their loyalty is more to their discipline than to the specific institution. In an earlier era in Canada, young faculty members and their families participated actively in the university community, both intellectually and socially. Their primary loyalty was to the institution, and the emphasis was on teaching and getting to know students both inside the classroom and beyond. Faculty matured with their institutions, as evidenced by the large number of professors who have been in their current university for thirty or more years. With the more cosmopolitan research orientation of younger faculty today and the less personal environment in larger and more complex organizations, academics entering a university are less likely to spend their entire career in a single institution.

This trend has clear implications for management. It reinforces the independence of individual faculty members and strengthens their mobility, shifting onto the administration the onus of demonstrating why a professor should stay at the particular university. If the classic definition of university management was "herding cats," it is even more the case today than it was in an earlier era when institutional loyalty among faculty was significantly greater and the institutional environment was smaller and more personal.

THE SIX CULTURES OF UNIVERSITIES

Were the modern university to be only about managing through the collegial culture, university leadership would be a much simpler affair, both to conduct and to analyse, hearkening back to the pre-1960s era when universities were smaller, less visible, and less complex organizations. In the revised edition of Bergquist's notable *Four Cultures of the Academy* (1992)[7], Bergquist and Pawlak (2008) have increased the number of campus cultures from four to six – the collegial, managerial, developmental, and advocacy (previously "negotiating") cultures, from the first edition, and the virtual and tangible cultures, from the second.[8] Knowledge of each of these cultures and understanding the way they are weighted and interact in a given institution are useful keys to successful institutional leadership.

The Collegial Culture

As already noted, the collegial culture is the foundational and still predominant culture of the university. According to Bergquist and Pawlak, it is a culture

> that finds meaning primarily in the disciplines represented by the faculty in the institution; that values faculty research and scholarship and the quasi-political governance processes of faculty; that holds assumptions about the dominance of rationality in the institution; and that conceives of the institution's enterprise as

the generation, interpretation and dissemination of knowledge and as the development of specific values and qualities of character among young men and women who are the future leaders of our society.[9]

Somewhat ironically, given that faculty are often portrayed as independent entrepreneurs loosely connected to the institution, the collegial culture emphasizes consensus building, collaboration, and shared forms of governance. It is manifested in the participatory nature of decision making through peer reviews and such bodies as departmental councils and senates. In this environment, the president needs academic credibility, excellent listening skills, and the ability to function effectively as a senior colleague in a fairly tight organization. This model is most prevalent in smaller universities, especially long-established ones with an emphasis on teaching.[10]

The collegial culture is also associated with the difficulties of academic politics, long memories, and resistance to change. It is often blamed for universities' lack of responsiveness to opportunities and the very long gestation periods for new academic programs. Most academics are familiar with a quote first attributed to W.S. Sayre: "[T]he politics of the university are so intense because the stakes are so low."[11] The culture has been fostered, in part, by the relative isolation of the ivory tower, an isolation that allows academics to pursue their scholarly interests without external interference and that is directly associated with the longevity and relative stability of the university organization. It is only in recent decades that this long-standing collegial model has been seriously challenged and compromised in most institutions.

The Managerial Culture

As defined by Bergquist and Pawlak, the managerial culture is one

that finds meaning primarily in the organization, implementation, and evaluation of work that is directed towards specified goals and purposes; that values fiscal responsibility and effective supervisory skills; that holds assumptions about the capacity of the institution to define and measure its goals and objectives clearly; and that conceives of the institution's enterprise as the inculcation of specific knowledge, skills, and attitudes in students so that they might become successful and responsible citizens.[12]

The origins of the managerial culture were in the natural limitations of the collegial culture, which tends to proceed very well until collegiality breaks down in the face of difficult decisions. This is particularly the case where difficult financial choices are inevitable.

I learned this early in my career when serving at Dawson College as vice-president, academic,[13] in the late 1970s. Dawson was the first English-language CEGEP,[14] and it prided itself on its strong sense of community, diversity, and communal decision making. By the time I arrived in 1973, it had already grown to over 7,000 students spread across a dozen facilities and three major campuses in the western, central, and eastern regions of Montreal. Following the college's very strong culture of consultation and collaborative decision making, the department heads in the faculty of arts at the east-end Lafontaine Campus were wrestling with how to cope with major budget cuts in a process that would inevitably produce winners and losers among the various units. After weeks of lengthy and often heated meetings, the dean of arts, who had always been a great champion of the faculty and its consensus model of decision making, came to me somewhat sheepishly to report that the department heads, after much debate, had finally come up with a solution. They unanimously agreed that I should decide what was to be done!

I was initially astounded by this decision but soon realized that it was the only way they could preserve their vaunted collegiality. This way, the department heads could not be held accountable. Even if they agreed with my decisions, they would not have to own them and their collegiality would be preserved. Of course, because they had an excellent dean, she quietly suggested where the budget cuts should be made. I naturally followed her advice, and the subsequent protests were more muted than they would otherwise have been.

The managerial culture is a natural outgrowth of the rising public profile of universities in Western society and the concomitant pressures for fiscal responsibility and accountability. According to Cohen and March, it is understandable why there is so much concern about this culture in academia when the overall goals of the institution are usually so general and even vague.[15] With the increasing size and complexity of universities in recent years, this concern has grown, especially as more and more of the larger institutions seek presidents with corporate leadership styles more akin to those of a chief executive officer than to those of the more traditional academic leader of previous generations.

This culture has also been enhanced by more frequent government interventions into the university sphere, many of them requiring significant responses to various societal needs. Good examples of intrusive legislation that has had a strong and direct impact on the activities of a university would be legislation for equity in employment and in the treatment of visible minorities and people with physical disabilities. For instance, the recommendations of Judge Rosalie Abella's Royal Commission on Equality in Employment were given considerable teeth by the Federal Contractors Program, which was initiated in 1986.[16] As a condition for bidding on large federal contracts, universities, among others, had to certify in writing their formal commitment to employment equity.

The 2001 and 2005 Ontarians with Disabilities Acts are quite intrusive in their formal requirement that many public sector institutions, including universities, submit written accessibility plans.[17] While these pieces of legislation were written in recognition of the need to move past platitudes to more formal action, they were not accompanied by additional funding for the institutions required to comply with their stipulations. Administrators quickly discovered that compliance with the legislation necessitated significant additional staffing and office costs and expensive renovations to public sector facilities. This forced senior managers to redeploy resources in ways that were not always popular on campuses.

Another manifestation of the growth of the managerial culture has been the significant increase in administrative positions in universities over the past few decades. Notable examples are the proliferation of vice-presidencies for such areas as research, advancement and development, and even government relations; other positions follow naturally from the development of such diverse areas as research support, employment equity, human rights, campus security, and special needs.

The rise of the managerial culture, however, has only compromised, not supplanted, the collegial culture. Perhaps this is best exemplified by the fact that the overwhelming majority of presidents still come from within the academic ranks and, as described earlier, many still prefer an academic leadership model to that of chief executive officer.

The Developmental Culture

The third culture evident in today's university has been termed "developmental" by Bergquist and Pawlak. It is supposed to build rational analysis and planning onto the collegial framework and, in the process, avoid political infighting.[18] The developmental culture is one that

> finds meaning primarily in the creation of programs and activities furthering the personal and professional growth of all members of the higher education community; that values personal openness and service to others as well as systematic institutional research and curricular planning; that holds assumptions about the inherent desire of all men and women to attain their own personal maturation, while helping others in the institution become more mature; and that conceives of the institution's enterprise as the encouragement of potential for cognitive, affective, and behavioral maturation among all students, faculty, administrators and staff.[19]

The developmental culture perpetuates the notion of "leader as server," influencing, suggesting, and informing rather than directing. While developmental leaders are sometimes perceived as idealistic and ineffective,[20] my interviews with some of Canada's most successful presidents suggest that they share such characteristics of this culture as a strong service orientation, a focus on institutional research, and a preference for "leading from behind."[21] As well, in specific instances, presidents have been brought in as "healers" to resolve conflict between the managerial and collegial cultures and between personal and organizational well-being, hallmarks of the developmental culture as originally described by Bergquist.[22] At the same time, the once-vaunted notion of "faculty development" has never really lived up to expectations, and the culture is probably not as strong in most universities as are the other five identified.

The Advocacy Culture

Bergquist and Pawlak's fourth culture is the advocacy (previously "negotiating") culture, centred on the notion that conflicts can be resolved only through confrontation and fair bargaining. It is a culture that finds meaning primarily in the establishment of equitable and egalitarian policies and procedures for the distribution of resources and benefits in the institution; that values confrontation and fair bargaining among constituencies, primarily management and faculty or staff, who have vested interests that are inherently in opposition; that holds assumptions about the ultimate role of power and the frequent need for outside mediation in a viable academic institution; and that conceives of the institution's enterprise as either the undesirable promulgation of existing (and often repressive) social attitudes and structures or the establishment of new and more liberating social attitudes and structures.[23]

Like the bureaucracy, the negotiating culture seeks the equal treatment of all. This outlook clashes directly with the collegial notion of recognizing individual achievement and excellence.[24] Like the managerial culture to which it is the response, the negotiating culture assumes that all things are negotiable, whereas the collegial and developmental cultures view academic freedom, for example, as non-negotiable.[25] It is interesting to note that, among the presidents interviewed for this book, those least comfortable with this culture were those who most strongly endorsed traditional models of academic leadership in the university.

The negotiating culture increases the influence of the board of governors by forcing it to determine how far it is prepared to go to meet faculty demands – that is, to take positions that are far clearer and often more confrontational than those that might be considered or adopted in a traditional collegial organization.[26]

The culture is very strong in Canadian universities, the vast majority of which now have unionized faculty. Its influence is particularly evident at times of collective bargaining or when personnel issues arise over the granting of tenure, performance evaluation, or cases of dismissal. However positive faculty/management relations may be in a given institution, they can never be taken for granted and are an important part of the cultural mix on Canadian university campuses.

The Virtual Culture

The virtual culture emanates from cultural and technological developments since the early 1990s. With its counterpart, the tangible culture, it is one of the new cultures identified in the revised version (2008) of Bergquist's original book (1992). It is a culture

> that finds meaning by answering the knowledge generation and dissemination capacity of the postmodern world; that values the global perspective of open, shared, responsive educational systems; that holds assumptions about its ability to make sense of the fragmentation and ambiguity that exists in the postmodern world; and that conceives of the institution's enterprise as linking its educational resources to global and technological resources, thus broadening the global learning network.[27]

The impact of the virtual culture has been stronger among American institutions, where the greater diversity, funding, and faith in technology of the US system have resulted in investment in sophisticated communications technologies at levels well beyond comparable institutions in Canada. Even Athabasca University, which has legitimate claims to being Canada's "open university," is a very small operation compared to such mega-distance-learning institutions as the University of Maryland University College and the private University of Phoenix, which serve students in the hundreds of thousands around the world. Nevertheless, almost every Canadian university offers some of its programs and services online, and the great majority of students who are taking one or more courses at a distance are campus based. While many of the initiatives in this field were inspired by the UK Open University and its focus on nontraditional and adult learners, distance learning has become part of the mainstream in most universities, as the convenience and flexibility of modern communication technologies cater to the needs of all learners.[28]

Anticipating the second edition of Bergquist's book (with Pawlak) and writing in the context of open learning and distance education, Latchem and Hanna responded to his first four cultures by suggested a fifth, the entrepreneurial culture, which closely resembles the virtual. It values the ability to respond quickly to market and other opportunities, to connect with and generate support from external constituencies, and to introduce new ideas, programs, delivery mechanisms, goals, and purposes.[29]

The important issue here is not the advent of new communications technologies but the cultural changes implicit in their influence.

These include new categories of learners, more open systems, and an associated rise in consumerism whereby students expect certain levels of service for their rising tuition fees and even develop a sense of entitlement that extends to faculty evaluations of their academic work.

The Tangible Culture

The "tangible" culture has emerged at least partly in response to the virtual culture. It is one

> that finds meaning in its roots, its community, and its spiritual grounding; that values the predictability of a value-based, face-to-face education in an owned physical location; that holds assumptions about the ability of old systems and technologies being able to instill the institution's values; and that conceives of the institution's enterprise as the honoring and reintegration of learning from a local perspective.[30]

The tangible culture hearkens back to the values implicit in the residential culture of earlier institutions and is most prevalent in the longer-established, more prestigious and selective universities. It values campus life, close faculty-student contact, and a more closed centre for free inquiry, research, and scholarship. It does not apologize for elitism and can thus be seen, in many ways, as serving as an antidote against the burgeoning virtual culture of the online learning universities by promoting academic status and prestige as the tangible benefits of an education at one of the better-known universities.

These six cultures are sufficiently established and different from those of most other organizations that they pose serious challenges to a university leader recruited from outside the academy, and this is why such people are so rarely appointed president of a Canadian university. Even in cases where they are recruited from politics or government, as in the recent cases of Lloyd Axworthy at Winnipeg, Alan Rock at Ottawa, and Dominique Giroux at Laurentian, the individuals have all had connections to academia in various ways and are not as foreign to the culture as would be someone whose experience was solely in the private or non-academic public sector.

DIFFERENT APPROACHES TO LEADERSHIP IN THE
UNIVERSITY CONTEXT

Each of the university cultures is represented to some degree or other on all Canadian university campuses, but the mix in a given institution will go a long way to determining its particular culture and, hence, the kind of person best suited to be its leader. While knowledge of these dimensions is central to effective management, the key concern is to determine their mix and integration in a given institution. One or more of the cultures will usually be predominant. For example, the collegial and tangible cultures are most apt to flourish in smaller and more elitist liberal arts institutions where the values coalesce around excellence in scholarship and teaching. The managerial and negotiating cultures are most evident in institutions that face critical issues of institutional identity, enrolment, and financing.

It is also helpful to recognize the polarities between the individual cultures identified by Bergquist and Pawlak.[31] The collegial and developmental cultures have many similarities but differ in their approach to disciplinarity, with the former emphasizing autonomy and the latter collaboration and interdisciplinarity. The managerial and advocacy tend to have disputes over their respective powers, while the tangible is a reaction to the openness of the virtual culture.

The quote from Ponder and McCauley in the preface to this volume reflects the ongoing conflicts between the collegial and managerial cultures, with the concomitant challenges to university leadership. Cohen and March reinforce these dichotomies and describe the elusiveness of the path through the cultural maze, citing contradictions across three predominant university orientations: "The logic of bureaucracy is the specification of objectives and technology. The logic of democracy is the organization of consent. The logic of collective bargaining is the discipline of conflict. The realities of higher education seem to be resistant to all three logics."[32]

Birnbaum addresses differences in the management of different university cultures by suggesting four frameworks for academic leadership – the collegial, the bureaucratic, the political, and the anarchical.[33] He sets these out as ideal types, with an illustrative prototype institution for each.

The *collegial institution* represents sharing power and group values in a community of equals.[34] An important condition for its maintenance is that it remain comparatively small. This institution is essentially self-governing, with a strong dependence on close personal relations and social history. It emphasizes thoroughness, deliberation, and caution in deriving findings or conclusions, all of which conspire to make its decision-making processes slow and ponderous. In the ideal-type institution Birnbaum describes, the president has considerable authority but only to the extent that he or she continues to support, and be seen as an effective player in, the prevailing collegial culture.

> Persons in leadership positions in collegial systems are expected to influence without coercion, to direct without sanctions, and to control without inducing alienation. They must provide benefits that other participants see as a fair exchange for yielding some degree of their autonomy. Their selection as leaders provides them significant leverage to influence their communities, their new status has been legitimated by the participation of their constituencies, and these constituents have certified, at least initially, both their competence and their commitment to group values.[35]

Birnbaum's *bureaucratic institution* exhibits all the dimensions of the classic Weberian bureaucracy – formal hierarchy and division of labour, impersonality and formal rules for the equal treatment of all. It is a rational organization with the president at the apex of the pyramid,[36] and it is better suited to administrative than to academic leadership. A president will fare best if he or she is seen as being fair and equitable in decision making.[37]

The *political institution* described by Birnbaum epitomizes the advocacy culture set out by Bergquist and Pawlak. Everything is negotiated among the various factions and special interest groups. The president acts as a political leader most of the time, paying more attention to power groups and personal concerns than institutional research. The leader's success will depend considerably on his or her knowledge of and appreciation for the institution's history, values, and key players.[38]

The fourth of Birnbaum's institutional typologies, the *anarchical*, closely resembles the perspective of Cohen and March (see section following). Institutional objectives and processes are vague and uncertain and presidential leadership is problematic, although Birnbaum's view is apparently somewhat more optimistic than Cohen and March's: "But while it is true that other organizational constituencies exercise influence that can prevent a president from achieving certain objectives, it is also true that ... on most campuses, most of the time, the president is the single most influential person. Presidents therefore can often make a difference, even though perhaps not to the extent that they themselves are likely to believe."[39]

The implication of the work of Bergquist and Pawlak, Birnbaum, and others is that a president needs to be very familiar with the prevailing academic cultures in his or her institution in order to determine how the institution can be most effectively led. This reinforces the notion that institutional "fit" is the key component of presidential effectiveness. As one might expect, there is considerable disagreement on this complex matter in the literature, with opinions ranging from the pessimistic to the more positive.

THE UNIVERSITY AS ORGANIZED ANARCHY

On the more pessimistic and even cynical side, perhaps the best-known publication in this respect is that of Cohen and March (1986),[40] who summarize their own work as follows: "Against a background of visions of leadership that tend to be rather more heroic, the book portrays colleges[41] as organized anarchies and their leadership as constrained by ambiguities of objectives, technologies and experience."[42] At the same time, they argue that while these ambiguities undermine conventional views of leaders, they do not undermine leadership itself.[43] Their analysis sets the stage for all further efforts to define leadership in the peculiar institution that is a university. What is it about a university that renders it different from and perhaps more difficult to lead than most other organizations?

To answer this question, one might begin by asking what it is about some organizations that makes them easier to lead than other organizations,[44] suggesting the following sorts of profiles:

1 The organization has a clear and measureable set of objectives against which its leadership can be evaluated. Examples include making a profit, increasing market share, raising the value of the stock, winning a sports championship, or providing consistent good and reliable service (such as for a dry-cleaning business).
2 The employees of the organization all share in these objectives and reap direct benefit from their realization. Their primary

loyalty is to the organization itself because they benefit directly from its success.

3 Organizational structures are simple and direct, with clear reporting lines and role differentiation closely related to the achievement of institutional objectives. There is little role ambiguity.

4 The authority and accountability of the leader(s) are clearly defined and understood by everyone.

5 The culture within the institution is entirely consistent with its purposes and objectives and is common to all employees whether executive or staff.

6 The institution's performance criteria are clear and easily measured – it is very apparent how it is doing at any given moment.

A university, however, shares none of these characteristics. Instead:

1 It has a multiplicity of purposes that are not necessarily mutually consistent, and even more problematically, there is ambiguity of purpose.

2 The institution is an assemblage of individual entrepreneurs whose loyalty is first to their own discipline and only secondarily to the institution. An individual's success may or may not be tied to that of the institution.

3 Universities are large and complex bureaucracies where process is as important as product and roles, at least on the academic side, are in many ways self-defined and somewhat independent of the overall institutional objectives.

4 The authority of the president and senior executive team is both acknowledged and challenged by the core professional staff, and it is most contentious where it conflicts with the professional authority of faculty.

5 The culture within the institution is multi-faceted, with a clear division between the academic and administrative sides.

6 The quest for clear performance criteria for universities has been prominent in recent years but has proven both elusive and at least in some cases potentially damaging to the institution's ultimate performance in that there are so many variables that the process becomes a "make work" exercise with diluted ultimate value.

All of these factors render institutional leadership complex and problematic, prompting Cohen and March to define a university as

an "organized anarchy," one characterized by three general properties in particular:[45]

1 Problematic goals – the institution has a variety of inconsistent
  and ill-defined preferences, many of which are discovered through
  action more often than they provide direction.
2 Unclear technology – the institution does not understand its
  own processes, which tend to be trial-and-error procedures
  emanating from past experience, imitation, and invention from
  necessity.
3 Fluid participation – the boundaries of the organization seem
  uncertain and changing as participants get involved to varying
  degrees according to the issue at hand.

These properties define an organized anarchy for Cohen and March,
who say this of the university: "It does not know what it is doing.
Its goals are either vague or in dispute. Its technology is familiar
but not understood. Its major participants wander in and out of the
organization. These factors do not make a university a bad organization or a disorganized one; but they do make it a problem to
describe, understand and lead."[46]

Cohen and March's analysis has considerable appeal for many
modern presidents struggling with the challenges and contradictions of academic politics. In its use of humour and in its depic-
tion of situations familiar to those trying to provide leadership and
change in highly politicized institutions, it has much the same time-
less appeal as the classic *Microcosmographia Academica: Being a
Guide for the Young Academic Politician*, written by F.M. Cornford at Cambridge in 1908,[47] or the British satirical television series
Yes Minister.[48] While depicting an institution that seems dysfunctional in many ways, each of the models essentially accepts the conflicts and complexities of organizational life and seeks to provide
guidance to those who need to understand and work through the
resultant politics. It is interesting that, notwithstanding the glaring weaknesses these three expose in their respective organizations,
none of them suggests changing them. In the complexity and even
in the dysfunction, there is a kind of love and appreciation for the
unique culture represented in each case. Such is the enduring history
of the respective institutions – universities and the English parliamentary system.

THE UNIVERSITY AS A LEARNING ORGANIZATION

Writing in the English context, Chris Duke takes a more optimistic view of university leadership. Only slightly ironically, he applies the ideas of Peter Senge to the university,[49] seeing its overriding goal as the development of a "successful, reflective and self-aware participatory learning organization."[50] The key to the leadership of such an institution is dramatically different from that defined more conventionally: "The learning organization is in fact far more responsive and swift-footed through effective, empowering delegation, than a centralized, tightly managed and controlled institution."[51] Duke advocates a less intrusive management style, one that leads from behind. He does not see this approach as *laissez-faire* but recognizes that it demands tougher self-discipline than controlling, directive management does. He envisions leaders who resist the pressures for relevance that threaten to rob universities of their essence but concedes that leaders "must live with inordinately high levels of role ambiguity and embrace paradoxical contradictions."[52]

Crowley presents perhaps the most complete overview of the American academic presidency, tracing it back historically and surveying not only the sociological literature but even depictions of the role in novels.[53] He quotes Balderston, who considered the job fascinating but only because it was nearly impossible to do it,[54] and Bennis, who recognized that at a time when they were never held in such low regard (during the Vietnam era), leaders were needed more than ever.[55]

TRANSACTIONAL AND TRANSFORMATIONAL LEADERSHIP

For the purposes of this book, the focus here is on the results obtained by university leaders rather than on the characteristics of individual leaders. Perhaps Burns developed the most useful concept in this regard: "that leadership is nothing if it is not linked to collective purpose; that the effectiveness of leaders must be judged not by their press clippings but by actual social change measured by intent and by the satisfaction of human needs and expectations."[56] From this perspective, Burns developed two types of leadership: the transactional and the transforming.[57]

Transactional leadership involves the exchange of favours between leaders and followers, and this is the predominant mode in most organizations. Transformational leadership is more complex but also more potent. It involves "a relationship of mutual stimulation and elevation that converts followers into leaders and may convert leaders into moral agents ... Moral leadership emerges from, and always returns to, the fundamental wants and needs, aspirations, and values of the followers."[58]

Bass and Riggio define transformational leaders as "those who stimulate and inspire followers to both achieve extraordinary outcomes and, in the process, develop their own leadership capacity."[59] They set out four core components of such leadership:[60]

1 Idealized influence – serving as role models for their followers
2 Inspirational motivation – motivating and inspiring by providing meaning and challenge for the followers' work
3 Intellectual stimulation – questioning assumptions, reframing problems and approaching old situations in new ways to stimulate their followers to be innovative and creative
4 Individual consideration – paying special attention to an individual's needs for achievement and growth by acting as coach/mentor

While these components of leadership can readily be identified in many university settings, including some of those described by the interviewees in this book, very few presidents, in Canada at least, would be described or would describe themselves as transformational leaders. According to Crowley,[61] while a few writers, such as Cameron and Ulrich, see transformational leadership as having been essential to meet the dramatically altered conditions for universities in the 1980s, the majority are less convinced, seeing transactional leadership as better suited to most campuses. They view the president as a facilitative rather than directive leader, taking full account of the cultural and symbolic components of leadership. This more modest conception of the president's role is more consistent with the previously cited views of Cohen and March and is especially relevant to Canada, where there is probably more suspicion of or hesitancy about giving too much power to leaders than there is in the United States.

Crowley cites Birnbaum's several reasons for the near impossibility of presidential leadership in a university.[62] These include the many constraints on presidential discretion, the unique characteristics of academic organizations, the problem of assessing effectiveness when the goals are so diffuse, and the sundry and conflicting limitations on the presidential role. After a thorough examination of the literature on the role of the academic president, Crowley concludes: "The president's job is necessary and important. It is illusory and impossible. It is transactional, transformational, managerial, marginal. It can be heroic. Heroism cannot prevail. Individuals can make a difference. Any difference will be minimal given the constraints and complexities, the ambiguities and uncertainties, of the university environment."[63]

He goes on to describe a series of models and typologies of the presidency, covering everything from pope, captain, statesman/politician to entrepreneur and even cybernetic administrator. In such a complex and ambiguous atmosphere, it is not surprising that many different leadership approaches are represented in our universities. As cited by Crowley,[64] McGill organizational theorists Frances Westley and Henry Mintzberg provide a useful typology of five types of visionary leadership:

1 The creator, who is driven by a single idea and has the single-minded need to realize it
2 The proselytizer, who has the foresight and imagination to build on the ideas of others
3 The idealist, a perfectionist whose vision must crystallize the dreams of a constituency
4 The *bricoleur*, a strategist, builder, and promoter who deals well with people and infuses the organization with intense personal effect and evocative symbolism
5 The diviner, an original thinker who focuses more on process than product and is a builder of organizations

While these typologies suit different personality types, they are also defined in part by the particular circumstances of the institution in question. And, as in politics, timing is everything. As typologies, they seldom exist in a pure form but do exist in combination for a given leader. The University of Windsor I inherited in 1998 needed talents closer to those of the *bricoleur* to build up its confidence and define clearer directions, whereas the creator might be more appropriate for a brand new institution like the University of Ontario Institute of Technology (UOIT) or for a Queen's or McGill where the focus is strictly on raising standards.

The truth of the matter is that, notwithstanding what is said in the advertisements for new presidents, most institutions most of the time want transactional, not transformative, leadership. There are several possible exceptions to this, although each depends both upon the particular institutional culture at the time and the personality, skills, and experience of the president.

1 *An institution in crisis* – because of plummeting enrolments, an undermining of the institution's academic reputation, major fiscal problems, or deteriorating labour relations (the four often go together). This situation calls for an interventionist leadership whereby the president may make significant management changes, take sometimes dramatic fiscal action, and work to build internal confidence and pride in the institution as it overcomes the components of its particular crisis. Rick Van Loon is often cited as a leader who used what was widely seen as a crisis at Carleton to transform the university's admissions standards and hence its academic reputation.

2 *An institution that takes on a new mission or mandate.* There are many recent examples in Canada of institutions that have taken on significant new roles (Ryerson evolved from a polytechnic to full university status, Mount Royal and Kwantlen from a college to university status, UOIT or Royal Roads to a new kind of university). These new missions require leadership that is fully cognizant of the challenges of the implicit cultural changes but that also has the confidence and skill to negotiate the tricky path between reaffirming all that is positive about the institutional culture and having the courage to change aspects of it.

3 *An institution that is taken to a whole new level.* In such cases, the president, rather than presiding over a comfortable status quo, champions a further level of attainment and does everything possible to transform the university in that way. This might involve achieving a higher rating in competitive tables, an exponential

change in research monies and awards, or significantly raising entrance averages and/or student enrolment.

It is interesting to note that while Bass and Riggio envision transformational leadership as being more effective than transactional in all kinds of organizations, when they address the issue of university leadership, they refer to transformational leadership as needed in a financial crisis. They compare two presidents, one transactional and one transformational, and conclude that the latter, who provided "interpretation, meaning, structure, and implications for the future" to faculty, was more effective than the other president, who concentrated on financial analyses. They go on to reinforce the point that transformational leadership in a university environment is needed primarily in times of crisis by referring to a study by Katz that finds transactional leadership to be all that is needed when an issue does not involve conflict.[65]

While the three exceptions outlined above may invite transformational leadership, it can be argued that the respective challenges can be met, and perhaps met even more effectively, through less dramatic transactional leadership. Many presidents may think of themselves as having been transformational leaders who have left a large legacy, but in most cases, at least in Canada, their contributions have been transactional, incremental, and not always permanent, given the tendency for their successors to change things substantially. Jim Downey, for one, does not see himself as a visionary or transformational leader.

> I believe that visions in universities are harvested, not manufactured. Except perhaps in a crisis, you must know the institution and know it well, know its culture, what its capabilities are, before you start deciding you want to do this or that ... I figured if I could be an effective administrator, if I could be an effective transactional leader, any transformation the place was capable of would probably happen naturally and I would discover it along with everybody else.

So, transactional leadership should not be seen in negative terms. As Peter George says, a steady and strong hand on the tiller can produce a first-class, stable institution where faculty and staff like to work and students like to study and participate. This sounds quite a bit like "peace, order and good government"!

THE CULTURE OF THE LOCAL INSTITUTION

However, it is not nearly enough for an incoming president to be well versed in the tacit assumptions of the academic culture described above. Even in a university culture as homogeneous as Canada's, it is dangerous for new presidents, the vast majority of whom come from outside the institution, to assume that they understand the cultural mix on a given campus. Indeed, learning the new culture quickly enough to capitalize on his or her position as a newcomer is one of the first and greatest challenges for an externally appointed president.

The issue is not only that each institution has its own particular mix of the six cultures defined by Bergquist and Pawlak, but also that the institution's history, both recent and distant, and the particular mix of individuals and leaders on campus contribute to a unique culture that may or may not be one to which the new leader can readily adjust. Schein notes that an organizational culture is a product of an institution's history, the values and beliefs of its founders and key leaders, and the degree to which it has been successful: "Culture is the sum total of all the shared, taken-for-granted assumptions that a group has learned throughout its history. It is the residue of success."[66]

When I was president of the University of Windsor, one of my biggest challenges was to get the institution to celebrate more, to recognize its very real strengths, and to believe in itself in the face of a low standing in a number of reputational surveys. Queen's was at the opposite end of the latter spectrum and therefore, I used to think, a much easier place to lead and manage. My opinion changed one day at an AUCC meeting when I jokingly chided Queen's principal, Bill Leggett, about how easy it must be to lead such a highly valued institution. He grabbed my arm and led me out of the seminar room we had just entered to the cafeteria, where he gave me a mini-lecture on how difficult it is to change the culture at as well established an institution as Queen's.

If there has been any doubt about the significant differences in individual campus cultures, it has surely been dispelled by several recent examples of presidents successfully completing one or two terms in one university and then running into conflict during and truncating their first terms at a second Canadian institution. While such incidents can sometimes be explained by personality conflicts, notably with the board chair, most cases are not that simple and may even be a product of an institutional culture that is relatively foreign to the appointee. The following are some of the factors that define a particular local culture in an institution:

- Memories of past presidents, strong or weak, and the consequent expectations for the most recent appointee[67]
- The recent history of the board of governors and the extent to which it has been involved in the management of the institution
- The style and interests of the board chair and whether or not he or she understands the difference between management and governance
- The profile and reputation of the institution
- The profile and history of labour relations in the institution
- The size and reputation of the immediate community served by the university

One influential writer gives an interesting twist to the discussion of organizational cultures. With the evolution of the "knowledge society," whereby managers are increasingly expected to manage those who possess more and more specialized knowledge, Charles Handy has predicted that private sector institutions will look increasingly like universities.[68] While this notion scared some of my corporate friends, who see the university as a sluggish bureaucracy of self-interests, the university practice of giving faculty the freedom and licence to pursue their own interests has become increasingly mirrored in today's companies. Some private enterprises have even borrowed versions of the university sabbatical leave, recognizing the importance of keeping their professional staff up to scratch in their areas of expertise. Of course, at the time of his writing (1989), Handy also recognized that universities could benefit from being more like businesses and this, too, has been a clear trend since then.[69]

In summary, the way to change the culture of a given university is first to work with it and to understand it, as opposed to confronting it from the beginning. I have observed a number of presidents getting into serious difficulty right from the start because they were too direct about wanting to change the institution and its culture. Instead of welcoming this "breath of fresh air," faculty, staff, and others reacted negatively to what was seen as the personal agenda of the new president. As Fullan and Scott note, "Many a president or dean has been run out of town for tackling directly the culture of the academy. Instead, our message is to start with the issue(s) the organization faces, refocus the agenda, use the considerable extant change knowledge, and then shape and leverage the strength of existing cultures and their leaders."[70] This observation helps explain why so few Canadian university presidents come from outside the academy and why those who publicly proclaim at the outset of their terms that they are going to change the institution in a dramatic way seldom succeed.

4

Setting the Direction: Institutional Vision and Strategic Planning

The first and greatest task of a president is to articulate the vision, champion the goals, and enunciate the objectives.

Frank Rhodes, former president of Cornell[1]

Like Frank Rhodes, many writers see the most important task of a university president as being to manage the "big picture" – to develop and communicate a mission, vision, and long-term objectives for the institution. There is a huge body of literature on strategic leadership, notably for the private sector. More than anyone else in the organization, the chief executive officer is expected to be preoccupied with the long term, to look at the strengths and weaknesses, the opportunities and threats facing the institution, and to forge an action plan that realizes the vision that emerges from the whole exercise.

Bargh et al. suggest that when the organizational context is "divergent" (goals and structures are increasingly inappropriate to the prevailing environment), the leader should challenge the status quo, and that, in contrast, when the context is "convergent," the leader should help optimize performance within existing structures and norms.[2] Universities are often on the divergent end of this spectrum, notably when they are searching for new leadership. Hence, in many cases, a university president is hired as a change agent by an organization renowned for its resistance to change.

Written in the American context of diverse institutions and cut-throat competition in some arenas, Richard Alfred's book *Managing the Big Picture in Colleges and Universities: From Tactics to Strategy* (the source of this chapter's epigraph) is one of the most comprehensive analyses of strategy in the higher education sector published to date. In his pithy foreword, Stanley Ikenberry notes that leadership and strategic planning are especially necessary in today's world of constant change, where universities are opening up to a much larger proportion of society and as their boundaries extend from local to global.[3] A key point is to differentiate tactics from strategy. Ikenberry believes that university leaders are too often seduced by short-term tactical questions (such as dysfunctional IT [information technology] systems, enrolment management challenges, budget shortfalls, and conflict resolution) that tend to crowd out the major strategic questions that will ultimately be more critical to the organization's future:[4]

> Strategic leadership is about long-term positioning, the successful execution of a multiyear strategy. Such leadership, and the strategy that drives it, evolves from the environment in which institutions find themselves, from threats and opportunities, and from a clear sense of core purpose and mission. It seeks to reposition the institution in new and fresh ways with stakeholders, it seeks differentiation not homogenization, and it seeks to thrive, not just to survive.[5]

Especially when they are appointed from outside, presidents tend to be preoccupied with assessing the strengths and weaknesses of their new institution, looking to forge changes in direction that will position it as a much stronger entity over the ensuing years. In fact, the very first significant thing presidents typically undertake is strategic planning. This poses a challenge for external appointees, who have to find an appropriate balance between acting quickly while they have maximum support for a change agenda and taking the time to learn the local culture and getting to know the key players in the institution – both critical ingredients for successful strategic planning.

The choice is a tricky one. There are many stakeholders, and some of them will move immediately to lobby the new president for their favourite project. It takes time to assess the credibility of various spokespersons and to determine how to evaluate conflicting perspectives. Even a president who has a pretty clear idea of what needs to be done has to take the time to ensure that his or her orientations and directions are seen to be in the long-term best interests of the institution and not just as the president's personal agenda. However, if the consultation period is too long, the excitement and support associated with a fresh appointment may wear off and the incumbent may be seen as indecisive or uncertain. Finding the right balance between consultation and decision making goes a long way to determining an individual's success in the job.

Hence, while most presidents agree that strategic leadership is fundamental to their role, there is significant disagreement about how this is carried out, both in the literature and in the reports of experienced practitioners. Alfred defines strategy as "a systematic way of positioning an institution with stakeholders in its environment to create value that differentiates it from competitors and leads to a sustainable advantage."[6] The emphasis here is on institutional positioning, competitive markets, and seeking specific advantage. The concept is that the leader would take the institution into new territory, forging a stronger identity and a better market position for the university, one that would benefit most or all of its stakeholders. This is very much the language of the private sector, which in itself is a challenge in the university environment.

Like Ikenberry, Alfred believes that many university leaders confuse strategy with tactics.[7] The latter are short term in orientation, addressing current problems rather than future positioning. A leader conversant with strategy would be able to answer the following question without hesitation: "In one sentence, what is your institution's unique 'signature,' and how does it differ from [that of] competitors in the minds of key stakeholders?"[8] A further determinant of how effectively an institution is poised strategically is the extent to which other key stakeholders (students, faculty, board members, alumni) are able to answer the question in the same way. Most of the presidents interviewed for this book share a healthy skepticism about the value of strategic planning. In part, this reflects the fact that they were academics long before they were administrators, and in some cases, it mirrors their personal experience.

Writing in the British context, Bargh et al. suggest that vice-chancellors' preoccupation with strategic planning is evidence of their struggles with the pressures of change and tradition: "[T]he present focus on strategic planning is really a manifestation of the wider failure to resolve the intellectual and cultural dilemmas posed by the transformations affecting the university sector in the late twentieth century. Mass higher education poses intellectual as much as managerial and organizational challenges, and so far the university world remains racked with ambivalence about its future(s). In that sense strategic planning can be seen as part of a debate about the core values which underpin higher education."

There are many examples of poor strategic planning across the university system in Canada. Especially in the 1970s and 1980s, it was easy to find so-called strategic plans for universities that were not much more than a compendium of all the wish lists on campus. As I have written elsewhere, Athabasca's long-range plan in the early 1980s was "strong on rhetoric but weak in establishing priorities or providing time-specific action plans for their realization."[9] A document that has dozens of goals and objectives is not strategic and is singularly unhelpful in providing any sort of guide to action. A plan that is not based on a clear vision and does not differentiate between alternate possibilities is not a plan at all.

Bill Leggett is not a proponent of formal strategic planning in its current state: "I had a very negative experience with strategic planning at McGill. It went on for a very long time and resulted in a great many recommendations imbedded in a very thick report. Six months later, few could remember more than a handful of the recommendations or who was responsible for what." As a result, Leggett took a different approach when he arrived at Queen's. He appointed David Turpin vice-president, academic, and told him he wanted a strategic statement of objectives and priorities no more than a dozen pages long and that he wanted it in three months. A committee of academic peers, led by Turpin, produced "The Document on Principles," which contained only four basic priorities and two or three recommendations for each. The document, which was approved by the senate by the end of Leggett's first year as principal, became the touchstone for academic decision making throughout his term of office.

Harking back to the earlier distinction between divergent and convergent institutions, Leggett concedes that there may be a role for more traditional strategic planning at younger institutions, but he sees the primary challenge for the leadership of a McGill or Queen's in terms of setting standards rather than strategic directions. In the context of those institutions, achieving significant improvements in quality through the application of clearly stated standards may be as transformational as efforts by younger institutions to establish niche positioning.

If one doesn't worry about whether the supporting exercises meet a theorist's definition of strategic planning, there is clear evidence of successful strategic leadership at the universities represented by the interviewees. Like Bill Leggett, for example, Martha Piper, Bonnie Patterson, and Dave Marshall all underlined the importance of the president having a very few key long-term priorities, always looking at the development of the university through the lens of these, and assessing institutional and his or her own performance against them.

Dr Piper used key elements of the institution's strategic plan to drive her daily management of the institution: "I'm a stickler for detail. I'm very focused. Take strategic planning. In my office, I always had a piece of paper on my in-box which stated my three or four priorities for a month or two. I would look at these at the end of every day and ask myself what I did today to advance those. You can ask anyone who worked with me, I always had these." For Professor Patterson, it was important to identify what she called the "big six" strategic directions that she felt needed to be pursued over what was initially an uncertain time period. This exercise led to a strategic directions paper for 2010 and then for 2014 in preparation for Trent's fiftieth anniversary.

Further to finding an appropriate balance between thorough consultation and rapid decision making, Paul Davenport took a somewhat different approach the second time around. As the new president of the University of Alberta in 1989, he waited three years before initiating a strategic planning process, wanting very much to understand the institution before he did. When he went to Western, he moved much more quickly, asking for special meetings of the board and senate within days of his arrival in the mid-summer of 1994: "I said that we were going to do a strategic plan – that was controversial in the first place. The university had said for years that the world was too uncertain to do strategic planning, governments were too uncertain. The economist in me responded that it was when the future was uncertain that you needed the strategic plan." Through the senate and board, a strategic planning task force of students, faculty, staff, and board members was set up with Davenport as chair. The subsequent plan ("Leadership in Learning") was approved in 1995. His swift action and subsequent concerted efforts at implementation were very successful. The priorities were broadly accepted across the institution, and he never missed an opportunity to reiterate them.

Peter George is particularly forthcoming about the challenges of strategic planning in a university environment, especially for a newcomer. He sees the system as driving the president to only minimally interrupt the way things are done. While it makes sense to build on present strengths and successes, it is difficult to move in new directions, partly because of inertia, partly because of resource constraints, and partly because of the very nature of our universities: "Just start with the basic premise that if you have a thousand faculty members, you start with a thousand individual contractors, each of whom thinks that their discipline, their research, their fourth-year class, their PhD program seminar is the most important thing the institution does. How do you move from that lack of institutional focus, a sort of chaos, to an academic vision/mission and set of priorities for the institution?" Against these challenges, the president is armed primarily with moral suasion and a bit of budgetary room to manoeuvre. It is a huge challenge. George continued:

> People like to talk about change; they just don't like to do it themselves – you're supposed to change the other guys ... It's impeded, too, by traditions like tenure, which is interpreted by some as "I can do whatever I want and you can't get rid of me," and academic freedom, which means for some faculty members that they can say whatever they like no matter whether it's true or not, or founded upon informed opinion. But you as president cannot do those things – you are bound by confidentiality and other norms of your position to be statesmanlike and rise above the fray. My approach has always been to identify opportunities and then look for local champions in our academic community who want to pursue the new possibility. That "bottom up" element is crucial to making things work and implementing changes.

Dr George emphasizes the importance of ensuring that resources are set aside to support strategic priorities. For example, in the major planning process he initiated in response to the huge cuts of Mike Harris's "common sense revolution," his university, McMaster, took more than was needed in order to establish a margin for reinvestment. The next step was to establish research priority areas. McMaster senior management set out three criteria to determine eligibility for investment as a priority area and then put the program out to faculty for internal competition. An eligible department had to demonstrate (a) research excellence, (b) a commitment to interdisciplinarity or multidisciplinarity, and (c) a commitment to extend its research and scholarly expertise to new learning opportunities for students, preferably undergraduates. The process thus tied research and teaching excellence together and led to the selection of four priority areas in the first round of competition and two others in the next. The winning areas received additional funding for faculty renewal and additional infrastructure costs. This initiative set the university up well for the subsequent CFI (Canada Foundation for Innovation) and CRC (Canada Research Chair) competitions and its own capital campaigns.

In my own career, it has always been important to set clear and strong academic priorities and to make sure that resources are directed towards them. The results have been mixed. Once as a vice-president, academic, and twice as a president, I have overseen major strategic planning initiatives respectively at Athabasca, Laurentian, and Windsor. In the first case, I was asked by the Athabasca University president to come up with a five-year strategic academic plan that would make specific and measureable the broad objectives of the long-range plan. As described in my 1990 book,[10] the exercise ran into serious difficulty when two of the three faculty members on the steering committee resigned (for different reasons) after months of consultation, debate, and the drafting of position papers. I realized that I had to be in a stronger position than that of chair of a planning committee, and thus we reformulated the process so that the faculties had more responsibility and I, as vice-president, academic, could then make the final recommendations based on my own assessment of the faculty submissions.

At Laurentian, I inherited the beginnings of a process that involved a huge strategic planning committee and a smaller steering group, a process that was stronger on participation than on authority for final decision. As incoming president, and given my experience at Athabasca, I made it clear that I would work actively with both committees, but I reserved the right to submit an independent report to the senate and board based on my own assessment of the process.

I took this a step further as the new president of the University of Windsor. I spent the first few months all over the campus and in the community, listening to everyone's opinions about Windsor's opportunities and challenges and where the university needed to go. The process started with my arrival in January 1998, and on the 1st of May I produced a draft document that reflected back to the various stakeholders what I had learned. It was quickly obvious to me that the institution was stretched much too thinly and that it needed to focus on a few areas of strength that I ultimately called "pinnacles." The community identified what these areas should be, and I fitted them into my framework, allowing only three at the outset ("automotive," "environmental," and "social justice").

After an extensive series of further consultations and visits to all areas of the campus and beyond, I wrote a final proposal, "The Best of Both Worlds,"[11] which was adopted with one dissenter at senate and unanimously by the board of governors. With this momentum, the document became the blueprint for a full-scale academic review whereby each academic department was to receive the same, more, or fewer resources based on their fit with the plan. This was a thorough and occasionally controversial process, but it made a significant difference to many areas of the university. Its impacts were ultimately positive, not only for areas that received new positions and other resources, but even for some that were under the gun. For example, after an initial uproar two departments (history and visual arts) that faced significant downsizing as a result of the process both subsequently strove to improve their performance to the extent that they are among the stronger programs at Windsor today. Results like these underline the importance not only of having a clear, widely supported, and workable strategic plan, but also of having the courage, fortitude, and ability to ensure it is fully carried out. A guide to action is only effective if the action is taken.[12]

An obvious prerequisite to success is the identification by institutional leaders of appropriate levels of resources to support the new directions. This is more easily done in good times, but it almost always involves the reallocation of resources towards areas of maximum potential strength. At Trent, for example, one of Bonnie Patterson's six priorities was getting the financial house in order. She notes that this was not so much a strategy as a prerequisite to being even able to dream of the other top objectives in her plan.

To this day, I am proud of the impact that "The Best of Both Worlds" had on the University of Windsor at a critical time in its history. The proposal gave a vision and a direction that not only encouraged and buoyed the morale of many on campus, but was frequently cited by newcomers as a key reason for their interest in coming to the university. An intensive reallocation process followed under the leadership of Vice-president, Academic, Neil Gold, which made an important difference in a number of academic areas. We were fortunate to be launching the new plan at a time when additional resources were available, and so "The Best of Both Worlds" provided the guide to action that was essential to maximizing the impact of these resources on the long-term future of the university.

I was less successful in my second term with the follow-up document, "To Greater Heights,"[13] There were a number of reasons for this. The first strategic planning exercise had taken place with a brand new administration at a time when the institution was foundering and almost any coherent plan would have been widely accepted. The bloom was off the rose the second time around, and the "To Greater Heights" document had been prepared with less thorough consultation and when fewer resources were available for redistribution to priority areas. As well, as a document that essentially reinforced the directions of "The Best of Both Worlds," it lacked the excitement of the former's newness, and although it was endorsed by both the senate and board, it generated far less discussion and/or sense of ownership than did the first exercise. The experience reinforces the perspectives of those who are more cynical about the value of strategic planning and suggests that I might have been more successful with a less pretentious exercise.

The cycle continued with the appointment of Alan Wildeman from the University of Guelph as my successor in July 2008. He had the opportunity to bring fresh perspectives to the plans and achievements of the previous decade and the challenges and opportunities of the next. He launched a new strategic planning process that will doubtless affirm some of the directions of the past and forge new ones. It is a pattern repeated in universities across the country that, when it works well, finds an appropriate balance between continuity and change, between building on the best from the past and ensuring adaptability to an ever-changing future.

This path is, however, fraught with peril. If the new plan is too general and too much like those of countless competitors, it runs the risk of being seen as a "make-work" exercise – the time and cost expended upon it resented by many of the faculty and staff whose very support is a prerequisite to its success. On the other hand, if it is too radical in its impact and contradicts many of the priorities of the previous plan, it may fail for lack of support or it may confuse participants, especially if the institution has a history of changing direction every time a new person occupies the president's office.

On balance, the most worthwhile strategic planning in the university setting focuses on academic standards. These standards are enhanced by ensuring the utmost rigour in the hiring and support of faculty, by establishing thorough review processes to ensure that tenure is fully merited, and by concentrating resources in the institution's areas of strength. Follow-through is equally important in building a culture that is never quite comfortable with the status quo, that looks outward in establishing criteria for top performance, and that builds on success to foster an atmosphere of achievement, teamwork, and celebration. Of such virtues are academic reputations made.

The president has primary responsibility for ensuring an organizational climate that encourages and builds these virtues, and most successful leaders have demonstrated by example how best to fulfil them. The president's role is not nearly as much about formal strategic planning as it is about identifying, through an open and thorough process, the strategic priorities that best represent the institution's mission and mandate and working tirelessly to communicate these priorities, to assign appropriate resources to them, to insist on the highest standards of performance, and to celebrate success. The presidential role has an even more powerful impact if there is consistency and continuity of leadership through two or more presidencies.

5

Academic Leadership:
Getting the Balance Right

Almost every book about the challenges of being a university president recognizes the delicate balance that a successful incumbent must find between understanding and respecting the academic culture that defines a university and working through and around it to initiate change deemed in the long-term interests of the institution. While such leadership should be easier for an internal appointee to the presidency, given that he or she knows the key players and understands how things work in the particular institution, this advantage is often offset by the much shorter honeymoon period that exists for an insider. It may be no accident that most of the internal appointees in recent years have been in the larger universities and that they are more apt to have come from a deanship (Rob Prichard and David Naylor at Toronto; Peter George at McMaster; Peter MacKinnon at Saskatchewan; and Elizabeth Cannon at Calgary) than from vice-president, academic, given the latter's closer association with the previous senior management team.

THE NEW PRESIDENT: LEARNING THE INSTITUTIONAL CULTURE

The first challenge facing a president appointed from the outside is to learn the culture of the new institution. I can speak of this challenge with some experience, having entered three universities at a senior level " cold" – that is, without knowing more than a couple of people in the institution or the community. The most immediate challenge in each case was to determine to whom I should listen; everyone with an issue wants the ear of the new president, and it is not always easy to separate the wheat from the chaff. And thus, the first response of a new president is to make him- or herself highly visible and available, both inside the institution and in its primary community.

In my experience, all stakeholders relish the opportunity to express both their pride in the institution and their prescription for its improvement. They quickly gravitate to a new president, seeing him or her, for a short time at least, as an open book, as someone who can champion their particular dream. While newcomers will ultimately rely primarily on members of the senior team, the board, and a few faculty members they have come to trust, the development of a very broad base of people to consult, including dissenters and critics, will pay rich dividends in the long term. Alumni, students, and long-serving faculty and staff offer very important perspectives that are taken fully into account by ambitious change agents.

Adjusting to the local culture was one of the issues discussed with the eleven presidents interviewed for this book, seven of whom were appointed to their first presidency from positions external to their current institution. The four presidents who had been internal candidates had a significant head start in that they knew both the culture and the key players of the institution from the outset. For example, while Rob Prichard had to adjust to a much larger playing field than had involved him at the law school, he already knew what he needed to do and many of the key players who would help him do it when he assumed the reins at the University of Toronto. Peter George had what he described as "the best of both worlds" in being an internal candidate with a long history as a faculty member and dean at McMaster but with the advantage of having the external perspective of someone who had been "away" for the four years immediately preceding his appointment while he served as president of the Council of Ontario Universities (COU). Dave Marshall grew up with Nipissing, moving from dean of education to president before it achieved independent status from Laurentian University; in his own words, he "learned on the job" as the institution grew. Myer Horowitz knew the University of Alberta very well by the time he became its president, having served as a chair, dean, and vice-president, academic.

Martha Piper represents a newer generation of university presidents with her emphasis on the external role. She faced an interesting challenge in moving from the University of Alberta to the University of British Columbia, an institution the former considered a major rival. Both because of UBC's very large size and because of Piper's determination not to play the role of vice-president, academic, she coped with the significant differences in culture, at least in part, by floating above them:

> What I didn't do and probably paid a big price for ... I said to myself very early in my tenure that I would not be VP academic. I think it is one of the biggest pressures on the president and I don't know how to resolve it. I think I failed in that regard. I purposely did not spend a lot of time with the deans who would have loved me to meet with them for breakfast or lunch. If I went down that path, I would have to do it with each of them and I would undermine the VP academic.

For Roseann Runte, a president best exercises his or her academic leadership by respecting the academic culture, listening, and being inclusive. This approach comes directly from her earlier experience: "When I was a junior faculty member, every time I tried to say something, someone would say that they didn't do things that way or that they tried it in 1929 and it didn't work. I always try to remember that when I am listening to others."

Bonnie Patterson also emphasized process when she addressed the question of the role of the president in academic leadership: "In the absence of process, you will get your best critics. If you shortcut the process side of things, then you haven't picked up on what is important to the academy." She cited the importance of respecting the rhythm of the academic year, noting that faculty are preoccupied with teaching and research during the two intensive thirteen-week periods in the autumn and spring semesters. Patterson also stressed the value of establishing a climate that encourages diverse opinions: "I found it very helpful to find champions on faculty who would support and be vocal and play a role in process, but I found it equally important to engage those who really believed something different. If you converted any of those who felt something was not quite right or doable or possible, then you knew you were on to something." Finally, she stressed risks of being visible in the community: "Things can go awry very quickly as you become increasingly preoccupied with all things external. The longer you are in the role, the less time you probably spend on the internal side of the house and you have worked with and developed other leaders on the academic front, like the provost, who address those issues. But, if you get too far outside and out of touch with the change agenda and processes, then you are in trouble."

A common theme among the presidents with respect to the issue of academic leadership was the importance of being very clear on a few major goals and of reiterating them at every opportunity. This was central to Paul Davenport's success at Western. He started with a mandate to improve the entering grades at a time when the university had fallen below the Ontario average. It quickly became apparent that a key aspect of attracting outstanding students was to improve the academic experience of those on campus and to combat Western's reputation as a party school. This approach led to a new "brand," the lynchpin in a strategic plan to offer "the best student experience among the research-intensive universities of Canada." The plan would play out differently in different faculties, but Davenport was determined to make it the integrating goal of each. He repeated it tirelessly, including it in every one of his public speeches.

While Bill Leggett views the notion of transformational leadership as more myth than reality in the university context, he made highly significant changes to the academic culture at both McGill and Queen's by focusing and being very clear on what was needed. His driving ethos went far beyond a passionate commitment to research: "There is no doubt in my mind, given my experience as a student, as a faculty member, and as an administrator, that, on average, by far the best teachers (not necessarily those who get the rave reviews but those who have the biggest impact on the lives of individuals) are those who are most deeply engaged in their discipline as teachers and scholars."

As chair of biology at McGill, Leggett refused to approve research grant submissions to the Natural Sciences and Engineering Research Council of Canada unless he had a prior chance to vet them. As dean of science, he took on a coasting mathematics department, refusing to accept a weak academic review and turning down a recommendation for a hiring, something that had never previously been done. As vice-president, academic, with a similar approach, he came close to shutting down the faculty of dentistry. In each case, he made it very clear that the standards were going to be much higher and that he would not compromise on that agenda. The results in each case were similarly impressive – demonstrably better departments in terms of research productivity and teaching and faculty morale. Leggett took this same approach as principal of Queen's. He found himself in a very new culture and took considerable time to figure it out.

What I didn't fully appreciate at the outset was just how intense the Queen's linkages are and how much of a community it really is. You've got 15,000 students all in residence or within a five-minute walk of the university, virtually no commuters. The students spend as many hours together outside the classroom as in it, intensively involved in university life, a student government that is exceptional in its responsibility and its delivery, an alumni base that grew up in that environment and whose partners and best friends come out of that experience. I didn't realize when I arrived just how intense that sense of belonging and community was. Fortunately, I took the time to study and understand it before I began to act.

As he had done on a smaller scale at McGill, Dr Leggett confronted a culture that had many strengths but was, in his view, much too comfortable and inward-looking for real competitive success. When he arrived, almost every vice-principal, dean, and departmental chair had grown up in the place, there were no more than a handful of woman among them, and very few faculty leaders were younger than their fifty-five-year-old new principal. He instigated open competitions for all positions and restructured the administration, creating the positions of vice-principal, academic, and vice-president, research, with the goal of ensuring focus and accountability for the teaching and research functions that form the heart of any top university. Leggett credits David Turpin, Suzanne Fortier, and Kerry Rowe, who filled these roles during his tenure, for much of the university's success in strengthening its teaching, international outreach, and research performance, and George Hood, who assumed the title of vice-principal, advancement, for his exceptional leadership in alumni relations and development.

Having a strong agenda coming into an academic leadership position can be a problem if the agenda is seen as a personal one by faculty or is not fully supported by the senate and board of the institution. Jim Downey emphasized the importance of getting faculty to "own" the plans if they are to be successfully implemented: "You can get the faculty to come with you if you are not too concerned to be seen as a leader. If faculty members suspect you have your own plan, that's cause enough to resist. I have often said that presidents have only two powers – to persuade and to nudge. You can get much further by nudging than by trying to persuade."

Given her experience as president of the Council of Ontario Universities and the influence of an experienced acting president, David Smith, and a report by two well-known academics, Harry Arthurs and Joyce Lorimer, Bonnie Patterson felt well prepared for her presidency of Trent, except for one thing:

What I really under-anticipated was, as someone who didn't know the culture or community at any level, the importance of having senior administrators who really knew the institution. The vice-president, academic; vice-president, administration; the director of human resources; and a new institutional analyst all came in with me on July 1st. Only the dean of arts and science was from within Trent but he was new to that post, too. We did a lot of learning together!

Ultimately, whatever the individual's leadership style, it is imperative that a president take full account of the university culture – its values, its priorities, its way of doing things. This explains why one individual can be very successful in a given institution and then bomb out in the next. The position is about more than skills and experience. Dave Marshall put it very well:

My approach is to find a common value. Forget all the artifacts – the structures, the organizational fixtures, the decision-making processes. Find a common value, find a common interest, find the thing the whole institution can coalesce around, and then judge everything else by whether or not it hinders the realization of that value.

If there isn't a match between the institutional values and those of the president, the president doesn't last. What institutional members want to see in their president, other than the givens of good, efficient management and the ability to work well with people, are your principles as the basis for your decision making. Other than that, your job is to articulate the institutional value set, not create it.

BUILDING THE TOP TEAM

Perhaps the most important element in a president's academic leadership is ensuring that the right people are in the right leadership positions at the top. David Johnston strongly endorsed this:

> I think this is a 95 per cent people game and a 5 per cent ideas game. You have to work very hard at appointing great vice-presidents and great deans and then, if you made the right appointments, reinforce them, love them to bits, and help them get on with it. Of course, you have to have the strategic plan to help people make the strategic choices, but it ultimately depends on the quality of people who share the agenda. I think that the positions of dean and chair are crucial.

Johnston seeks out individuals who are sometimes unconventional, who will take risks and challenge the status quo. When recruiting for the position of dean of law at McGill, for example, he found great resistance to hiring a young dean by long-serving faculty members on the committee who wanted to perpetuate the status quo. Like Bill Leggett, he brought in a renowned outside academic to demonstrate to the search committee that the law school was in danger of going straight downhill if it did not recruit fresh new leadership. This argument led to the appointment of Rod MacDonald, who was still in his thirties and who turned out to be an outstanding recruit.

While all of the presidents interviewed agreed that the building of the top team is critical, some of them played a much more direct role in senior appointments than others. One determining variable was the size of institution. University search processes are detailed and elaborate and involve large committees and much consultation. In the largest institutions, this renders direct presidential involvement in all senior searches problematic. Nevertheless, while he did not chair all the search committees, Rob Prichard, for example, played a very active role in the selection not only of vice-presidents but also of deans and college principals on campus. Reflecting the importance he attached to such appointments, Prichard invested a great deal of his own time into searches to fill seventeen dean and ten principal positions. Unlike previous practice, where a committee's recommendation had been a *fait accompli* by the time it reached the president's office, Prichard met with every decanal and principal search committee to give his assessment of the priorities for the job and the qualities needed in the appointee. He also met with the leading candidates. Thus, by the time the recommendation came to him, he was in unison with it.

Prichard went even further for vice-presidential appointments, taking the position that the committees were not formal search committees but rather were advisory to him:

> There are different points of view as to how assertive the president should be. I was convinced that, in a place as big as the U of T, we needed great leadership in all the faculties, all the colleges, and in the vice-presidential positions. If we got great leadership in all those places, the place would just sing.
>
> If I look back at it, the principle was absolutely borne out. Each time we set the bar just a bit too low, we paid the price for five or seven years. When we made fabulous appointments, the place just took off!

Peter George believes that his greatest asset is his ability to pick good people, and he takes great pride in the McMaster vice-presidents who have gone on to leadership positions elsewhere in Canada. However, he only chaired vice-presidential searches and wonders whether he would not have been better off chairing the dean searches as well.

Paul Davenport emphasized that it is not only the question of the "top" team but, at least in a larger institution, of a number of key teams throughout the university: "What you find in universities is not one team but many teams. The president's job, in part, is to set out a vision of how his or her institution can be better that appeals to a critical mass of academic faculty and staff who will then constitute teams in their own right." In a smaller university, the president is more easily involved in the daily academic leadership. Bonnie Patterson noted that she had only two deans at Trent and met every fortnight or so with all the academic directors, something that would be handled by a vice-president or even a dean at a much larger institution.

In reflecting on my own career, I recognize that it is a rare senior administrator who can boast a superb hiring record. I chaired many search committees and also had many opportunities to turn back recommendations from a vice-president for a senior appointment.

Early on, while vice-president, academic, at Athabasca University, I made a controversial appointment to a senior position despite the advice of many people I respected not to choose that particular person. I believed that I knew best, that I could work with the individual to ensure a successful appointment. I was wrong. This individual's style, which had so frustrated others when he was a faculty member, had an even greater negative impact from his new position of greater responsibility and authority.

At the beginning of my presidency at Laurentian, I reluctantly accepted a recommendation for a faculty position even though the candidate – a popular sessional instructor – lacked the formal credentials required of an external candidate. I had the impression that the hiring was based more on faculty friendship than credentials, but I let it go, in part because I felt too new to the culture of the place. The individual was a competent teacher but did not produce the research and scholarship that would have enhanced his academic department. We could have done much better. In retrospect, this was an ideal opportunity to send a strong message about quality to the academic community and I missed it. I didn't repeat the mistake when confronted with a similar situation in my later position at Windsor. In that case, we hired a very well qualified minority candidate over the objections of the dean, who wanted to hire someone with a significantly inferior curriculum vitae but a profile more like that of most the faculty. The appointee continues to be a very productive member of faculty to this day and is a great example of the value of employment equity policies in universities.

On at least two significant occasions at Windsor, I bowed to the judgment of a vice-president when my "gut" told me that the decision was wrong. In both cases, I preferred an alternative candidate but went along with the vice-president on the grounds that he was the primary contact for each individual. Neither case worked out well. I regret to this day that I didn't take a stronger stand and insist that my preferred candidate be selected. If I had a chance to do it over again, I would trust my own judgment and, of course, take full responsibility for the subsequent outcomes.

Overall, I would repeat most of my selections of those reporting directly to me (with only a couple of significant exceptions). I always worked closely with search consultants, taking special care to ensure that our search was wide, and I avoided "rubber stamp" searches in which the preferred candidate was a foregone conclusion. While the committees usually came to a consensus, this was not always the case, but the selected candidate was always the one I preferred.

While some argue that awarding tenure is the most important management decision, I believe that the initial hiring is even more crucial. It takes a lot of time and effort to recruit the best people, but hiring the wrong people is even more costly. In every case that I can think of where a senior appointment didn't work out and the incumbent resigned or had to be let go, the aftermath was extremely difficult. In some cases, this was because the person had supporters who disagreed with the negative assessment and didn't hesitate to make their views known publicly. In others, even where there was widespread agreement that the appointment had been a mistake, there was a tendency to blame the university leadership, and it could take quite a while for the community to be brought back together and a new search to be completed successfully. Such situations occur fairly frequently in universities, as evidenced by the number of "acting" or "interim" positions in institutions that have had some turmoil over leadership. The cost in such cases is not only internal strife but also lost opportunity, given the natural tendency for those in interim appointments to be cautious and unwilling (or to lack the support) to make changes to the status quo.

Sometimes, a president can provide academic leadership simply by recognizing when someone has a great idea and doing everything possible to see that it comes to fruition. Such was the case at the University of Toronto when Dean of Arts and Science Marsha Chandler approached Rob Prichard early in her deanship.

With all the big classes in arts and science, she wanted to guarantee every student in first year arts and science a seminar with twenty-five or fewer students in it, with our full-time faculty and ideally our very best faculty members. I said that it was the greatest single idea I would hear in my ten years as president.

To do that, she had to move heaven and earth to reorganize teaching schedules, with resistance everywhere. She was utterly determined to do it. She backed off a little and did it in eighteen months instead of the six she had initially said. It transformed the undergraduate student experience, my son's included. He said it was the best single experience he had at the U of T.

Every one of the presidents interviewed for this book underlined the critical importance of having the right vice-presidents, deans, and departmental chairs in place. There were many success stories like that of Marsha Chandler, and they reinforce the notion that the best presidents are those who can assemble the strongest teams of leaders and then give them the inspiration and leeway to get on with the job in their individual ways.

TENURE AND PROMOTION

Every university has formal tenure and promotion review systems. In most cases, they offer the university the final opportunity to review just how well a promising appointment has turned out. Normally, the president receives recommendations from a vice-president, academic, or provost based on an elaborate system of departmental and university-wide committee reviews informed by external referees. He or she will have the opportunity to accept or reject the recommendations, or refer individual cases back.

I always took this role very seriously, recognizing that once tenure is awarded, it is extremely difficult and time-consuming to dismiss a faculty member on the basis of their subsequent performance, however mediocre. In my entire career in academic administration, I was successful in winning dismissal of a tenured professor for cause on only a couple of occasions. In each case, however, the attempt was well worth the time and effort, as it is critical to uphold standards of performance and integrity in an academic institution. But there is another reason why it can be important to take steps to dismiss a tenured professor for cause. Critics of universities like to cite tenure and sabbaticals as key components of a soft and cushy professorial lifestyle. While both can certainly be abused, they are at the heart of the academic freedom that is the very definition of a university and their value is tremendously enhanced by rigorous performance criteria and procedures. To the extent that there are legitimate concerns in this area, they are about individual failures to uphold standards, not about the standards themselves.

As president, I reviewed any case for tenure or promotion that was even slightly contentious. In most instances, I found that the formal processes had been thorough and thoughtful, and I ultimately upheld the recommendations. On a number of occasions, I found significant procedural errors and referred these back when there was time for further process or reconsideration. I paid special attention to dossiers in which there was a difference between departmental and university committee recommendations, usually with the latter refusing to accept the positive recommendation of the former. In every case but one, I upheld the negative recommendation, recognizing how critical it is that the president ensure the highest academic standards. On one occasion, I agreed to uphold a positive recommendation from the university-wide committee even though the department itself had voted against it. These contrary decisions were not taken easily, and I went to particular lengths to clearly express my reasoning in writing to the respective committees. While I regret a small number of my hiring decisions, I have no regrets about the tenure and promotion decisions I upheld or overturned. Processes and presidential styles vary, but the single most important priority is to make it clear to everyone in the university community that these are among the most important decisions taken in a given year.

For most of my career, I worked with collective agreements that had provisions whereby the time allowed for a tenure decision could be extended if the committee or president was uncertain. In retrospect, I believe that this too often let everyone off the hook, allowing them to avoid a tough decision by postponement. After working for more than ten years with the Windsor provisions, according to which a decision had to be made one way or the other in the final year of eligibility, I recognized that this latter approach was more effective and, ultimately, fairer. Everyone involved knew there were no escape clauses, and they were thus motivated to do a thorough and effective job from the outset.

FACULTY UNIONIZATION

Faculty unionization is well established in the vast majority of Canadian universities, whatever the variances in provincial legislation and context.[1] Even though the presidents selected for interview enjoyed positive faculty relations for all or most of their terms, the majority of them see faculty unionization as problematic. There is some irony in this, given that unions usually want management, and specifically, the president, to have considerable power. In the terms set out by Bergquist and Pawlak, the advocacy and managerial cultures reinforce each other. In a more collegial culture, union leaders are frustrated by the relative lack of authority of management and

by the challenges posed by disagreements with those of their members who favour more traditional forms of academic governance. It
is thus not surprising that the presidents who are most concerned
about faculty unionization are those who see a university president
as being more an academic leader than a chief executive officer.

Whatever their primary orientations in governance may have been,
many of the selected presidents faced challenging labour relations
issues and, in most cases, coped extremely effectively with them. Jim
Downey, for example, found himself in a difficult position at UNB,
where the faculty had recently gone through the unionization process. In the 1970s, he had been through the same certification process as a faculty member at Carleton, one of the first institutions to
unionize; he remembers the experience as terribly bitter and divisive,
and believes unionization transformed the culture of the institution
in a very negative way: "They were still trying to negotiate a first
collective agreement and I arrived at UNB in the midst of that. I
knew instinctively what was expected of me to help the institution
through that. Nobody talked in those days of being a change agent,
but I knew instinctively that we had to change that climate of mistrust and that we had only a short period in which to put Humpty
Dumpty back together again."

Downey and his administration took several steps towards reinfor-
cing the university's culture of collegial decision making, which was
seriously threatened at the time. They scrapped a plan to develop a
manual to ensure that all managers interpreted the collective agreement the same way and persuaded the board to offer the faculty
binding arbitration: "On the manual – or 'the interpreter's bible,'
as I called it, I was afraid it would lead to a fundamentalist attitude
to the collective agreement, that we would become slaves to it. I
thought it better for us to make mistakes and to lose the occasional
grievance or arbitration and to have to say we were sorry, rather
than take this very bureaucratic approach."

The results were positive, a settlement was reached over wages,
and labour relations were good for the rest of Downey's tenure at
UNB. He gives the faculty union equal credit for the labour peace, as
they responded by electing good academics and reasonable people to
the executive. Downey concedes that one can keep peace at too great
a cost, but he is proud of the ten good years of amicable relations
that existed during his UNB presidency. He sees his role as having
been, in part, that of "pastoral leader," of ensuring that the mistrust

wasn't institutionalized and that the university wasn't transformed in a negative way to undermine the collegial relations that were at the heart of the academy.

Many presidents share concerns about the impact of faculty unionization on the culture of a university, especially the collegial and developmental cultures. Paul Davenport noted how disruptive and destructive a faculty strike can be for an institution, undermining its commitments to students and the leadership of a president. That faculty have tenure and yet can threaten an institution with a strike suggests a potential imbalance in labour relations in the university sphere as compared to labour relations in the private sector.

Peter George attributes what he believes to be an unfortunate loss of the sense of family and community at Canadian universities to the growth in size of the universities and the polarization resulting from labour issues and the unionization of staff.

As more faculty associations become faculty unions, collegiality becomes more and more fractured. In the worst cases, they become more and more self-centred. What collegiality means to some faculty and the unions and faculty associations is putting faculty interests first and co-management if possible. It doesn't necessarily mean consultation with all the stakeholders, who would normally be involved with making some decisions in a truly collegial decision-making process.

George also believes that there has been too strong a move towards a more corporate style of governance and leadership, but he is encouraged by recent counter tendencies: "The American literature seems to suggest that, now, there are beginnings of drifting back to emphasizing collegiality and mediation skills – there's a happy medium in there somewhere."

Bill Leggett's biggest disappointment at Queen's was the faculty unionization that occurred within months of his appointment. While taking some satisfaction from the cooperative spirit in which all involved developed the first collective agreement and the positive administration-faculty relations that prevailed throughout his principalship, he still sees unionization as counter to the ideals of academia.

I don't believe in academic unions – I think they are totally inconsistent with the idea of an environment of free inquiry and individual accomplishment, which, for me, are the cornerstone of academia. I fear that they create a gradual eroding slope. With every contract, some new limit to the creative potential of the university and its constituent parts becomes imbedded, often inadvertently. Fortunately, at Queen's, this has not yet become an issue but I fear that it will.

Dave Marshall blames the increase in class size in recent years, at least in part, to the unionization of faculty associations. Unrelenting financial pressures mean that universities are faced with annual hard choices. Given budgetary shortfalls, the options are of the nature of reducing the number of faculty, lowering faculty pay, or increasing class size. Marshall noted, "Over the past 15 years, the average class size in Ontario has gone up ten students because faculty associations, not presidents, decided they would rather have higher class sizes than a reduction in pay (and presidents are essentially powerless to fight against this). It is the result of a union mentality that is more compatible with General Motors than it is with academia."

The above concerns notwithstanding, faculty unions are well established in almost all Canadian universities. While they may not be the preoccupation of most professors in between contracts, no university president can afford to underestimate their power in negotiations when times are tough or when there is a controversial issue on campus. When the chips are down, faculty will almost always rally around their union. This puts immense pressure on the leadership team if a strike is imminent. Strikes can be tremendously disruptive to a university, especially in their aftermath. Prospective students may be wary of an institution known for its difficult labour relations, particularly if they feel that the school year is threatened in any way, and faculty may worry about their research careers. Strikes often leave bitter feelings, not only between faculty and administration, but among faculty members themselves. The resulting climate of distrust can seriously affect an institution and undermine relationships for years to come.

I used to believe that managers got the unions they deserved. Experience has taught me that labour relations are more complicated than that, with past history and institutional culture playing significant roles. A president should do everything possible to find a way through difficult negotiations, but sometimes he or she must stand up for a particular principle or for financial integrity even if the result is a strike. At such a time, more than any other, the strong support of the board of governors is crucial for both the future of the institution and the position of its president.

In addition to contract negotiations, there are always other hot issues on university campuses for faculty associations to address – issues around academic freedom, human rights, governance, and the outsourcing of teaching or related support services. A recent example on many campuses is the increasing reliance on non-tenured, part-time sessional instructors. Financial savings are the primary motivation for their engagement, since they tend to be paid far less, proportionately, than full-time faculty and do not require the same levels of infrastructure and support. Their hiring can lead to morale problems for both groups – sessional and part-time instructors, who feel exploited and unappreciated, and regular faculty, who worry about the trend away from full-time, tenure-track appointments. This is an important issue for faculty associations, one that has a high potential to attract significant student interest and concern on many Canadian university campuses.

Given the increasing financial pressures on our institutions and such responses to these pressures as major budget cuts, increased use of part-time instructors, greater demands for accountability, and the introduction of more corporate approaches to university management and governance, there will be no shortage of issues around which faculty associations might rally the troops. In this context, it is more important than ever that presidents communicate issues and challenges openly and honestly and find ways to persuade faculty and their associations to work with them in the best interests of the institutions and their students.

THE CRITICAL IMPORTANCE OF INSTITUTIONAL FIT

While the best predictor of an individual's success may be his or her previous performance in similar or related positions, the style, values, and priorities of a new president must match those of the institution at the time of appointment if he or she is to be successful. A good fit with the environment of the institution, and especially its academic culture, is crucial to success in strategic planning, in labour relations, and in ensuring the support of the board and senate, all critical factors in presidential performance.

Usher et al. strongly endorse the importance of institutional fit: "From the university's point of view, the biggest single consideration in the final selection of the top candidate is institutional fit. An individual must be perceived as a good match for the university's needs, culture, and challenges. Similarly, the institution and opportunity must match the individual's expectations, competencies, and career stage."[2]

The implications are clear – the search committee needs to do everything it can to assess a candidate's compatibility with the university's culture, and even if the committee's choice is being brought in to change the institution significantly, the appointee must have considerable confidence of his or her ability to work within that culture.

PART THREE

Key Issues for Today's Presidents

6

Student Access and Success: Confronting a Declining Undergraduate Experience

One of the inherent dangers in the role of a modern Canadian university president is that the incumbent becomes so preoccupied with government and community relations, fundraising, collective bargaining, research productivity, institutional reputation, and governance issues that he or she overlooks the crucial issue of the evolving student experience on campus.

The issue of the quality of today's campus experience is seen in a variety of ways by such different constituencies as students, faculty, alumni, board members, the general public, and the president.

For the most part, today's undergraduate students inhabit a campus that is much larger and less personal than the one my generation remembers from the 1960s. First-year classes, for example, are huge in all but the smallest universities; the average student-to-faculty ratio across the country has risen steadily, from a low of 11.3:1 in 1978 to 17:1 by 1997 and to well over 20:1 by 2008.[1] Today, it is over 25:1 in many institutions, with little evidence of a freezing or reversal of the trend.

Today's students are much more numerous, are in much larger classes, and are more apt to live off-campus than their counterparts of a couple of decades ago. They tend to lead very busy lives, combining part-time or even full-time jobs with their studies, and are more likely than yesterday's students to be commuters with far less time for the extracurricular activities that were so much a part of the earlier campus life. They are from more varied social backgrounds and are of every nationality. Because they are more anxious about future employment than their earlier counterparts, whose job prospects were far more promising, many of today's students are more instrumental in their approach to their education, attending university primarily because it enhances their employment opportunities.[2]

Full-time faculty worry about heavier workloads associated with larger classes and higher expectations for research publication. Many feel that they do not know their undergraduate students as well as formerly. They are concerned that burgeoning enrolments do not seem to be accompanied by comparable increases in tenure-track appointments, while more teaching assistants are engaged to teach undergraduate classes.

The university known to today's faculty and students is a far cry from the one viewed through the rose-coloured glasses of many loyal alumni who support an institution primarily out of nostalgia for their own on-campus experience and the consequent network of friendships and acquaintances they have developed. Canadian universities have changed dramatically over the past few decades. The campus life remembered by many alumni – a homogeneous and socially elite student body, almost everyone living on campus, mostly full-time students without jobs during the school year, small classes, high participation in extracurricular activities, and highly accessible faculty and even senior administrators – scarcely exists on most campuses today. I frequently have wondered if today's students, many lacking the intense experience of earlier, more personal campus connections, will be as loyal to their institution in the future as those who graduated a few decades earlier.

Members of the board of governors see the university primarily in financial and reputational terms. They are far less likely to leave the running of the institution to the president and senior team if the institution is facing enrolment, funding, and reputational challenges. They are interested in such key performance indicators as entering averages, scholarship and endowment levels, reputational surveys, and, of course, balanced operating budgets.

According to any number of surveys in various Canadian provinces over the past few years,[3] the general public has a very positive view of the university, even though the institution itself is not always well understood. There is widespread recognition of the positive effect of higher education on regional and national economies and enthusiasm for the leadership roles that faculty, staff, and students play in the local community. Such a viewpoint, however, is a double-edged sword for university presidents. While a successful image is what they strive to create, it tends to be more difficult to raise funds or to persuade governments to invest more money if the general perspective is that universities are thriving. Campus expansion and research successes mask such fundamental resource problems as dramatically larger classes and long-deferred maintenance for decaying physical plants.

While presidents are always concerned about the quality of teaching and learning on-campus, they find it hard to admit publicly that these standards are declining in their own institution. As head cheerleaders, they must always present the institution in the most favourable possible way to recruit the best students and faculty, to encourage alumni and corporate contributions, to develop government and local community support, and to build strong private sector connections, locally, nationally, and internationally. All of this must done with integrity, especially since presidents must be more aware than most of the weaknesses in the institution.[4] How could a president extol the virtues of attending his or her university while knowing that tuition fees were steadily increasing at the very time that the quality of the average undergraduate student's experience was declining?

During my tenure at COU, there were endless discussions among Ontario executive heads about the dilemma of persuading taxpayers and governments of our funding problems when we were individually extolling the virtues of each of our campuses. How could we persuade anyone that the system was crumbling when we were very actively talking about our own booming institution for marketing purposes? I have a vivid memory of one such discussion that went on and on until David Atkinson, then president of Brock University, said, "I've got it! Brock ... the best of a bad lot!" It brought the house down because it crystallized the discussion so beautifully.

Jim Downey believes that it is almost impossible for a president to persuade the general public of the financial plight of the university because the institution has become the modern version of the medieval cathedral.

The truth is that you have too little credibility, finally, with those who make the decisions because the real indicators they are looking at (Are employers happy with the graduates? Are graduates happy with the experience they've had?) are very positive. Then, there's the outward appearance of our institutions. We really are the medieval cathedral. Walk around a university campus and behold the architecture and the academic, social, and athletic facilities. How do we make the case for our poverty? For this reason, it is generally easier and better to get people excited by our possibilities than to feel sorry for us.

I asked each of the interviewees if, amidst all the great aspects of campus development and expansion and activities in their extremely busy lives as chief executive officers, they worried that the average day-to-day undergraduate experience was deteriorating and that they weren't doing enough to address it. The responses covered a pretty wide spectrum, with the challenges seen as greatest in the largest institutions.

Martha Piper said that she has always been concerned about the distance between the positive message and the worst aspects of the undergraduate experience. She had monthly breakfasts with UBC's top students and recognized that the institution just wasn't providing them with what they deserved. While she initiated many efforts to do something about this, she is not satisfied that enough was achieved and appreciates the efforts of her successor, Stephen Toope, in that regard.

Piper feels more successful at the graduate level. She was incredibly impressed at Stanford when a mentor, Dick Taylor, himself a winner of the Nobel Prize for Physics, invited six Nobel laureates to a lunch with her. She was startled that all six had stayed at Stanford, given that institutions like Harvard or Princeton would go to great lengths to lure them away. They all agreed that they had chosen to remain at Stanford because of the quality of the students, which helped her realize that great research and great students were intricately enmeshed.

Similarly, Rob Prichard concedes that he gave the matter too little attention and applauds the priority given to it by his successor, David Naylor. He also cited Paul Gooch's leadership at Victoria University, a constituent of the University of Toronto, for its very successful "Vic One" program, which features small group seminars and an interdisciplinary focus.

However, for Paul Davenport at Western, also a large research-intensive institution, the undergraduate student experience was a preoccupation: "I would say 'that's my particular brand.' If you could compare the allocation of my time compared to my fellow presidents in the G13, you would find that I spent more time on campus and less on, say, federal government relations. It's not a question of what's right or wrong but what you are good at so it is no accident that I have invested an awful lot of my time in the student experience." While he had considerable success in promoting and making real his mantra for Western to give "the best student experience among the research-intensive universities of Canada," Davenport conceded the difficulties of the challenge:

> Despite the best efforts of faculty and staff, the dramatic increase in student-faculty ratios over the last two decades in most Canadian universities has had a negative effect on the quality of education and particularly on the interaction between undergraduate students and full-time faculty. In my way, I have tried to do something about it beyond just complaining to government. I've put a lot of time and energy into the issue of the student experience and may well have neglected other things.

Jim Downey, president of three "comprehensive" universities, was less apologetic for not giving more time to the quality of student experience issue: "I was confident enough in my institutions and the people who staffed them to believe good things were happening. The real proof to me was not that class sizes were getting larger, although that was of some concern, but what our graduates and their employers were saying. We seemed to be meeting the needs of our society, not just our economy, but our society."

Peter George shares the concerns about the growing student-faculty ratio and its detrimental impact on opportunities for individualized mentoring and the close association of a student with a faculty member. He looks longingly at top American universities with their 10:1 ratios (compared to Canadian universities' 25:1 or larger) and believes that the quality gap is very real. While not seeing any easy responses to this challenge, he does point out that, underneath the broad aggregates, there are still small-enrolment senior undergraduate courses that are fiercely protected by the faculty and provide wonderful learning opportunities for students.

Myer Horowitz had always been concerned about, but frustrated by, the lack of resources to provide the level of student experience to which he aspired for his institution. He felt significantly reassured by the quality of the vice-presidents, academic, during his tenure (George Baldwin and Peter Meekison), both of whom worked hard to improve the undergraduate learning experience on campus.

David Johnston is another who believes that burgeoning student-faculty ratios have lessened the quality of the undergraduate experience. While he saw diversifying the university's income as a key way to ameliorate the situation, he admitted that his institution has not done as well on this indicator as he had hoped. As president, however, he worked hard to make the student experience more personal, taking the time, for instance, to personally address and sign 50,000 letters a year, including 10,000 scholarship letters. He tried to meet with students and encouraged his deans and others to follow his lead in developing a more personalized institution.

Bill Leggett sees the issue very much in financial terms. When the Harris government deregulated tuition fees for professional programs, the changes in quality that the new funding helped to achieve were dramatic, and he fought hard, but unsuccessfully, to achieve similar tuition relief for arts and science. At the same time, he recognized Queen's responsibility to ensure that those who needed financial assistance to attend the institution received it, and he worked tirelessly to build at Queen's one of Canada's largest and strongest student aid endowments.

Leggett advocates a sea change in the attitude of Canadians, away from the view that post-secondary education is a right to be provided by government to one that recognizes it as the highest return on investment that most individuals will ever experience. He does not understand why students worry about graduating with a $20,000 debt load when they would not think twice about taking out a $20,000 car loan. A more liberal tuition regime, coupled with effective financial aid targeted at the truly needy student, would help university leaders ensure a higher level of undergraduate learning experience on campus.

The rapidly growing demand for university places raises the issue of who should attend university, as governments and taxpayers worry about the costs associated with burgeoning enrolments. For example, it is interesting that one of the responses of the Ontario government to the huge enrolment pressures spurred by the "double cohort"[5] was to seek further information on entering averages of first-year students. The premise that universities were lowering their standards to raise student numbers in an enrolment-driven funding system was belied by the reality that entering averages actually went up over the period in question. Nevertheless, the issue of who should go to university has been part of the dialogue over the past decade or so.

With higher tuition fees have come stronger student demands for accountability, for better teaching, and, in some cases, even for higher marks. Many professors worry about a growing sense of entitlement among university students in both Canada and the United States, manifested in a more consumer-like approach to higher education ("we're paying for it and we are owed the credential"). This sense of entitlement is exacerbated by the cutthroat competition to get into professional schools, such as medicine or law, where the admission decision is almost completely dependent upon undergraduate grades. Faculty have felt increasing pressure to grant higher marks to students who feel they are "owed" them. There is much discussion about the "new student" of the twenty-first century, though very little conclusive evidence that the changes are as dramatic or as sudden as often portrayed.[6]

As someone who has long believed in equality of opportunity and has seen first-hand the success of open admissions at institutions like the Open University and Athabasca University, I would not deny qualified students access to a publicly supported university. On the contrary, I believe that both individuals and the country would benefit tremendously from the further expansion of what is already one of the highest enrolment rates in the world. While the Open University has received international acclaim for the success of its students, I credit this less to the institution's educational technology and much more to the fact that its open admissions policy has given so many capable people the opportunity to study at the post-secondary level they were previously denied. Nevertheless, I don't believe that the traditional Canadian university is necessarily the right place for every current student but I do believe that those admitted take on a serious responsibility for their own performance.

We have seen that Canadian universities are relatively homogeneous in structure, aspirations, and processes compared to the universities in most other countries. Academic standards are high, but the country lacks the diversity of the institutions elsewhere, notably in the United States. The participation rates in universities continue to grow, as students, with strong support from their parents, see the university as their best ticket to future economic and social success. The result may be that many of the students on university campuses would do better in institutions more specifically geared to their own talents and interests. While this speaks to a better array of community colleges and technical and vocational institutes in all provinces, it also suggests the need for great diversity within degree-granting institutions. I explore this issue in detail in chapter 12.

Creating a broader array of degree-granting institutions would be an important first step to improving the post-secondary experience of many Canadian students, but it would have to be accompanied by much better advising and guidance to help individuals find the institution best suited to their needs. As a regular participant in the Ontario Universities Fair between 1991 and 2008, I was regularly astounded by how little research many students did in selecting their university. Instead of really looking into the programs and educational experience best suited to their particular interests, needs, and abilities, they relied on the advice of one or two friends or were easily influenced in their decision by a chat with a particular professor. As one who believes that there is no such thing as a best university, only the best institution for a given individual, I regret that students are not better informed in making their choices and too often lack the diversity of choice available to students in other countries. If there were greater student mobility across Canada and a larger array of purposeful degree-granting institutions, students would have access to more appropriate choices and a better university experience.

Much more needs to be done on every university campus to improve the quality of undergraduate teaching and learning.[7] The most commonly cited concerns about the undergraduate experience on our campuses are the following:

a) Class sizes are getting larger each year; faculty are less accessible than previously; and the student experience is consequently less and less personal and engaging.
b) In the crucial first year, too many courses are taught by instructors, notably teaching assistants, who are not actively involved in research and scholarship in their discipline and often have almost no experience as teachers.
c) Faculty teach the way they were taught, which was too often by "talking head" lecture and too little student engagement.
d) Grade inflation over recent decades is clearly documented, and too many students have a consumerist sense of entitlement that

extends to their grades and a concomitant lack of responsibility for their own performance.

e) Too many students take a disjointed selection of courses, their choices driven by availability in the timetable rather than any explicitly prepared curriculum.

f) With the rapid expansion of university access, more and more students (and often their parents) take an instrumental view of their education, seeing it as preparation for a job rather than, more traditionally, as learning for its own sake.

g) A number of factors conspire to limit or lessen the student's experience beyond the classroom, potentially undermining the very purpose of a university education.

Each of these is addressed in turn.

a) Class Size

Burgeoning class sizes are frequently cited as one of the key factors in the declining quality of the undergraduate experience. They are associated with providing passive rather than active learning, giving students far less personal attention, and offering them with too few opportunities to challenge what is being presented.

Too often, large classes just happen. Class numbers are determined by the combination of booming enrolments, restricted academic budgets, and a fixed physical plant, with the result that rooms are too often overcrowded and under-equipped. In theory, the problem is not necessarily large classes per se, especially with today's communications technologies; it is more that no forethought is given to coping with or using them constructively. As long ago as 1964, for example, I was exposed to a superb teaching model at the Institute of Education at the University of London, where I was doing the Post-Graduate Certificate in Education (PGCE). Every Friday morning, we had three one-hour lectures in Beveridge Hall, a large auditorium that housed almost 500 students. When we were not practice teaching, we attended follow-up small group seminars the following Monday led by tutors and faculty at the institute. This worked extremely well, for me, at least. By and large, the lecturers on stage at Beveridge Hall were superb communicators. I particularly remember the philosopher R.S. Peters, who inspired in me a lifelong interest in "authority," which was the subject of both my master's and doctoral theses. I always felt that he was speaking directly to me, personally, even though I never met him.[8]

I learned a very important lesson from my experience of this model. I remember going to a Monday seminar after one of Peters's lectures with very clear ideas about what he had said. There were about a dozen students in the room, and because it was the University of London, they were a rich mix from all over the world. After giving my views, I was quite taken aback when a self-proclaimed Trotskyist from Pakistan told me that I had completely missed the point of the lecture. As much as I argued back at the time, I went home with serious doubts and reread my notes and modified my viewpoint somewhat (although never going as far as the Trotskyist). I learned how differently the same presentation can be heard, filtered through each person's own culture, experience, and philosophy. It was a wonderful learning experience, one that not only had an impact on my views of teaching but also helped make me a lifelong champion of international education and diversity in the classroom.

The Institute of Education model lends itself readily to today's technologies, provided that the classrooms are designed to accommodate such large numbers. Once a class contains more than seventy or eighty students, it becomes far less personal and not significantly different from one with an enrolment of a thousand or more. Huge, well-designed lecture halls, supplemented by good-quality audiovisual support, can be used to replicate the Beveridge Hall experience. The secret of the model is to assign the best communicators to the very large lectures or video programs. This frees up faculty and tutors to oversee and support the small group seminars where students get to test what they have learned in a dynamic and stimulating environment.

The institute model also lends itself to online learning, through which students have ready access to a well-qualified tutor and can interact in asynchronous time frames with their fellow students, who, in the largest and most international distance education institutions, may be dispersed all over the world.

In these ways, the disadvantages of large classes can be overcome and even turned into an advantage. However, classroom renovation is expensive, and many universities lack the enrolment base needed to generate the financial resources necessary for an effective online program in distance education. This issue is discussed further in chapter 12.

b)   The First-Year Experience

A student's first year at university is crucial. Many students are ill-prepared for the freedom of choice and association that defines a university, and they may need learner support systems that are over-stretched or unavailable on many large and overcrowded campuses. A strategy commonly practised in some institutions is to have relatively open admissions and then allow a kind of Darwinian self-selection to take place during the first year. In such cases, drop-out rates are high and many leave campus very disillusioned with the whole process and, more damagingly, with themselves.

I have always argued that a university admission decision cuts two ways. It demonstrates the university's confidence in the student, who then has a concomitant responsibility to live up to expectations, but it also obliges the institution to take on the responsibility to do everything possible to help the student succeed. That is why, in my "White Paper on Teaching and Learning"[9] and the associated strategic plan, "To Greater Heights,"[10] both produced at the University of Windsor, the emphasis was on providing learner support, especially for first-year students.[11] This approach led to a concerted "first-year experience" program at Windsor that focused on both the academic and the social experiences of new arrivals on campus and that was ultimately successful in improving retention rates, engagement, and satisfaction among first-year students.

A related concern on today's overcrowded campuses is the growing proportion of first-year classes taught by sessional instructors and teaching assistants. While the primary motivation for this trend has been to save money, it does have some positive elements. Many sessional instructors are actively engaged in their area of study, notably in the professional programs, and they bring life experience to the classroom to the benefit of students. Teaching assistants gain valuable experience in their areas of interest through teaching, and they also depend on such opportunities to finance their education.

On the other hand, it can be argued that first-year students are the ones who most need the best academics, teachers who bring current knowledge of and passion for their discipline to the classroom.

The first-year experience is absolutely pivotal to students' success or failure at university, and they deserves the best teaching the institution can provide. The first-year classroom is not the place to try out graduate students. Early exposure to highly motivated, engaged academics is a critical component of a successful university experience. This approach may also be more cost-efficient. Instilling a love of learning and imparting the requisite skills early in a student's university career will subsequently pay rich dividends in the form of a highly motivated, independent learner who requires far less attention and support. It will also reduce student dropout rates to the financial benefit of the institution.

c)   How Faculty Are Prepared for Teaching

The position of university professor is almost unique among professional roles in that the incumbent is seldom trained for a core activity that engages much of his or her time – teaching. Indeed, many university faculty simply teach the way they were taught, and some of the methods go back centuries. Some methods are tried and true (the small group tutorial), some were always poor (rote lecturing and passive note taking), and others that may have worked with highly motivated elites are less successful in meeting the challenges of mass higher education.

Almost all Canadian universities have recognized the need to help faculty establish better learning conditions in their classrooms and labs by setting up centres for teaching and learning, running regular seminars and courses for faculty and teaching assistants, and establishing awards and other forms of recognition for teaching excellence. These initiatives have doubtless improved the quality of much of the teaching on campus, but a bigger challenge for a university is to really put recognition for good teaching on the same level as that for good research.

It is, of course, notoriously difficult to define good teaching. While student evaluations of teaching (SET scores) are the main tools used, some studies have shown a correlation between student evaluations of faculty and higher grades, suggesting that any effective evaluation of teaching must encompass other measures as well.[12] Good teaching is ultimately about instilling a love of learning in the student and in encouraging the development of independent learning skills. This involves a host of learning styles and teaching techniques, from problem-based to experiential learning, and the impact of a particular faculty member may not always be appreciated until years later.

Giving as much importance to teaching as to research is to confront a firmly established academic culture – something that has always been recognized as difficult. An effective president and senior management team should make this a top priority and address the issue from many perspectives. Good teaching must be as strong a criterion for tenure and promotion as is research productivity. Faculty should be encouraged and rewarded for developing innovative practices in the classroom and distance-delivery learning systems. Students should be encouraged to be as active in lodging complaints about poor and indifferent teaching as they are in complaining about their own marks.

While I believe that the best teachers are often the best researchers as well, some individuals are naturally better at and more enthusiastic about one or the other. It thus makes sense to offer considerable flexibility in teaching loads and research expectations so that the institution takes maximum advantage of the talents and interests of its faculty and staff.

d)   Grade Inflation and Students' Sense of Entitlement

University of Toronto professors James Côté and Anton Allahar have documented significant grade inflation at both the high school and university levels in the United States and Canada.[13] Several factors have conspired to strengthen this trend – well meaning efforts to build student esteem in schools, institutional financing that rewards student persistence, student evaluations of faculty that reward those who mark more easily, and huge pressures to get the highest possible grades on students aspiring to such professional schools as medicine and law.

A related phenomenon is the increased incidence of cheating on university campuses, exacerbated by the ease of access to knowledge via the Internet. This has been well documented in the United States,[14] and there is little evidence that things are much better in Canada. Professors deal regularly with issues of plagiarism even thought students know that teachers have access to search vehicles such as turnitin.com that can quickly identify material parachuted in from the Internet. Many universities now have academic integrity offices and officers to work against such deception both through policy and education.

As higher education has expanded to a broader educational cohort, more students bring an instrumental approach to their university studies, posing new challenges for faculty whose primary orientation has always been to produce scholars. This phenomenon has been dubbed "the student as reluctant intellectual" and the "professor as reluctant gatekeeper" by Côté and Allahar.[15] What is most disturbing about their analysis is their assertion that while the problems they cite are well known in university circles, there is very little evidence that anyone is doing very much about them.

It is not difficult to understand why the status quo prevails. Administrators are concerned about institutional reputations and keeping enrolments and success rates up for funding purposes. Faculty members feel burdened and overwhelmed by their relatively new gatekeeper roles, especially when efforts to uphold academic standards go unrewarded or are even punished through student evaluations. Students come to university with a history of success and take umbrage at being told that their work is not up to standard. They are not used to such criticism and tend to blame the instructor rather than accept responsibility for their need to improve their performance.[16] Parents, the general public, and governments are buoyed by higher rates of accessibility and degree completion but are apparently less concerned about the quality of the credential.

There are no easy antidotes to these trends, but the university president must confront them if the integrity of a university degree is to be preserved. It is critical that students be deeply engaged in their studies and take responsibility for their own learning. This puts the focus on undergraduate teaching and learning and, again, on the president doing everything possible to provide a more differentiated university system, one that recognizes different approaches for different needs. The president has the formidable responsibility to mobilize the university community to identify, discuss, and resolve these problems. At stake is the very integrity of the institution he or she purports to lead.

e) Curricula: What Students Learn

The amount and kind of attention faculty members pay to curricula in our universities varies tremendously. It ranges from undertaking ongoing reviews and detailed collaborative assessments in some professional programs to leaving almost everything up to the individual professor in many others. In the best case scenario, there is, across the institution, an appropriate balance of carefully regulated programs, such as medicine, engineering, law, and nursing; fairly integrated collections of courses in areas of concentration in arts and science; and a broad array of interesting courses for students who are still trying to discover their focus areas or who have a broad range of interests. In the worst case scenario, over-regulation and rigidity dominate some of the professional programs, while a laissez-faire approach – characteristic of arts and social sciences programs, in particular – leaves students with a grab bag of courses and very little depth in any area. The latter concern is exacerbated by our crowded institutions, with one of the biggest challenges in the year being to put together a timetable that works. The result, too often, is that students take a course only because it is available, not because it really interests them or is appropriate to their area of concentration.

Following earlier successes with graduate programs, a welcome trend in Canada has been the development of full-scale, external program reviews at the undergraduate level. Typically, a given academic program is reviewed every seven years through a process of self-assessment, scrutiny by a broader university-wide committee, and formal visits from a team of external experts in the field. This process is critical in ensuring the high quality of academic programs across the country, especially in its encouragement of thoughtful introspection about the courses and processes to which students are exposed.

A critical component of a president's academic leadership is ensuring that regular and effective processes are in place to review curricula and the quality of the student experience and that all members of the community, especially faculty and students, are directly involved in them. Curricular reviews must go far beyond the content of programs and courses. Especially in an age when knowledge is so readily available on the Internet, a university graduate must be an independent learner, someone with an insatiable curiosity and the research skills to seek out knowledge, distinguish among competing facts, and apply what has been learned to the problem at hand. From this perspective, a review of curricula must consider not only the information presented but also the philosophy behind the approach to learning and how the student is thus engaged with the materials.

There are those who argue that market forces and the rise of consumerism in higher education will doom traditional university approaches to teaching and learning.[17] These are useful threats to the extent that they spur universities to take such issues more seriously. At the same time, the university academic model has prevailed for many years and outsiders can sometimes underestimate its ability to incorporate external innovation in communications and technology while preserving the best aspects of its traditional approaches.

f)   An Instrumental View of the Purpose of a University

More and more students see an undergraduate education in instrumental terms, the focus being primarily or even exclusively on finding a good job. While universities have long been important conduits to better-paying jobs, this orientation has become much more prominent in today's knowledge society.

This is not surprising. In earlier eras, when only a small proportion of the age cohort went to university and well-paying jobs were so much more accessible, it was easier to take a more esoteric approach to learning. In a well-documented research report,[18] Rick Miner convincingly presents a looming demographic and labour market crisis arising from the intersection of what he terms two "mega-trends" – an aging population and an emerging knowledge economy. Miner concludes that not only will there be a huge shortage of available workers over the next twenty years, but Canada will need 77 per cent of its workforce to have post-secondary credentials by 2031, a proportion significantly higher than today's 60 per cent level.[19]

Miner's paper merits serious consideration, especially for its emphasis on better funding for higher education and the development of a more seamless system of post-secondary institutions so that the country avoids the double problem of "people without jobs and jobs without people."[20] While the challenge runs across the whole spectrum of higher education, including vocational training and apprenticeships, tomorrow's economy will demand more worker flexibility and creativity than ever. From this perspective, the vast majority of jobs will require workers who are creative, flexible, and are independent learners – that is, workers with skills and orientations that are developed at least as much by a liberal arts education and cooperative programs as by narrower approaches to job preparation and training.

g)   *The Whole University Experience*

So much of what one learns at university emanates from outside the classroom, lab, or seminar. When graduates recount their university days, they are apt to cite the values of social networking, extracurricular activities, team sports, and residential life as crucial components of their experience. To them, a university education is about more than just learning facts. It teaches people how to think critically and independently and how to use knowledge and develop collaborative social skills to work with others for a better society.

Proponents of the tangible culture believe that today's students have nowhere near the richness of experience of students in earlier eras when institutions were smaller and there was a greater opportunity to take full advantage of university life. Indeed, many commuter students experience today's university almost entirely in the classroom, lacking the time, finances, or inclination to get more involved in campus life. They are seeking their degree as a passport to a better job or to qualify for entrance into a professional school. They bring a consumer orientation to school, expecting value for their money.

In comparing the small residential university of 1960 with today's mega institutions, it is easy to decry the changes. However, there is much about today's university that is better. No longer serving primarily social and economic elites, it provides opportunities to a far broader cross-section of the population. Urban universities, in particular, have a rich mix of nationalities and cultures, and their students are exposed to a much larger world. Research is at the heart of the academic endeavour, and today's faculty and students are more exposed to new ideas and different perspectives. Modern communications technologies are opening up access to knowledge and viewpoints as never before. Campuses are more egalitarian, women are in the majority, and family background is no longer as important as it once seemed to be.

While we should celebrate the opening up of our universities, we need to do more to preserve and build upon the best features of the earlier institution. A good teacher can always marshal resources to ensure that students are challenged and fully engaged in their studies. University may not be for everyone, but it is for a much larger proportion of the population than it used to be. The country will thrive to the extent that it can provide students with an appropriate range of institutions across the educational system that cater to their various aspirations, needs, and talents. Institutional differentiation is addressed further in chapter 12.

One further critical factor influences a president's ability to foster a strong climate of student support on campus, and that is the extent to which he or she has regular personal contact with students. While this is much more easily achieved in smaller institutions, it is perhaps even more appreciated in larger ones. Such contact can take many forms – having monthly meetings with student leaders; initiating and playing an active role in recognition ceremonies for academic, athletic, extracurricular, and voluntary leadership; attending as many on-campus events as possible (debates, intercollegiate athletics, plays, concerts, and visual arts displays); hosting social events for students on campus and at home; and holding open meetings to canvass student opinions and to give students the opportunity to pursue matters of concern. Students also appreciate being invited to represent the university at community events.

In all of these and related situations, there are multiple benefits for a president. He or she will develop a much better understanding of the perspectives and concerns of each new intake of students (and each class has its own identity and culture), and students who have an opportunity to interact with the university's leaders will usually feel better about their institution. Most importantly, the vibrancy and enthusiasm of the university's primary clientele are infectious and rewarding, and contribute immensely to the president's own morale. Furthermore, continuing contact with individual students and alumni is a particularly gratifying part of one's post-presidential life.

7

International Outreach

We have seen that most Canadian universities were relatively small and even parochial in both their clientele and outlook until well into the 1960s. While there is considerable variation on campuses across the country, almost every university today has made a significant commitment to internationalism through the recruitment of international students and faculty, faculty and student exchange programs, research partnerships, and even mandatory overseas components for specific degree programs.

Like many of my contemporaries, I benefited tremendously from international experiences as a student. In 1964 I graduated from Bishop's University, a wonderful institution that was so small (550 students), homogeneous, and parochial at the time that it would scarcely be recognized as a university by today's standards.[1] However, the relative lack of program choice with only two or three professors per discipline was more than compensated for by the personal contact we had with faculty; the high participation of students in clubs, seminars, and sports; and the overall atmosphere of discussion and debate.

In 1965 I went to the University of London for the Post-Graduate Certificate in Education program, and my first class had over 500 students. During the long Easter break, with thirty-five other people from seventeen different countries, I went on a comparative education tour of the Soviet Union. The trip transformed my life, opening my eyes both to the similarities and to the differences across cultures in languages, art, politics, and everyday life.

I returned to London in 1971 to do my doctorate in comparative education and have had wonderful academic travel opportunities ever since – "tier one" Canadian International Development

Agency (CIDA) projects in Thailand and China and a "tier two" in Jordan; projects in Sri Lanka sponsored by the World University Service Canada, of which I was chair at the time; visiting professorships at the Open University in Britain and the Open Polytechnic of New Zealand; travel in South and Central America as founding chair of CREAD,[2] a distance education consortium for all of the Americas; meetings hosted by the Association of Commonwealth Universities (ACU) in Cypress, Malta, Swansea, and Birmingham; as vice-president for North America in the International Council of Distance Education (ICDE); and through conferences, meetings, and student recruitment in many other countries, including India, Bangladesh, Dubai, Australia, Costa Rica, Venezuela, many European countries, Cuba, and the United States.

It is my firm belief that, as much as it is fulfilling to learn about people in other countries, the strongest benefit of international travel is learning about one's own country and oneself. When I became president of Laurentian University, I inherited a program called Université Canadienne en France (UCF) that afforded university students from all across Canada the opportunity to study for a year in France. The campus was situated in a rather remote enclave high up above Villefranche-sur-Mer, sandwiched between Nice and Monaco, a rich environment for learning if there ever was one. Ironically, while the motive for most of the students was to improve their French or learn more about Europe, the isolated mountain venue meant that what they learned more about than anything else was their own country. They met others from across Canada and learned to appreciate both the regional differences and national similarities that characterize Canadians. As is so constantly the lesson, the message was that their international experience helped them better understand themselves.

By the time I got to Windsor, I was driven by more than a conviction that international experiences are tremendously valuable; I saw a global perspective as being a fundamental component of what a university education must offer. I questioned whether a person could consider him- or herself a university graduate without being exposed to other ways of thinking, other ways of looking at the world. A broad perspective seems particularly important for students in Canada, a country whose vast geographical reach limits opportunities to interact with other nationalities in the way that Europeans, for example, increasingly take for granted. At the same time, Canada's steadily increasing urbanization, immigration, and multiculturalism provide unprecedented opportunity for participation and interaction across cultures.

We were extremely fortunate at the University of Windsor to become the primary clients of Bazaar 2000, later renamed Higher Edge, a Canadian leader in international consulting. With ever-expanding offices and services in key locations in Asia, Africa, and South America, Higher Edge offers expertise in international credential transfer, visa requirements, and cross-cultural sensitivities, all vital components of the increasingly complex and competitive market for international students. Founded by York alumni Mel Broitman and Dani Zaretsky, talented friends driven by a passion for internationalism, the firm quickly helped the University of Windsor become one of Canada's most international universities. Windsor went from having 428 full-time "visa" (international) students in 1998 (4.6 per cent of its total full-time enrolment) to 1,459 in 2008 (11.2 per cent).[3] The initial influx of students came from India, Bangladesh, Pakistan, Nepal, China, and later Nigeria, and now they come from over seventy countries. The new crop of international students have very high academic standards, and they will increasingly provide the university with an outstanding group of alumni in well-placed positions all over the world.

The integration of international students is an important challenge if local students are to benefit as well. One of the most important consequences of the much higher numbers of visa students was that the university was pressured, by the students and Higher Edge itself, to provide them with much better services and support. With a significantly multicultural local community enhanced by such a large influx of international students, the commitment to developing a multinational student base has had a major impact across campus. This multicultural base has provided a more welcoming environment for overseas students, it has enhanced academic standards in many areas, it has sensitized faculty, staff, and students to many different ways of looking at the world, and it has fostered dialogue, debate, and friendships across many countries, languages, and cultures. I always urged our students to make friends with as many people as possible from other countries – apart from all the other benefits, it would later give them a free place to stay in locales all over the world!

We quickly built on these successes to expand dramatically the number and type of student-exchange program as well. In our model, Windsor students spent one or two semesters in parallel academic programs in sister institutions around the world, and students from those universities came to Windsor for similar time periods. In 1998 there were only a few such programs. By 2008 Windsor had exchange arrangements with forty institutions in thirteen countries.[4]

As previously noted, one of the great Canadian champions of international education has been Bill Leggett, former principal of Queen's University. He is unlike most of his contemporaries with similar interests in that his conviction of the vital importance of international education was not based on his personal experiences as a student or faculty member: "I had never studied or travelled outside North America. In fact, by modern standards, I had never really travelled at all. Mainly, I had this gut sense that the world was getting increasingly smaller and that the future leaders of Canadian business, government, and society would require a broader perspective on Canada and the world if they were to achieve success."

For Dr Leggett, the principles of internationalism are central to the building of Canada as a country. He does not favour building more universities to keep up with the demand for local access but would strongly prefer that federal funding be used to encourage and support students to travel to universities in other parts of the country. He argues that if more Canadians had the experience of living in other parts of the country, it would help break down the barriers that have long plagued its politics – the enmity between East and West, the lack of understanding in the rest of Canada of the aspirations and culture of the people of Quebec, and the need for much better relationships with Aboriginal peoples. He commented:

> I think we made a huge mistake as a country in devolving authority for education to the provinces. As a result, we failed to create the mechanisms of financial support (cheaper travel, scholarships, and other incentives) that would encourage and assist students from one region of the country to study in another.
>
> If, as a nation, we had created that sense of the importance of using the university system as a vehicle for knowing one another, its citizens and leaders would come to understand that, in general, the aspirations of citizens in every part of this great country are, at their core, essentially the same.

For example, regarding a student aid program that provided matching funds for private donations, Leggett decries the Ontario government's decision that out-of-province students were ineligible for support from the resulting scholarships. The Quebec government's refusal to allow holders of its graduate scholarships to study out-of-province is another case in point:

> These [decisions], to me, were totally counterproductive. It would be so much less expensive, and so much more effective, to facilitate the creation of real centres of teaching and research excellence in specific disciplines in both small and large institutions across the country and move students to them than to build less-illustrious, resource-starved institutions in every community just so students could live at home. We have inherited a system that lacks a national sense of what we are about as a country and how post-secondary education contributes to that end. This is completely counter to my sense of where we need to be as a nation.

An illustrative case study is Leggett's struggle to make Herstmonceux, the English castle given to Queen's by benefactor Alfred Bader, into the successful and creative academic entity it is today. His fundamental challenge was to overcome the bureaucratic obstacles at home. Students who wanted to attend for one semester were unable to secure accommodation in either Queen's residences or Kingston-area apartments for their return in mid-year or, alternatively, were faced with having to pay a full year's accommodation at home despite being away half the time. Moreover, almost all the courses in the arts departments were for a full year, which meant that many students going abroad for one semester were forced to delay their graduation for at least a semester and perhaps a year for the privilege.

It took several years for these problems, once identified, to be resolved. Once accomplished, however, the seeds of Herstmonceux's success were sown. More importantly, the problems' resolution also opened up the opportunity for students to participate actively in the myriad of other international exchanges that had been theoretically, but not practically, available at Queen's. To this day, Bill Leggett links the changes that led to Herstmonceux's success with the evolution of Queen's impressive leadership position in international study at the undergraduate level.

The value of an international experience for a student is most graphically represented by an incident Leggett recounted that occurred at Herstmonceux when he was hosting a meeting of the presidents of Canada's G-10 universities, the top research institutions in the country. A Herstmonceux student was asked to talk to the assembled presidents about her experience there, which she did very eloquently. One of the presidents then stood up and challenged her, suggesting that she had spoken beautifully but that what she had experienced, in reality, was little more than a wonderful vacation at her family's expense. Anything but intimidated, the young woman looked him right in the eye and said, "Sir, I grew up in Burlington. I thought I would live my entire life in the Hamilton area. Since coming here, I have visited five countries and learned that I can cope in every one of them. I have seen what Canada is and my eyes have been opened to how everyone in this part of the world admires it and wants to be there. I have become so proud of my country and so aware of the opportunities in the world around me that, while I am going back to Canada, I intend to make the world my oyster."

Her response validated everything that Leggett believed in – the sense of self-confidence that came from her experience, the "can do" attitude, and the new ability to see Canada from other perspectives. He noted that "as Canadians, we have a tendency to criticize and devalue our leaders and our country. When you view Canada from another dimension, suddenly it becomes important to value and preserve it."

Leggett's experience at Herstmonceux was echoed annually in experiences of my own at Windsor, where we had two receptions a year for exchange students, both local and international. Each was asked to talk about his or her experience, and each said and conveyed much the same thing. The transformation in the students was highly visible and often startling – the confident, outgoing, and enthusiastic returnees were almost unrecognizable from the slightly reticent and shy students about to go off to a new institution and a new country. This personal development is enhanced by the networking opportunities and broad range of new interests that an international experience inevitably fosters.

I believe that even a somewhat negative international experience contributes to personal development in ways that cannot be duplicated in one's local environment. Furthermore, if one has been away long enough in a culture significantly different from one's own, a common experience upon return is reverse culture shock. I have never forgotten how a good friend was almost physically ill at the commercialism in Canada at Christmas time when he returned after working for several years in a youth program in poor regions of Africa.

Promoting a strong international perspective in Canadian universities is a critical issue for the country as a whole. By geography, Canadians are an ocean away from most of the world's population and are separated from the Spanish and Portuguese countries of North, Central, and South America by the massive United States. Undergraduate students have nothing resembling the opportunities for travel to countries with different languages and significantly different cultures that their European counterparts take for granted. Summer visitors to Europe are always astounded by the mix of young people in a particular nation – the French in London, the English in Paris, the Germans in Amsterdam, and the Italians in Berlin. Now that they are joined in the European Union, these nations provide students with cheap and easy ways to travel – networks of inexpensive youth hostels, exchange agreements, and fast trains. For Canadians, exotic foreign places are much further away than they are for Europeans. In fact, the parochialism goes much deeper than that because it is even a challenge to travel to other provinces, given Canada's geography and great distances between cities. It is further to fly from Victoria, British Columbia, to St John's, Newfoundland (5,078 kilometres) than from Halifax, Nova Scotia, to London, England (4,623 kilometres).

Bill Leggett's leadership represents a challenge to all Canadian universities, especially those without the resources or wealth of a Queen's. While these institutions might find it more difficult to sponsor and support as many international exchanges, many of the benefits can be realized by attracting more international students than would otherwise be the case and then doing everything possible to integrate them into the activities of local students. Of course, the Canada that universities serve today, especially in the urban regions, is a far cry from the white, homogeneous country that existed a few short decades ago. Toronto and Vancouver are very cosmopolitan today (respectively 42.9 per cent and 41.7 per cent visible minorities in the 2006 census and 43.7 per cent and 37.5 per cent foreign born in the 2001 census)[5] and, relatively speaking, so are many of the smaller centres served by universities such as Calgary (22.2 per cent visible minorities, 20.9 per cent foreign born), Windsor (16.0 and 22.3), Hamilton (12.3 and 23.6), and Kitchener (13.8 and 22.1).[6] Indeed, at Windsor, faculty and staff were often unable to distinguish between local and international students because so many of the former were part of very recent immigrant families from all over the world, and the pressure on the administration at places like York and Windsor to provide better prayer space for Muslim students comes as much from Canadians as from students from the Middle East and Africa.

There have been many overtures to the federal and some provincial governments to provide better funding for international programs for Canadian students and faculty. The country has a rich history of youth organizations dedicated to giving our best students international opportunities and exposure – Canada World Youth, World University Service Canada (WUSC), Canadian University Students Overseas (CUSO, now partnering with Voluntary Service Overseas), and the Centre for International Studies and Cooperation (CECI). However, it has not been as easy to increase funding for student travel beyond Canada in these current tougher fiscal and more conservative times. I have strongly supported the initiatives of many of my fellow presidents to try to persuade the federal government to increase the financial support for these sorts of programs, believing that the rewards would be enormous, not only for the personal benefits to the individuals involved but for what they bring back in the form of ideas, talent, networks, and the will to make Canada a leader in international relations. I am disappointed that these efforts have not been more successful.

Especially among the more research-intensive universities, international connections are increasingly important. While individual faculty have worked closely with disciplinary peers in other countries for a long time, many institutional leaders have only recently begun to recognize the value of international partnerships in research and are now actively seeking opportunities that will enhance the quality and reputation of their university through strategic alliances. The effectiveness of this approach is enhanced by today's easy and rapid communications technologies and by the preoccupation with institutional prestige that drives the world's top universities. Martha Piper appreciates the significance of these developments and the importance of personal relationships in international success, citing the leadership of Steve Sample of the University of Southern California, who established the Association of Pacific Rim Universities:

I was a bit sceptical at first, worrying that it would just be an old boys' country club. But Steve looked me right in the eye and said, "Don't underestimate it. If these people are your friends, you can pick up the phone and get things done. They will go to bat for you, they understand you, they're your only real friends in this world." He was right. Whether it was Fudan University in Shanghai or the National University of Singapore, I could pick up the phone and call the president and get an instant response. It was tremendously helpful.

A related trend is collaborative academic programming whereby a Canadian university is linked to an American, European, or Asian university in an effort to enhance the prestige and reputation of both. Early examples of this kind of collaboration were York University's Schulich School of Business, which offers an MBA degree in tandem with Chicago's Northwestern University, via its Kellogg School of Management, and the joint Windsor/Detroit Mercy JD/LLB law degree. There has been an explosion of such agreements in recent years.

In summary, international outreach has become an important component of almost all Canadian universities. The significant increases in the numbers of international students attending Canadian universities and the proliferation of international exchanges have greatly enhanced the openness and quality of higher education for Canadians. At the same time, the lack of a national strategy for – and accreditation of – post-secondary education undermines Canada's efforts to compete; the country seems comparatively passive in its international recruitment efforts compared to such competitors as the United States, Australia, Britain, and even New Zealand and Ireland.

Glen Jones has suggested three reasons for Canada's relatively passive approach to internationalization in recent decades – the country's preoccupation with itself that was spurred by Expo '67 and the increase in the number of Canadian studies courses in universities; the limits and challenges of the country's federal-provincial model and jurisdictional boundaries, as discussed above; and the fear of displacement whereby international students and efforts would hamper domestic provisions.[7] While acknowledging the increasingly global outlooks of individual universities across the country, Jones advocates a more pan-Canadian approach to this important issue: "We need to find an approach that builds on Canada's strengths and values, and moves us forward in terms of improving post-secondary education in Canada."[8]

A much more aggressive, comprehensive, and better-funded approach must be adopted if future generations are to succeed in competing effectively in the international economy and in promoting such strong Canadian values as multiculturalism, peaceful coexistence, and environmental sustainability. Without this, Canada's former advantages in higher education will continue to erode and its economic and social leadership will lessen.

8

Financial Issues: Underfunded or
Fat Cats?

No discussion of presidential leadership among Canadian public universities will last very long without the matter of money coming up. In terms of time investment, no issue is more preoccupying for a president, both in terms of ensuring the revenues and carefully managing the expenditures.

THE PRINCIPAL CHALLENGE: THE BATTLE FOR PUBLIC SUPPORT

On the revenue side, the president's challenge starts with having to persuade governments and taxpayers of the vital importance of investing in universities for the future economic and social health of the country. On the expenditure side, it means tight fiscal management and doing everything possible to make optimum use of the resources available. An important component of persuading government of the need for more money is to demonstrate how effectively the university is using existing funds and what it could do with additional resources.

Most presidents believe that the post-secondary educational sector is significantly underfunded, that the quality of university education in Canada is in serious decline, and that a major financial crisis is looming for our institutions. They are strong advocates of better per capita funding and more flexible (higher) tuition fees. While they accept their responsibilities for fiscal management, they also tend to uphold the prevailing model of the research-intensive university, notwithstanding its greater cost per student than alternative approaches.

On the other hand, studies have shown that the general public (and therefore most government leaders) believes that universities are doing very well, especially compared to competing issues of more immediate impact, such as the availability of health care, the size of elementary school classes, and the state of roads and sewers. Canadian universities are, in one sense, victims of their own marketing success. The general population's positive view of the sector has grown even more positive over the years, perhaps at least in part because of presidential advocacy.[1]

Taxpayers are not necessarily persuaded that the institutions are underfunded or that they need more resources. Our universities have been through a major growth era, with crane-strewn campuses manifesting ambitious building projects. They look prosperous and seem to be booming, complicating the case for additional governmental support. It is difficult to persuade politicians to increase grants when at least a segment of the general public thinks you are "fat cats." The public's expectation, instead, is that universities should find new, more efficient ways of operating and that their fiscal problems should be resolved from within and not at the additional expense of the taxpayer or fee-paying student.

Are our universities facing dire financial straits, or are they relative fat cats in public sector funding? What can university presidents do both to make their case for more resources and to ensure that these would be used to optimum advantage? The responses can be considered from a number of viewpoints:

a) The declining quality of the undergraduate experience
b) Government and community relations
c) Internal fiscal management
d) Research infrastructure and endowment funds
e) Management by crisis
f) Major technological change
g) International examples: block grants, tuition fees, and income-contingent repayment plans

a)   The Case for Declining Quality

The quality of the undergraduate student experience is particularly difficult to establish in objective terms. For the general public, the primary policy issue is "accessibility" – ensuring that there are sufficient places for all who aspire to them. There was never more public interest in the universities than during the "double-cohort" challenge in Ontario, when parents and politicians were much more concerned about the number of student places than about the actual quality of the student experience.

The students themselves would describe the university experience in different ways. First, as previously noted, the intensity of the students' engagement with faculty and with each other is arguably significantly less in the current era of mass higher education than in earlier more elitist times. Not only are faculty more oriented to their graduate students, but it can also be argued that undergraduates have lower expectations for their university experience than their predecessors and that they have become more accepting of large classes. While there are creative ways to use larger classes effectively, a consistent increase in student-faculty ratios inevitably frustrates the quality of the student experience in ways that go far beyond the classroom. Especially in the first couple of years of undergraduate study on most campuses, accessibility to faculty is far more limited than it used to be and the overall experience is too often an impersonal one. In this environment, too many students fall by the wayside, and even those who persist may not have the quality of academic and social experience of the previous generation.

The second problem has become pervasive and is attracting increasing attention. The practice of assigning sessional instructors and teaching assistants to first-year classes has gone way beyond any pre-planned model. In their 2009 book *The Transformation of Ontario's Postsecondary Education System,* Ian Clark et al. expose the weakness of the Ontario universities' argument that undergraduates must be taught by full-time faculty who are actively involved in research: "Ironically, while the universities have opposed the idea of having any university-level institutions in Ontario whose mission is primarily that of teaching, many of them employ large numbers of faculty whose job consists solely of teaching. In some universities, part-time and temporary faculty now do half or more of all of the undergraduate teaching."[2] The case can be made that today's reliance on what Clark et al. call the most expensive type of post-secondary institution (research-focused universities) is not sustainable and that significant change is both necessary and urgent.[3]

One response would be to define our universities more narrowly and encourage them to do fewer things better. Hence, the large research-intensive universities, such as those in the G13, would concentrate much more on graduate programming, leaving more and more of undergraduate education to the rest. The smaller universities would focus on providing the highest quality of undergraduate student learning experience. The middle-sized comprehensive and regional universities would worry less about offering a full range of programs for their respective catchment areas, instead striving to attract top students from all over the country by developing a reputation for the quality of their particular specialties.

Such reforms assume a more market-driven system, one that encourages more student mobility, a greater variety of institutions, and a more entrepreneurial and national approach to student recruitment. With less pressure from the local region to offer the full range of university programming, a given institution could benefit financially by divesting itself of undersubscribed or unduly expensive programs to focus on what it does best. Of course, this might result in most institutions competing for the same popular and more lucrative programs, with consequent winners and losers. The concomitant risks would include being perceived as being less responsive to local community needs and losing the enrolment base that had previously sustained the institution. As well, the higher costs of graduate programming would mean that the research-intensive universities would require better funding or much higher tuition fees to replace their current reliance on undergraduate student revenues.

On balance, while there are very strong arguments for greater institutional diversification in Canada (see chapters 12 and 14), the case for financial benefits to a given institution is less clear and one dependent upon significant national reforms of the whole postsecondary system.

b)   Government and Community Relations

As public institutions, Canadian universities rely heavily on two sources for their base budgets, both under the direct jurisdiction of the appropriate provincial government: annual operating grants and student tuition fees. Presidents spend a lot of time on both of these issues, starting with lobbying government for more resources.

Lobbying involves much more than simply advocating for one's institution, since higher education must compete with many other sectors for funding, such as schools, health care, and municipalities.

The first task is thus to work with colleagues to make sure that the university sector as a whole gets at least its share of the provincial pie and then to fight for a fair and equitable piece for one's own institution. This requirement has led universities to endeavour to present a strong collective voice formally through member associations in most provinces. The two largest, the Council of Ontario Universities (COU) and the Conférence des recteurs et des principaux des universités du Québec (CREPUQ), are somewhat different in makeup but play similar roles in representing the universities collectively to their respective ministries. All of the established public universities are also members of the Association of Universities and Colleges of Canada (AUCC),[4] a national body that focuses its representation on issues of direct concern to the federal government, notably the support for research and scholarship across the country.

A central dilemma for executive heads is trying to persuade taxpayers and governments of the magnitude of university funding problems while individually extolling the virtues of their respective campuses. Challenges like the following must be addressed directly:

1 As institutions relatively unknown to many people, universities are not well understood and often presumed to be overly bureaucratic, wasteful, and poorly managed. While most faculty work extremely hard, often six or seven days a week, a few take advantage of the freedom of the job and the relatively laissez-faire management structures in ways that can undermine public confidence in the profession.

2 The deterioration of operating funds is less obvious to the public than to the major competitors for public funds – elementary and secondary education (whose large classes are better known to the public and have a greater impact on parents than large classes in universities),[5] municipalities (roads and sewers), and, especially, health care, where long waiting times in emergency rooms or for a needed operation have a huge public profile and impact.

3 The average person does not appreciate the important distinctions between capital and operating funding. Beautiful new buildings can go up while the university is strapped for the base operating funds that support the core operations of the institution, from teaching and learning to maintenance of the physical plant. Government per capita funding has been declining for many years, and student-faculty ratios have soared to well over 20:1 or

even 25:1 in some cases, more than double what they were thirty years ago.[6]

4 Presidents may be seen to deliver a mixed message. Attempts to establish how difficult the financial times are for a given institution can be undermined by the same person's claims for the wonders of the place when recruiting students, speaking to alumni, or fundraising.

5 Bill Leggett suggests that part of the problem is that fewer of the newer generation of political leaders have had the kind of university experience that most presidents remember and aspire to recreate.

> It is tragic, frankly, and deeply disturbing that governments don't seem to be able to understand the importance of investing for quality in our universities and that the general public is not concerned with this reality. As a consequence, the gradual decay we are seeing now becomes a self-perpetuating legacy because as each new group of students goes through institutions where they haven't had the opportunity to get to know the professor except from the back of the room or to fully engage and test their creative ability and then graduate to pursue their careers, the view that there is nothing more to a university education than this becomes perpetuated and intensified.

6 Other highly visible spokespersons for higher education are less apt to be in synch with university presidents. Faculty and student associations (and their provincial and national bodies) often deliver messages to the public that differ from those of the institutions' presidents, all of which complicate the clarity of the case. While there have been many efforts on all sides in most institutions to seek ways to coordinate the messages coming from their diverse constituencies, there are genuine differences in the perspectives and interests of presidents, faculty, and students on some issues (tuition fees, for example) that may render a common message unrealistic.

Given their prevailing notion that the core problem is underfunding, presidents may be open to the criticism that they are never happy, even when governments respond to their entreaties. It is probably true that presidents do not thank politicians enough for the funding announcements and increases that they do get. For example, the McGuinty government made a huge investment ($6.2 billion) in Ontario's colleges and universities through its "Reaching Higher" program starting in 2005, establishing post-secondary education as the clear funding priority for that particular year. This bold step reflected the premier's passion for education, and he used up considerable political capital in taking it given the other very strong claims for increases, especially from the health care sector. While reaction among the universities was very positive, it did not take long for the presidents to be pushing for more, and the government never really got either the results or the recognition the premier expected. When government leaders get poorer results than expected for bold investments, they are less likely to make them the next time around. One of the key tasks of the president of an institution like COU or CREPUQ, then, is to tutor university presidents in government relations, something most of them have very limited experience of when assuming the presidential post.

My own conclusion from my many years of experience in government relations is that presidents are almost always more effective, both individually and collectively, when they take a positive approach to government. Those with experience in the corridors of Ottawa and Queen's Park almost always counsel their universities to try to understand the politics around what they are seeking, to see the issues from the government's and voters' perspective, and to frame their arguments in that context. This has very much been the approach of past successful leaders at AUCC, COU, and CREPUQ, each of whom brought extensive government experience to the post. I don't mean to suggest that presidents should never criticize government policy. On such occasions, however, it is essential that their points be well supported by demonstrable data and that their support base be broad, extending well beyond the universities themselves.

Even that may not be enough. In 1998 the university presidents of Ontario expressed their concern to Premier Harris that Ontario stood last among the ten provinces in per capita student funding. After a forceful presentation on the issue from Rob Prichard, the chair of COU at the time, the premier immediately turned the argument upside down by congratulating the universities for having the "most efficient" system in Canada. The presidents persisted with their representation, however, and it later found more traction with the McGuinty government.

Of course, presidents are not the only ones who speak for the universities. Their cause can certainly be helped when board chairs and chancellors speak up, and it can be even more effectively served when those less directly connected – mayors, foundation heads, corporate leaders – extol their virtues.

Whatever the message, Dave Marshall stressed the importance of keeping it clear and simple. He subjects it to a litmus test: "If I can't explain our financial case to a Rotary Club in a twenty-minute speech, it's too complex. It won't be understood." For Marshall, being able to differentiate among institutions is a key component of a president's ability to persuade business people of the value of investing in the local university. The general public will buy the importance of teaching and learning and will appreciate the university's role in research and development, but people will only support a given institution to the extent that they are persuaded that it is striving to be the best in one area or another. No business can be all things to all people, and corporate success depends on identifying the right niche and doing it better than anyone else. It's the same for universities, says Marshall.

Most of the presidents interviewed felt that Canadian universities were seriously underfunded, especially given the decade-long decrease in per capita funding in most provinces and the concomitant increases in the student-faculty ratio. David Johnston is particularly adamant, not only that universities are significantly underfunded, but that the education sector at all levels deserves much greater investment in the competitive global knowledge society. Not apologizing for consistently seeking more funding, he quoted Robert Browning: "Ah, but a man's reach should exceed his grasp, or what's a heaven for?" Notwithstanding his strong advocacy for better funding, Johnston believes that presidents could use better tactics than the whining and complaining that is too often the public perception of what they do:

> We should be doing more in the intelligent, thoughtful public
> discourse as to what is the role of public education in our coun-
> try. We are often so busy managing our institutions and trying
> to find the time to be strategic and do planning that we don't
> spend enough time entering into that public discourse about the
> importance of public education. To me, that's the great oppor-
> tunity for Canada, even in this crisis – to say that we will be the

knowledge capital of the world, that we would be able to generate and use knowledge better than any other society and that would be our destiny for the twenty-first century. That's the kind of thing a university president should be saying.

Myer Horowitz didn't apologize for having been a strong public spokesperson for better university funding throughout his career. He emphasized that even when university grants went up, they were almost always short of increased costs (inflation) and that the only institutional response over and over again was to cut, cut, cut. While the latter exercise led to some improvements in the way universities function, he conceded that, by and large, university leaders believe that their institutions are organized appropriately for the roles they perform and that most of the answer to their challenges lies in better funding.

During the past two decades, a number of leading presidents, including most of those interviewed for this book, achieved stronger support for universities by persuading political leaders of the direct correlation between investment in them and both local and national economic prosperity. Paul Davenport, an economist, has been a particularly influential proponent of this argument. Like many in the larger, more research-intensive universities, he favours more freedom for universities to set their own tuition levels, and he was an early advocate of income-contingent plans that would not require graduates to repay their government loans until their incomes reached a specified level.

Peter George, another economist, shares Davenport's enthusiasm for a freer tuition regime and income-contingent provisions for student loans. As a former president of cou, he has a unique perspective on presidential lobbying and government responsiveness. He finds that politicians and others are much more cognizant of the importance of universities to the economy – and, hence, more apt to listen – than they were ten years ago:

In terms of resource allocation, there have been peaks and valleys, but at least you can now talk to politicians in terms of their own stated commitments around the importance of higher education to prosperity. It is a huge step forward, but is not yet evidence in changes to the funding regime, despite the additional resources committed by Ontario in its Reaching Higher initiative.

The problem is that accessibility and increasing enrolment invariably crowd out quality considerations for government.

One of the most successful Canadian university presidents in government relations, Martha Piper of UBC, has a different perspective on funding issues from that of most of her colleagues. When she moved to the University of Alberta from McGill in 1985, she found an institution in a "land of milk and honey" compared to the situation in Quebec and was shocked to hear university leaders complaining publicly about the levels of funding. She points out the relativity of university funding, noting from her extensive international experience how much Asian universities do with so much less. Piper decries our tendency to always want more, to say that we need more classrooms, offices, and labs when we are not making optimum use of the ones we do have. She believes that universities have a lot to learn about the management of their resources:

> We don't have the discipline that most big corporations do and yet we are big businesses! How many of us have really had the discipline to examine our cost structures, our costs per student, whether or not we are above or below the mean, and what we are paying and how we are paying ... we just don't have the discipline. We don't have "earnings per share" or "total shareholder return," but we should be able to measure what the value is for the money that is coming in. People say that we are lean as we can be, but I'm not convinced that is always the case.

And so the debate will continue. Presidents make a very good case in tying the fiscal health of their institutions to the future of Canada, but they will be more tested than ever to prevail in times of escalating government debts, shrinking tax bases, and cutthroat competition from other public sector institutions.

c)   Internal Fiscal Management

The gap between public perceptions and fiscal realities has its internal dimensions as well. It is important to keep faculty and staff informed about the financial position of the university and to involve them directly in the annual budget exercises. While part of the role of the president may be to protect faculty from external pressures so that they can get on with their academic work, Dolence and Norris have observed that shielding employees too much from fiscal realities may mean that they don't buy into the consequent strategies.[7] Presidents will naturally dramatize financial difficulties when they are trying to convince others of the institution's needs or to impose significant cuts or constraints, but they have to be very careful to avoid hyperbole that might undermine their internal credibility if the case turns out to be less serious than originally depicted.

Universities are much more sophisticated in budget management these days, increasingly delegating both responsibility and authority to those closest to the core activities of teaching and research. A common tactic has been to build annual cuts of from 2 to 5 per cent right into the budget process. After the resulting revenues have been used to the extent necessary to cover projected shortfalls, the balance is reallocated to the current priority areas. By establishing this as the standard budget process, presidents can avoid a crisis mentality and help instil a stronger performance culture in faculties and departments anxious to win back at least their share of the institution-wide cut.

While the majority of presidents still see the significant underfunding of their institutions as the primary issue, universities have made major gains in cost-efficiency over the past two decades, primarily on the administrative side. Working through the Canadian Association of University Business Officers (CAUBO), vice-presidents, finance, and their colleagues have established all sorts of provincial and national consortia to realize cost savings through collaborative group purchasing of supplies (technology) and services (insurance). CAUBO is a great source of ideas and has played a leading role in encouraging universities to invest in more efficient energy sources, the result being significant long-term savings in such areas as lighting, insulation, heating, and cooling.

On the academic side, consortia of university libraries have collaborated on investments in technology that have led to the establishment of some of the most sophisticated and effective electronic library resources in the world. Such cooperation is particularly beneficial to smaller institutions, allowing them to give their students and faculty access to academic materials through the largest university libraries at levels not previously imagined.

Years of cutting have left very few areas of universities with much discretionary spending ability. Given that 80 per cent or more of operating revenues go to faculty and staff salaries, any significant reductions in allocations to a given area must involve position reduction. This, of course, is a major concern for labour relations and a test of the ability of the senior administration to persuade others of the seriousness of the situation and the need to take the recommended action.

The burgeoning cost of presidential compensation has already been addressed, but faculty salaries, too, have increased dramatically in recent years. This is a result of several factors: an overall "sellers' market" during a time of rapid expansion, accentuated by faculty shortages in such key disciplines as accounting and finance; the elimination of mandatory retirement in most North American jurisdictions (which used to lead to significant salary savings when a full professor was replaced by a much cheaper lecturer or assistant professor); and the strengthening of faculty unions on campus.

As also noted earlier, administrations have coped with financial pressures by using increasing numbers of sessionals, part-time instructors, and teaching assistants rather than by attempting to reduce the compensation of full-time faculty. Given the damage that labour unrest can do to an institution's reputation, this response is understandable, but the trade-off may be a significant decline in institutional quality over the long term. Another common response to budget cuts in universities can lead to longer-term difficulties. Many departments and faculties continue to offer programs and services even when the support funding has been cut totally or severely. Managers preach "doing more with less," and employees are proud of their ability to sustain services. Their dedication and commitment are commendable, except when they lead to burn-out and an unacceptably low quality of service because human and financial resources have been stretched too thin. Often, it is better to cut a program or service than to offer an inferior product.

d)   Research Infrastructure and Endowments

So far, the discussion about funding has focused on base operating budgets and their primary sources, provincial government funding and tuition fee income. Today's university president is heavily involved in private fundraising as well, and major private contributions to universities are regular news stories in many communities.

However, most of this money goes into new buildings or endowment funds in support of student scholarships and research, with little impact on regular operating funds in most cases.

Very recently, however, there has been an exception to this norm, one widely experienced by many Canadian universities. The global financial crisis, coupled with record low interest rates, resulted in a sharp and sudden decline in pension and endowment revenues. Scholarships from endowment funds at most universities are based on an assumed approximately 5 per cent return on investment. When interest rates have fallen below this threshold, institutions have usually responded, not by cutting the number or value of scholarships but by skimming the necessary top-up funds from the regular operating budget. There is even less choice with pensions. Those universities with defined benefit plans are especially likely to face massive shortfalls in their pension funds, which they are required by law (with some differences by province) to fund even though most of the actual payouts will not be made for years to come. This has been a very serious issue for some Ontario universities where the provincial government, not wanting to set a precedent for other public sector organizations, has not acceded to requests for greater policy leeway.

A related and often controversial issue is the institutional costs of research. These have grown dramatically in recent decades as universities endeavour to provide the requisite labs, libraries, and computer networks; manage grantsmanship and intellectual property; and ensure such regulatory requirements as animal care, environmental assessment, and ethical aspects of human research. These costs are covered in part by the federal indirect-costs program, but at less than half the rates paid in the United States, the United Kingdom, and the European Union. At the time of writing, the funds provided amounted to less than twenty-five cents on the dollar notwithstanding a concerted AUCC campaign to achieve at least 40 per cent of the direct costs of research.[8] Again, if the institutions are unable to secure the balance from the research contractor (and they have often been forced through the competitive process to understate the costs), the shortfall has to be made up from regular operating funds. The issue can also be a bone of contention between the administration and individual researchers who often wonder where the infrastructure funds go.

e) Management by Crisis

Although Canadian universities have never been in greater demand, a good case can be made that they are facing an imminent financial crisis. The government share of their revenues has steadily eroded since the early 1990s,[9] and faculty salaries have escalated at the same time. While tuition fees have risen to compensate, they have been closely regulated by governments nervous about the political backlash from too rapid an increase.

Canadian presidents have regularly cited the funding of major American universities to make the case for our relatively resource-starved institutions. While the argument still holds for the top American institutions where per capita revenues, notably including much higher tuition fees, support a more personal and resource-rich learning experience for students than is possible in Canada, the picture south of the border is not nearly as rosy as it used to be. In his widely publicized report *Higher Education Budgets and the Global Recession*,[10] John Aubrey Douglass of the University of California – Berkeley, provides a very discouraging picture of American public higher education. He notes that, as of September 2009, thirty-four states had made recent major cuts in higher education spending. The most acute case is California, which boasts one of the largest and most successful higher education systems in the world. He contrasts the American cuts with the sustained or increased investment in higher education in most other countries, one result of which is that the United States, which had led the world in both tertiary access and degree attainment rates only two decades earlier, has fallen out of the top ten in both categories.[11]

When he was minister of education and training in the Harris government in Ontario in 1995, John Snobelen was caught on a leaked departmental video extolling the virtues of "creating a crisis" in the educational system to facilitate its reform. Notwithstanding the political heat and embarrassment this caused him, it can be argued that some changes are much easier to make when there is a widespread perception of crisis. From this perspective, I asked the interviewees whether it would be better for presidents to declare a crisis and use it to change the way their institutions operated than simply decry the lack of adequate public funding.

David Johnston disagreed strongly with this approach, arguing that crisis management is never as effective as longer-term planning:

"I think crises are hard to manage. They take a lot of energy and you often lose people to somewhere more comfortable. Good presidents try to avoid crises and try to ensure that the energy of change can be built into the institution without having a burning platform to do it." Like Myer Horowitz, he believes that the current model for universities will be with us for some time to come and that it is important to find new ways to fund and make it work.

Dave Marshall believes that a delivery crisis is definitely coming in post-secondary education and wonders when it will be recognized: "I think you are starting to see it in the larger universities – 1,200 student classes in Intro Psych or Intro Biology are an indication. What do they have to be before we get to the General Motors situation – 2,000 students ... 2,500 students?" He worries about universities using their own private sources of revenue (such as those from continuing education, international students, and other profit-making areas) to cross-subsidize the delivery of credit programs. He also worries about the dilution of the Alberta public system, decrying the province's practice of awarding private, faith-based institutions 80 per cent of the public grant: "Universities are not sufficiently funded. The proportion of our operating expenses that comes from government grants has been declining for two decades and it should go back up. Universities are a public trust."

It is clear to all the presidents interviewed that the continuing trend to higher faculty salaries and flat university funding is just not sustainable over the longer term. Paul Davenport's view is representative:

> The settlements in Ontario since the turn of the century for full-time faculty members have been as high as 6 per cent. From time to time, you get some relief from turnover, but we're going to have little turnover in the coming recession. So, in my view, our current situation is unsustainable. Our faculty in Ontario are highly educated, work hard, and deserve to be fairly paid. Nonetheless, I see a bleak few years in Ontario as universities discover the only way to balance the budgets with those kinds of settlements are layoffs and closure of positions, which have a negative impact on the quality of education. The difference with the hospitals is that the general population are very worried when they see layoffs at hospitals, but they're much more able to accept it for universities as class sizes go up.

On balance, taking heed of David Johnston's concerns and the earlier quote from Jim Downey that "it is generally easier and better to get people excited by our possibilities than to feel sorry for us," presidents would be well advised to avoid a crisis approach to their funding challenges. In any event, if the decline in undergraduate education continues to the point of crisis, it would be better if the alarm bells are rung first by students, parents, and the general public.

f) Major Technological Change

For many, the explosion in communications technologies offers the best hope for more accessible and cost-efficient education around the world. However, especially compared to American and European responses to the same fiscal pressures, Canadian universities and their leaders have not seen major technological changes in teaching and learning as central to their ability to cope. While every campus-based university now offers some form of online teaching and other forms of distance education, these are usually complementary to the existing mode of operation rather than something that might replace standard classroom teaching in the future.

David Johnston has shown a particular interest in this field, serving on a number of commissions and advisory groups on the information highway and chairing Ontario's Advisory Committee on Online Learning and its Task Force on Learning Technologies (of which I was a member). The latter group produced the report *A Time to Sow*,[12] which advocates significant investment in new learning technologies and the development of a much more supportive environment for such initiatives. This report highlighted the teachings of Tony Bates, an internationally recognized leader in the management of technological change; while seeing new technologies as a fruitful response to challenges such as those set out above, Bates is concerned about the high cost of the initial investment in them and emphasizes the critical importance of embedding them within a wider strategy for teaching and learning.[13]

Bonnie Patterson reinforces the notion that more technology than ever is being used in the classroom but believes it would be too expensive for Ontario universities to use the new technologies in a really big way. The evidence around the world supports this view. On a large scale, distance education can be very cost-efficient, but overall the costs of online learning and the concomitant student support can be prohibitive. The initial investment in the requisite infrastructure (course design, computer systems, support networks, course materials) is usually higher than most presidents anticipate, and the systems are only cost-effective for the mega-universities.[14]

Again, the prevailing enrolment-based funding systems in Canada tend to discourage innovative approaches to teaching and learning. When he first came to Mount Royal, Dave Marshall mused about partnering with Athabasca University to create a hybrid institution – half distance, half residential. The concept never got past the casual idea stage, but he still believes it could have merit. He also dreamt of Mount Royal taking advantage of the best distance education courses from around the world, delivering, for example, Haifa University's world religions course, which Haifa had spent $500,000 developing. He quickly realized, however, that this would mean losing that proportion of Mount Royal's enrolments for funding purposes, a classic example of the reward system frustrating an interesting idea. Nevertheless, he continues to develop blended learning at Mount Royal, the driving criterion being advantages to students.

Perhaps the principal reason that Canada's universities don't accept open and distance learning more fully is that it clashes with the prevailing academic culture. This issue is pursued further in chapter 12.

g)   International Examples: Block Grants, Tuition Fees, and Income-Contingent Repayment Plans

So far, the discussion of financial challenges has anticipated difficult times but not a sea change in university funding. As previously noted, Canada's very decentralized system has tended to mitigate against the more dramatic government intervention into university affairs that one has seen in the United Kingdom, Australia, or New Zealand. However, there is considerable evidence from those jurisdictions and from the budget cuts in the United States that things might be changing.

The most recent and dramatic example comes from the United Kingdom in the aftermath of the 2010 Browne Report,[15] which advocated radical changes in university funding, ones that went further than the other jurisdictions in implementing the principles of income-contingency repayment plans (ICRPS). An ICRP is based on the notion that a graduate should not have to repay his or her educational loans until the investment has paid off in terms of higher earnings.[16] Browne's principal recommendations are for the elimination of the long-standing practice of allocating block grants to universities, the removal of ceilings on tuition fees (although an initial standard fee of £6,000 is proposed), and an ICRP program. Students would not pay tuition fees directly but would have loans applied on their behalf to their chosen university. Graduates would not have to start paying back until they are earning at least £21,000 a year. If they had not repaid the loan in full in thirty years, the balance owing would be forgiven.

Under very difficult financial conditions, Prime Minister David Cameron's coalition government is in the process of implementing most of the Browne recommendations, although it has maintained a £9,000 annual limit on tuition fees. As a case study, the UK initiative is a fascinating one for Canadian advocates of a more open tuition regime, not only to see how the mechanisms of an income-contingent repayment scheme work, but to judge its effectiveness in political terms. There has been widespread and volatile public reaction to the changes, with students protesting the corresponding tuition increases vigorously and even violently across the United Kingdom. Notwithstanding the positive benefits of an ICRP approach to students, many see the reforms as an excuse for raising tuition fees and increasing student debt in the process.

The UK reforms will be of considerable interest to Canadian provincial government leaders challenged to fund the post-secondary education sector in a period of increasingly difficult financial conditions. However, the challenges for Canada would go beyond selling such an approach to a skeptical public. An effective ICRP scheme requires very large numbers of participants[17] (so that the many good risk students compensate for the fewer bad risk ones, thus keeping loan rates affordable), and so the most effective approach in Canada would be a national one. This would require common agreements between each province and the federal government, a daunting challenge in the constitutional minefield of higher education.

Like Paul Davenport and Peter George, I find much that is favourable in an ICRP approach and will watch the UK experiment with great interest. There is one element to the scheme, however, that I find deeply disturbing and that is the disproportionate support for "higher priority" courses in science and technology.[18] As discussed in the section on instrumental views of education in chapter

6, I strongly believe that the humanities and social sciences are as important to our economic, political, and social futures as science and technology, and am therefore very concerned about such direct government intervention in labour market planning that discourages liberal education.[19]

WHERE DO WE GO FROM HERE?

In considering where Canadian universities might be heading as they confront continual financial challenges, we turn again to Tony Bates. Originally from the Open University, Tony came to Canada, first to the Open Learning Agency and then to the University of British Columbia. Internationally known as a knowledgeable observer of and consultant on educational technology and its effective application to learning, he is often critical of today's mainstream universities. In a year-end submission to his internationally popular blog, Dr Bates listed a number of options for universities facing the almost inevitable further budget squeezes in 2010 and beyond:

1 More of the same – larger classes, more adjuncts, higher tuition fees, poorer service
2 Enrolment cuts
3 Greater institutional differentiation, with some elite institutions prevailing and the others bearing the brunt of the cuts
4 A multi-tiered and increasingly differentiated faculty – a very few research-only professors, slightly more teaching-only professors and many more adjunct faculty, but with poorer pay
5 Closing of various educational support units and services
6 Exploring new models for post-secondary education that focus less on expensive buildings and more on virtual learning[20]

It is difficult not to be cynical in considering these options. For any given year, it is highly likely that governments and institutions would respond as they usually have. Both have a vested interest in increasing enrolments, so it is unlikely that there would be cuts there under the existing funding formulae. Some attempts might be made towards the differentiation of institutions and of faculty roles, but these are more apt to be discussed than carried out. Support units and services would be shaved further but would soldier on with fewer resources. Thus, Bates's first option – the status quo – is still the most likely in the short term, but the cumulative impact of too many years of this approach would ultimately require a dramatic response as the quality of undergraduate education in particular deteriorates beyond acceptable levels. In such a decentralized system, it is not clear who would provide the leadership on this issue.

Given the exponential progress of technology, Duderstadt et al. foresee dramatic changes in the basic character and structure of the university over the next few decades, but they concede that the changes in the short run will be less obvious. They see procrastination and inaction as the worst responses and urge presidents to do everything they can to mobilize their campuses to consider the implications of new technologies and new learners and to prepare for the significant changes to follow.[21] Making or adjusting to these changes will not be easy, as they run against the prevailing culture of the university. Writing in another context, Duderstadt underlines this point: "Although information technology today is used primarily to augment and enrich traditional instructional offerings, over the longer term it will likely change the learning paradigm. It will likely change the methods of scholarship. And it will certainly change the relationship between faculty and staff and the university."[22]

In the meantime, university presidents will have to continue to deal with financial difficulties, cutbacks, layoffs, and sometimes difficult labour relations as their universities struggle to meet the many roles set out for them in the knowledge society. Notwithstanding the growing public recognition of their importance, universities will be hard pressed to compete with other government spending priorities (such as health care) and with demographic changes (post–"echo boom"), both of which reduce the revenue base. While university presidents will continue to lobby governments for more money, they will have to find better ways of using existing resources if institutional quality is to be maintained or improved.

There will never be sufficient funds, and whatever the revenues emanating from government grants and tuition fees, the choices as to how to best spend the existing budget will only get tougher and tougher. Such is the challenge facing the new generation of university presidents in Canada. It will be taken up again in the concluding chapter of this book.

9

Presidential Leadership and Day-to-Day Administration

Many want to be president, but few want to do president.
Steven Sample, president, University of Southern California[1]

It is one thing to develop great plans for change in a university and quite another to see them through to full implementation. There are many books on university leadership but far fewer on the day-to-day administration that is necessary to ensure its effectiveness.[2]

While leadership styles are many and varied, every university president has to be effective in the day-to-day administration that comprises so much of his or her role. As reflected in cross-section of presidents selected for this book, almost none of Canada's executive heads had significant management training before assuming the presidency. Most learn to be leaders on the job, starting as a department chair and working up through a vice-presidency or deanship to the top post. In the words of Dave Marshall, this experience is invaluable in learning how to deal with the "alligators in the swamp."

While there are variations on the theme, the common experience in Canadian academic culture has been the influence of shared mentors and the examples of colleagues, both successful and unsuccessful, and such experiences have apparently produced a pretty strong consensus about how our universities should be led. For example, his appointment as president of the Council of Ontario Universities had a major influence on Peter George and prepared him well for the McMaster presidency: "I learned a lot simply by observing the presidents at cou. I am surprised in retrospect how much freedom they gave me to set and act on priorities when I had only been a dean. It is better to ask forgiveness than permission – I always felt I responded more positively to someone who said, 'It's your job, go and do it,' and so the people who were the chairs of COU at the time were very empowering."

Like most successful leaders, Dr George has tried to manage in the way he would like to be managed himself. He said that one of the advantages of university administration is that you learn that if you dig a hole for yourself, you had better know how to get out of it. This comes from experience and especially from having supportive supervisors who encourage instead of blame and only read you the riot act in private. He observed that "there is a style of leadership, including supervision, that is empowering and there's one that is disempowering. If someone is micro-managing and always looking over your shoulder and blaming you when things go wrong, it doesn't work. I have been fortunate over the years to have the encouraging kind of supervisor – it doesn't mean they pat you on the back every day but that they were always supportive."

At the same time, none of the presidents, George included, felt truly prepared for the challenges of the presidency before taking on the role. Knowing what needs to be done and organizing to do it are very different functions. To start with, most people aspiring to leadership positions are Type A individuals, those with very high energy levels and a propensity to action. They are used to succeeding and may want to do everything themselves. This may be effective at lower levels in the hierarchy, but it can prove unworkable in a position with as wide and complex a range of responsibilities as the presidency of a university.

A classic positive example is Rob Prichard's experience at the University of Toronto. He was chosen at a relatively young age as the new president in part because of his success as a dean. The university needed exactly the kind of leadership that had raised the profile and academic reputation of the law school – and consequently helped with fundraising – under Prichard's watch, and he charged into the presidency in much the same way he had started as dean. However, he quickly found the difference in complexity and scale to be overwhelming. The law school had a $3 to $4 million budget and thirty faculty, while the comparable university figures were over $1 billion and 7,000 professors. He realized that he was not as well prepared for the presidency as he had been for the deanship. Well served by his training in economics and the law, he soon saw that he could not operate as he had at the law school, where the deanship was essentially a one-man show.

What I didn't have going for me was any sense of how you operate on a large scale and how you translate successful leadership on a small scale, which I had at the law school, how you go from basically single-handedly doing things to having to do everything through other people ... The lack of preparation for me was the scale change. It wasn't that I didn't know the issues.

It took me three years before I felt I knew what I was doing, how to do it, and had assembled the core of the team to get it done. When I think of ten years as president, I think of three years learning the job and preparation and seven years of doing it.

He cited the example of the university budget process, noting that in his first year he made about 250 calls on the issue, whereas by his third year, when Adel Sedra was in place as provost, he made only half a dozen. He believes, however, that the initial two-year experience was worth it, not only because it exposed him to all aspects of the institution but also because the front-line knowledge he thus garnered gave him more credibility with his vice-presidents.

TIME MANAGEMENT, TEAM BUILDING, AND DELEGATION OF AUTHORITY

The job of president is all-consuming – and increasingly so – with days full of meetings, evenings and weekends given over to entertaining and attending innumerable community events, frequent travel, and no end of regular and electronic mail and telephone messages. The president is always in demand. There are so many constituents wanting just a piece of his or her time – faculty, staff, students, politicians, alumni, parents, community members, the media – it never ends. At a minimum the job requires someone with tremendous energy and vitality. In the words of David Johnston, "There is a Darwinian selection for this kind of position. You really have to be robust psychologically and physically to do these jobs. Once you're in the job, you have to organize it so it is doable. You have to manage strategically so that you don't always work the long, long days."

In this frenetic environment, one of the key challenges is learning how to best use one's time. Given the huge range of expectations and opportunities for a president's involvement, this task goes beyond traditional issues of time management. Rob Prichard quoted one of his mentors on this (who, ironically, did not mention the issue in his own interview): "David Johnston has a great expression which is that the trouble with being president of the university is that you could fill about six days every day with *good* things to do with your time. The real trick is to pick out the one-sixth that are the *best* things you can do as president."

Once socialized into the job, the new president may find it all too easy to settle into the routine of the academic year. The cycle starts in September with the incoming classes, the welcoming speeches, athletic and cultural events, and the start-up of all the board and senate committees of which the president is an *ex officio* member. The fall semester, punctuated by convocations, goes incredibly quickly, and after a brief Christmas break, the cycle continues through the spring semester with its emphasis on budget preparations and government lobbying. May and June bring celebrations, awards, and events in recognition of staff, along with personnel reviews and the major convocation season. Going on throughout the academic year are important but time-consuming searches to fill vacancies in deanships, vice-presidencies, research and institute chairs, and critical staff and management positions. The summer is not a slack period either, as it is frequently given over to international conferences and visits, professional development, community and alumni relations, and personal research and writing.[3]

Throughout the September to June period, a plethora of social events can fill every president's evenings and most weekends. These range from community and charitable events (important for ensuring good relations with the immediate community); through alumni and fundraising affairs; faculty, staff, and student recognition events; events in support for athletic and cultural programs; attendance at seminars and academic colloquia; keynote speeches to service clubs and at countless conferences; student and faculty recruitment; and welcoming many visitors to campus. These activities are all over and above an impressive range of external demands on a president's time: fundraising; government and community relations; meetings with provincial, national, and international associations and their committees; conferences, writing, and research in the individual's own areas of interest; and general networking activities on behalf of the institution.

The literature is full of anecdotes from former university presidents who speak of arriving back from a fundraising trip to find their daily calendar jammed with appointments, morning, noon, and evening, seven days a week. Indeed, it is very easy to fall into the routine of simply following the schedule prepared by the office staff in response to the multiple demands for the president's time. One of the more candid responses to the time management question came from Jim Downey, who acknowledged the huge challenge of managing to avoid having the job run the president rather than vice versa: "The phones ring, memos and emails arrive, meetings are called. In that sense, being a president is easy – there's a structure, a rhythm, a schedule, all of which tell you what to do and when to do it. There's great comfort in that. The hard part is to find the time and the distance to reflect on what it all means for the character and culture of your university." The danger is that the incumbent will confuse participation in all these activities with providing the leadership the institution needs. The following are three of the toughest challenges a president faces in deciding how to use his or her time:

1   *Wanting to say "yes" to almost every invitation on the premise that the president's visibility on campus and in the community is a fundamental part of the job.* This was a particular trap for me, primarily because I have always enjoyed public speaking and participating in academic seminars and celebration events. This kind of involvement can be very stimulating, but it may also rob the president of valuable time for reflection and longer-term planning.
2   *Letting routine take over.* I can readily acknowledge that there were many periods during my presidencies when the weeks just flew by and I was just too busy to stop and think about whether I was using my time wisely.
3   *Favouring what one likes to do or does best as opposed to what should be done.* Presidents need to be very conscious of this danger and at least delegate responsibility for the things they enjoy less or don't do as well so that those things do get done.

Dave Marshall put it well: "Being president of an institution is not a status quo job. Anyone who takes the job as president just to maintain the status quo is doomed to failure – it's not like running a high school." Indeed, an important component of the job of president is to challenge the status quo, and this means taking the time to think and act "outside the box," a cliché that is too seldom made real. Jim

Downey referred to Robert Birnbaum's classification of academic presidencies into three groups according to their performance – the modal (50 per cent), the exemplary (25 per cent), and the failed (25 per cent).[4] A critical aspect of an exemplary presidency is the ability to use one's time strategically while ensuring the effective day-to-day management of the institution.

Most presidents believe that they are in the exemplary category. They see themselves as being strategic in their use of time, focusing on the major things they want to achieve while leaving much of the day-to-day to other members of the senior team. A recent English study challenges that belief. Starting from the perspective that most theories of leadership are conceptual frameworks not well grounded in empirical research, Bargh et al. interviewed a broad cross-section of vice-chancellors in the United Kingdom to test how they thought they spent their time against how they actually did. The results suggested a significant mismatch between the self-perception of roles (as reported in interview data) and the objective description of those roles (as recorded in observing what vice-chancellors actually did): "The most common [mismatch] is that vice-chancellors define their role as predominantly strategic while spending most of their time on routine management."[5]

Such conclusions are not to denigrate active campus management. Peter George's view is that presidents can be strategic "intermittently." He places a premium on being visible and available, what he describes as "throwing myself into the job."

> People in the community want to know that there is a hand on the tiller. There's the port side and the starboard side. One side is external activity and the other is internal activity – custodian of the academic mission. Faculty especially get worried if the boat seems to be drifting, and they get really worried if it is overbalanced, especially towards the external relations side. It always seemed to me that the key thing was that you had to have a hand on the tiller that people believed was pointed primarily at the academic mission of the institution.

He stresses the importance of presidents being active on campus and not sequestered in their offices all day: "There's more and more pressure to be externally oriented because of the relentless pressure to secure additional resources to support the academic mission.

Balance is hard to maintain, and the president is often seen as remote from the internal community because he/she is spending too much time off campus."[6]

While at Waterloo, David Johnston was more systematic than most in his approach, even to the extent of charting how he spent his time and giving this record to the Senior Officers Evaluation Committee. He commented, "Even though I'm conscious of trying to be strategic, I slip into doing instead of leading. What we've done here is to try to build some buffers, some insulation." The Waterloo model assigns primary responsibility for the operation of the university to the deans' council, which is chaired by the provost and meets weekly. The president attends when he is in town. However, Johnston placed a very high priority on the external role of the president and wondered if the two-thirds of his time allocated that way was sufficient: "If I had my druthers, I would spend even more time externally. I think the leverage role of the president is felt much more externally than internally. If you manage the institution properly, it can function internally without you chairing all the committees."

Similarly, Dave Marshall has great faith in the ability of the institution to function in the absence of the president. He believes that it is important to have confidence in others and not try to take on every aspect of the job alone: "If I have the right processes in place and the right people, I have confidence in that. When they need me, I'll be there, and when there's an emergency, we will deal with it." All those interviewed recognized that assembling a strong senior team was key to getting things done. As described above, Rob Prichard's early experience in the job convinced him that he had to recruit the best possible team and delegate much more than he had ever done as a law school dean. In the great majority of Canadian universities today, the president's job is too complex and too broad to be handled effectively in any other way.

Assembling a strong top team and delegating much of the internal management to its members is easier said than done. A new president usually inherits most of the vice-presidents and deans, and it takes skill, determination, and patience to forge one's own leadership group. Nothing is more important to a president's effectiveness than a good team. I had my own best periods of leadership when we had a talented top team that worked very well together and in whom I could comfortably and confidently delegate major areas of responsibility. Unfortunately, there were also significant periods in my career when I stayed too long with a key senior person or had difficulty breaking a lifelong habit of trying to do too many things myself.

While almost every manager will confess to some poor appointment decisions, the most effective leader assembles a diverse group of people who are better than he or she is in their specific areas of focus. A president unwilling or unable to work closely with challenging colleagues will not last long in the position,[7] and it is highly unlikely that someone whose top team consists entirely of "yes" people will be very effective in the long term. I have seen plenty of examples of shortcomings in this respect – a president who only wanted to hear the good news, never the bad; vice-presidents or deans who seemed to assume on all occasions that they were the brightest people in the room; other people who were so busy trying to impress everyone that they never listened to the advice being proffered; micro-managers who were unwilling to relinquish any authority; and people who quite openly played favourites.

Perhaps the most misplaced university leader is the person, however talented, for whom it is always "all about me." Such people want daily recognition and tend to take credit for everything positive that goes on around them while finding someone else to blame for any shortcoming. This sort of narcissism quickly undermines an individual's authority and ability to work with others, and it is not only logical but also fortunate that such people are rarely appointed president.

There is another team, a smaller one, that is absolutely crucial to presidential success, and that is the staff in the president's office. Where finances permit, an executive assistant can represent the president at social functions, do research and intelligence gathering on key issues, and, perhaps most importantly, serve as a pipeline to the president for institutional politics, ensuring that the incumbent knows what is going on in the various communities inside and outside the university and thus keeping him or her from being increasingly isolated from these communities.

No position is more important than the president's executive secretary, the person who is the face of the office to the faculty, staff, board, students, and external public. He or she must deal with a very broad range of issues and concerns personably, efficiently, and with great integrity and loyalty. I had terrific such support over the years but none better than I received from Chris Charlebois during the whole of my more than ten years at Windsor. The office team, as well, is an important asset in the transition to new leadership, and incoming presidents should ensure that there is at least some overlap in staffing to help them appreciate their institution's history and learn its organizational culture.

A common approach to administrative leadership is to remind oneself constantly of the strategic priorities and to ensure that they are prominent factors in time management. For example, Martha Piper chose to invest a lot of her time and energy in the preparation of the annual operating budget of UBC. While she would not usually question the priorities emanating from each vice-president, it was she who ultimately decided how much would be allocated to each overall area: "In today's complex university, while the academic priorities are paramount, there are many others, including student programs, student services, and residences, which are more important than the academic community may see them. The only one who has the overview of putting it all together is the president."

Martha Piper's time investment in the annual budget exercise was considerable. She had a very complex computer model of revenues and expenses and would often take it home to try out various scenarios. She personally took the budget through the various committees of senate and the board, and she always made the final presentation at the board and defended the budget decisions. She made the deliberate choice to invest a large part of her time in activities more often the domain of the vice-president, academic or finance and administration. While acknowledging that this might have been seen as undermining the power of the vice-presidents, Piper saw it as a critical piece of her leadership strategy.

For Paul Davenport, a particular emphasis was getting the communications right, notably with the faculty and the members of the board of governors:

When you first get involved as president, you underestimate the amount of time you should give to communications as opposed to the time you give to getting the management decisions right. So I just focused on getting all my decisions right and assumed that if I did that, everything would work out fine. Well, the world is not like that.

Particularly as president, you have got to spend a lot of time explaining to people the reasons for the decisions you take, both before and after they are taken. To the degree possible, you've got to get the complexity of those decisions offloaded to your vice-presidents so you have time to communicate to the myriad of groups who work and study at the university and who support it externally. You don't know that your first day on the job as president, but I did know it by the time I arrived at Western and I have been a better president here for that reason.

Notwithstanding how easy it is to let the job run the office-holder, presidents should not beat themselves up too much about spending so much time on routine administration. Roseann Runte was particularly clear about the interrelatedness of everything one does as president, stressing the importance to sustainability not only of what is achieved but how it is achieved.

I don't think that you can get from point A to point B without encountering people and things along the way. If you just run through and knock them all down on the way, you might get to your goal but it's not going to be sustainable or well received. On the way to a goal, there are many things that you do that are not visibly part of what you might be able to say or part of the goal but which are actually very strategically part of that goal. I don't know if those who haven't been there can understand that.

Runte cites the example of fundraising, disagreeing, for example, with those who say that presidents should only deal with $100,000+ donors:

If, along the way, you don't take an opportunity to be really nice to a small donor, you miss a chance for the university to be perceived as a caring, wonderful institution and to show the staff what kind of community you want to create. It is because everything is linked – the academic excellence and the kind of community you want. What the president has that almost no one else has is the knowledge as to how everything fits together.

Another characteristic that would well serve a president determined to bring about substantive change in an institution is patience. Experience suggests that change inevitably takes longer than initially anticipated by a new president. David Johnston, for example, recounted being very disappointed after two years with the slow progress of his own objectives at McGill, until he was reassured by noted Harvard president Derek Bok. Bok had started his presidency by writing down ten objectives on his first day, and he'd almost resigned after the first year because of discouragement with the lack of progress. The same review three years later, though, was more fruitful: "He said that two of the ideas were dumb ones and had been discarded. Three of them were wonderfully successful, but none had been associated with him because they had been taken up by other champions. The other five were moving along but the ones that were going best had other champions."

Bok told Johnston that he came to a conclusion that is frequently voiced by successful presidents – you will be much more effective if you never take credit for anything and are never seen as a champion of something. This conclusion is antithetical to the "president as hero" notion promoted in some American literature on university leadership, but it had an impact on Professor Johnston and his subsequent leadership style: "My definition of leadership is recognizing your total dependence on everyone around you. I found that, unconsciously at McGill, to get anything done, I needed to reach out to others. By the time I came to Waterloo, it was not an intuitive notion but a rational thought, and I worked more consciously at building a team of champions."

COPING WITH THE SEEMINGLY TRIVIAL AND THE UNEXPECTED

One of the most commonly repeated laments of experienced presidents is that they end up giving too much time to issues for which they could not have prepared or that had initially seemed to be little but had somehow grown to be big. Every year, there will be a number of completely unexpected challenges – they may be opportunities, crises, or annoyances, but how the president handles them will go a long way to defining how positively he or she is seen in the job. These can be divided into several categories: crises, niggling concerns, missed opportunities, and "little" things.

Crises

While, by definition, crises cannot always be predicted, an effective university administration must have emergency communication procedures and clear protocols for how to handle everything from a major disaster (fire, earthquake, extreme violence) to more common "crises" such as power shutdowns, burst pipes, and significant issues involving personal relations and human rights on campus (alcohol, drugs, depression, racism, sexual abuse). In recent years, a whole new industry devoted to crisis management has grown up, providing realistic disaster simulation workshops that can prove extremely valuable in a subsequent crisis and provide an opportunity for team building in the process.

Niggling Concerns That Can Grow into Major Issues

Every year, many of the issues that seemed small at the outset grow into time-consuming and frustrating problems for the president. Many of these problems can be averted if specific policies for handling them have been developed through widespread consultation with those most affected by them. A Canadian favourite is "snow days" – deciding when to close the university because of inclement weather. Having come to the University of Windsor from such wintery places as Montreal, Edmonton, and Sudbury, I was not very sympathetic to concerns about Windsor's winter weather and, in fact, never closed the university in the ten and a half years I was president there. While I might like to be remembered for more positive things, at least some staff will always remember me as the president who never gave a snow day.

Another favourite issue is the parking problem. I am not sure there is a university in Canada where students, faculty, or staff are happy with the parking arrangements. The parking lots are always too expensive, too far from classrooms and offices, and unfairly distributed. It will be interesting to see whether or not the growing interest in environmental issues finally changes the assumption of many that it is a basic human right to drive one's own motor vehicle onto campus and to park it within a short walk of one's office or classroom.

Missed Opportunities

Sometimes the most important decisions in a year are the ones that were not taken – the opportunities that were missed because the president was too busy attending to routine administrative issues. Experienced presidents are always looking for opportunity, recognizing that it can come from the most unexpected sources and activities. One's capacity to think creatively and take advantage of these can be stimulated by deliberately associating with people not connected to the university, by reading novels instead of pop management literature, and by participating in activities well outside the job's routine.

Of course, it is one thing to have big ideas and another to see them implemented. Some presidents drive their staff crazy with their frenetic advocacy for new ideas, while others make very effective use of their colleagues to filter out the best and plan collaboratively for their implementation. It is difficult to evaluate an individual's performance in this area, but a president who has the confidence to seize opportunities when others either don't see them or are wary of them, and the sensitivity to consult appropriately before leaping ahead, is much more likely to transform at least part of his or her institution than someone less tactically and strategically oriented.

"Little" Things That Are Really Very Important

There are a lot of small things that a good president should do that are behind the scenes but will ultimately make a huge difference to the way many feel about the institution. Roseann Runte emphasized these in her interview, and I would add a few from my own experience – dressing up in academic robes to bestow a degree on a student in his hospital bed a few days before he died, even though he was a few credits short; taking in a refugee student from Berundi when he was isolated in residence over Christmas without any money; or befriending a student who used to race around campus very deftly in her motorized wheelchair.

Sending messages of care and concern contributed to the value of the institution, but I reaped at least as many benefits as I sowed. I will never know if the dying student was conscious of the ceremony, but it made all the difference in the world to his family and gave me a special feeling of pride in his achievements. The refugee student became a very good friend to my wife and me, we acted as parents at his subsequent marriage to the bride he brought from Berundi, and today they are a thriving family of seven in Ottawa. The wheelchair student story is more bittersweet, as she passed away in January 2010 after a lifetime of championing the cause of the physically handicapped. She involved me in wheelchair simulation exercises that enhanced my understanding of the particular challenges so many of our students faced, and I will be ever grateful to her for her care, courage, and commitment.

COPING MECHANISMS

Presidents run on adrenalin, and if our sample of presidents interviewed is anything to go by, they don't tend to acknowledge how stressful the job can be, except perhaps during those rare periods when everything seems to go wrong all at once. Nevertheless, every president has his or her coping mechanisms, and these can be grouped into several categories – personal traits; family and colleague support; and interests, activities, and diversions outside the job itself.

Personal Traits

A significant number of the presidents mentioned the ability to sleep soundly, to compartmentalize, and to leave the problems at the office. In my own case, I have come to realize that sleeping may be what I do best in life. No matter what the pressures, I was inevitably asleep within a few minutes of my head hitting the pillow and almost always woke up the next morning refreshed and ready for another day. This talent was usually a huge plus, but it had its downside in my tendency to forget yesterday's crisis. The others around me would still be caught up in it and thought me insensitive when I was all too cheerful the next time we met.

Of course, a strong belief in and commitment to the job makes a huge difference to one's ability to cope with its stresses and strains. For example, echoing themes of the developmental culture identified in chapter 3, David Johnston spoke of his faith and the purpose that it gives to his life: "My faith has been important as a refuge and a rock but also because I believe we have been put on earth for a purpose and that is to serve, and we have to judge how well or poorly we perform. I think that helps me to do this job. I believe that it is a calling and that I should measure myself on when I'm performing well and not."

A personal trait fundamental to effective leadership is a sense of humour, the ability to enjoy even the most difficult parts of the job and not to take oneself too seriously. A leader's ability to keep things in perspective is also essential to effective team building. Conversely, nothing undermines those in leadership positions more quickly than losing their cool under fire or putting their own profile and reputation ahead of those of their colleagues.

Support Groups

The position of president can be a lonely one, and this underlines the critical importance of the personal support of family, mentors, and friends, many of them from outside the university environment. This kind of support is often about bucking someone up when times are tough, but it is also about keeping the job and its challenges in perspective. Martha Piper drew attention to the latter: "My family was critical to me. People asked how I could do the job while married with children and I responded that I could not do it without being married with children. I couldn't imagine doing it as a single woman. It just wouldn't work because you would lose perspective. There's nothing like kids to bring you back to reality and make you humble."

A vital component of leadership that comes from partners in particular is confidence to do the job. No one has had more faith in my ability than my wife, Dr Jane Brindley, and her confidence and support were the difference between success and failure for me on many, many occasions. I could not have done any of the jobs without her, and she helped me get through the roughest patches relatively unscathed.

The president's job makes huge demands on the partner, especially in the overwhelming number of cases where a woman is supporting her husband in the role. Even when it has been clearly established that the female partner has her separate career and will not play the traditional role of chatelaine, she is subject to the stresses of being married to a high-profile and extremely busy individual, with all the expectations around the couple's entertaining and visibility that this entails. The stresses are strongest where the president lives in a university house. While there has been a trend away from such a provision, a significant number of Canadian university presidents and their families still live on or very near campus in houses in which they are expected to entertain as part of their responsibilities. The reactions of spouses range from enthusiastic acceptance of the role to rejection of the notion that one should take on social responsibilities just because of the position of their partner. The majority play a significant role, not only in entertaining but also in representing the university in the community, and, of course, in supporting their spouse. Still, it is not surprising that there are tensions associated with the role of spouse, especially when it comes unexpectedly to a partner who originally married a young academic and not someone who was or even aspired to be a university president.

When I was about to go to Sudbury to be a university president for the first time, Myer Horowitz gave me a couple of important pieces of advice, based on his experiences at Alberta: (1) if they offer you a house, don't take it; and (2) however much entertaining you think you should do in your first year, do half. This was good counsel, but I chose to ignore both points. Instead, we accepted the huge seven-bedroom house that came with the job and did lots of entertaining, hosting over a hundred people at a time on many occasions, sometimes several times a week. We also accepted the smaller university house at Windsor but entertained there more rarely, primarily because the adjacent campus itself was much better served by various dining and assembly halls, but also because we wished to preserve more of our private lives within a very active schedule of public appearances.

When Bob Birgeneau left the Massachusetts Institute of Technology (MIT) to become the president of the University of Toronto, the U of T governing council agreed to pay a salary to his wife for her services on behalf of the university. While this was standard practice in some American universities, the announcement of the contract provoked strong reaction in Canada and has not apparently been emulated elsewhere in the country. While there are good arguments that the spousal role is demanding and deserving of such remuneration, these are usually trumped by such political considerations as having the position formally defined and open to public competition (for the chatelaine role, not that of spouse!) and by the assertion that a president's salary already includes such responsibilities, leaving it to the couple to determine the degree of the spouse's involvement.

The many issues swirling around the president's partner are so common across the country that they became the rationale for the creation of an AUCC partners group that has met for many years in conjunction with the biannual assemblies of presidents. At these gatherings, a social program for the partners, their participation in some of the presidents' meetings, and their own discussions of common problems stimulate good ideas, provide personal support, and generate broader perspectives. Just as for the presidents themselves, one of the best ways the partners feel supported is to find out that many others face the same challenges that they do.

Presidential colleagues are invaluable contacts, notably through the federal, provincial, and international associations that bring executive heads together to discuss common issues and concerns.[8] New presidents look to experienced colleagues for ideas and wise counsel and, sometimes, nothing more than a bit of empathy. Presidents talk to each other all the time, and some, such as Saskatchewan's Peter MacKinnon, are regularly consulted by colleagues on matters presidential. More than any other group, fellow presidents are peers and, notwithstanding the significant differences in the size and mandates of their respective institutions, have many common challenges. Presidential organizations help presidents develop informal networks of support and friendship and are frequently a source of good ideas.

I can easily identify personal examples of each of the advantages of presidential associations. The first is learning from others how common some of the challenges we face are. On the personal front, it was tremendously valuable for me to be walking alongside the president of one of Canada's most respected universities one evening after a COU dinner and to hear him say, with some frustration, that never a year had gone by when some faculty member had not told him that morale was at an "all-time low." If this could happen at a celebrated institution under the leadership of one of the country's most successful presidents, it certainly helped put my own similar experience in perspective. I never took such comments as personally after that interchange.

On the ideas front, I shall ever be grateful to one I got from John Stubbs, then president of Trent, relating to his practice of hosting informal lunches for a randomly selected cross-section of faculty and staff, the purpose being to chat about the institution, what they liked most about it, and what needed improvement. I emulated this practice at both Laurentian and Windsor and enjoyed it immensely. If a president only meets professors and staff in formal departmental meetings, the agenda inevitably focuses on their concerns. This is understandable, since a formal meeting may be one of the few occasions they get to confront a president directly on such issues. It can be an effective forum, but it might leave the president with an overall view of unhappy faculty and a failing institution. My experience with the Stubbs-inspired luncheons was the opposite. We would share quick personal resumés, which had the benefit of allowing us to make all sorts of connections, and then talk about whatever anyone wanted to bring up. Most of the time, I heard about the great things that were happening on campus, and even the complaints were offered respectfully and constructively. I always left the lunches buoyed by what I had heard and by the connections the faculty and staff participants had made across departments.

Close friends, chancellors, community leaders, and others also contribute to an individual's ability to cope with the presidency, not least because they are outside the immediate university community and can provide objectivity, levity, and humour, which sometimes may be lacking among colleagues who are too close to the issues at hand. It is critical for presidents to recognize the importance of such support and to cultivate those who are positive influences in this respect.

Diversions

The interview sample produced a wide range of diversionary activities that had the common benefit of removing the individual from the issues of the moment. In many cases, the purpose of the activity was primarily to allow the president to get away, to tune out – Peter George's fishing, Bonnie Patterson's boating, and Bill Leggett's country retreat. Physical activity is an important plus for the job, not only for the obvious relationship between physical shape and energy and stamina but also for its social aspects.

Myer Horowitz, for example, exercised regularly with an "early birds" group in Edmonton that he still belongs to today, even though he lives in Victoria. He also retained a graduate seminar throughout his presidency and was able to share some of his dilemmas and challenges with students. Not only was this an invaluable teaching tool, it gave him many opportunities to think out loud and to bounce ideas off bright people not directly involved with the concerns under discussion; I imagine that Bill Leggett's weekly visits to his lab and his graduate students yielded some of the same benefits. In a further example, one of the fringe benefits of my strange propensity for trying to play old timers' hockey without any of the requisite skills was that I was able to associate regularly with people who had nothing to do with the university. This gave me a fresh perspective and a better sense of how the institution was viewed in the wider community.

Of course, some of the diversions are built right into the job, contributing to its appeal. Roseann Runte noted that the very variety of activities in the position made it easier to cope: "One of the joys of a university presidency is that there are so many parts of the job that one part balances another. If you go on a walkathon, for instance, it's almost a holiday."

Our universities have outstanding athletic teams, writers, musicians, actors, visual artists, dancers, and other talented performers, and the daily schedule is full of stimulating visitors, seminars, debates, demonstrations, and speakers' forums. A visit to a research lab or institute or a chat with a creative scholar is inevitably energizing and rewarding. While the pace may be frenetic, the obligatory presidential attendance at so many of these is almost always more a pleasure than a chore, and it greatly enriches the work environment.

POST-PRESIDENCY

As one might expect, all the presidents interviewed loved their job. They spoke of its wonderful variety, the opportunities it gave to meet and work with interesting and talented people, the international connections, the joy of seeing faculty and students thrive and develop, and the intellectual stimulation of identifying and solving problems. Even the most reluctant administrator in the group, Bill Leggett, is just grateful that others talked him into doing a job he hadn't really aspired to in the first place. He considers the ten years he spent at Queen's as principal the richest, most rewarding period of his thirty-five-year career.

Some who have left the university presidency are as active as ever, facing new challenges and opportunities. In his appointment as Canada's twenty-eighth governor general, David Johnston has taken on a role with a much higher public profile than any he has had before, with huge implications for his family and the conduct of his daily life. Nevertheless, the legal, diplomatic, social, and communication skills he has honed during his academic years will doubtless serve him and the country well during his tenure in the post.

Leaving the presidency of the University of Toronto at a relatively young age, Rob Prichard moved fairly quickly into other challenging positions, first as chief executive officer of Torstar, then as president and CEO of Metrolinx, and more recently as chair of both Penguin Canada and the international business law firm Torys LLP. He remains very active in the academic community through a number of board appointments and by co-chairing the Canada Excellence Research Chairs Program, but has thus far managed to resist the temptations of politics despite much speculation by others about his suitability for the field.

After completing her terms as president of Trent in 2009, Bonnie Patterson wanted to take time to consider her future before making any move. However, she was a logical choice to succeed Paul Genest as president of the Council of Ontario Universities when he was appointed to a senior position in the Government of Ontario late in 2009. It was a job she had already done well in years past, and as a just-retired president, she was cognizant of the challenges facing Ontario universities at the time of her appointment. Initially temporary, the job has now been confirmed as a three-year appointment.

As much as they enjoyed the role, the presidents who have retired do not seem to have had much difficulty with the transition. One of the characteristics of academia is that its members make far less of a distinction between work and leisure than do people in most occupations. A benefit of retirement, then, is that one can keep doing what one loves without having to do the parts of the job that were less pleasurable – the endless meetings, the crises, and the frenetic schedule.

Bill Leggett has been retired for five years and, as much as he loved the role, doesn't miss the position at all. He continues with his lifelong research interests and spends more time with his family, travelling and enjoying their country cottage. He did not give up all related activities immediately, as evidenced by his appointment in 2007 as the chair of the Canada Foundation for Innovation.

Dave Marshall, who will be stepping down from the leadership of Mount Royal in the summer of 2011, looks forward to the opportunity to pursue his own interests: "I would like to do over the next twenty years all the things the presidency never let me have the time to do – write a dirty novel, play in my blues band, ride my motorcycle across Canada, play golf with my wife, Sheila, play with my grandchildren. I honestly don't think I need the adrenalin of the position or that I draw much from the power of the position so that I will feel empty."

Jim Downey has faced the post-presidency period twice, in 1990 after his presidency at the University of New Brunswick and again in

1999, post-Waterloo. He readily found interesting work after each, and while he did not really miss the job, he missed being captain of a team. "If it's only what you, yourself, have done, it's often not very much. But if you can lay claim to some of what the team has done, there's nearly always something to point to. That, existentially, is what I missed most." At the time of writing, Dr Downey had just completed a successful three-year term as president of the new Higher Education Quality Council of Ontario and looking forward to his first real retirement.

Similarly, Martha Piper misses the people but not the job and is delighted to have more time to spend with her family and on hobbies like exercising, reading, cooking, and quilting. Not wanting to quit "cold turkey," she has retained her membership on a number of private and public boards because she enjoys working with smart people to solve problems. However, she is very happy to leave the follow-up details to others. She misses the people but not the limelight.

Myer Horowitz has been retired the longest (twenty years at the time of writing). The transition was initially difficult, especially because he stayed on campus when Paul Davenport took over. He now recognizes that it was both unfair to his successor and not good for him that he had remained on campus after retiring. I have heard many other presidents reflect on similar situations when an outgoing president was still on campus when the new person came in. These experiences were instrumental in my own decision to leave the Windsor community at the end of my ten and a half years on the job, not only in the interests of my successor but also in the interests of my own personal health. Horowitz has since moved to Victoria with his wife, Barbara, and they are happily settled there. He is an adjunct professor at the University of Victoria and served as chancellor of University Canada West.

Paul Davenport's retirement plans include moving to France, writing a book on collegial leadership, and continuing to lead bike tours of Western students in the Loire Valley. He will also be returning to Western for six weeks each fall to teach his popular courses on nineteenth-century Paris, and he intends to continue his involvement in Rwanda as a volunteer.

Peter George has no specific plans for his retirement, although he hopes to find ways to use his experience to assist good causes. He is heavily engaged in volunteer activities. He likes the idea of a part-time job, perhaps running a foundation. He expects that something attractive will come along, much in the way it always has for him. I wouldn't bet against it.

Roseann Runte is the furthest from retirement, very much enjoying her first term at Carleton University, her fifth institutional leadership position in twenty-six years. Her own academic interests continue and she writes.

The External Roles of the President

As previously observed, the role of university president in Canada has evolved swiftly in recent years away from on-campus leadership to an increasingly busy and important external function. There are mixed feelings about this trend, both within the institutions and among the presidents themselves.

David Johnston, well known for his many community activities, would have spent more time outside the institution if he could have, while Bill Leggett and Myer Horowitz regret the trend towards president as CEO, preferring the older model of president as academic leader. This is not to suggest that the two styles are mutually exclusive; I simply want to emphasize the different ways the job can be viewed. Even the interviewees favouring on-campus leadership spent at least as much time in off-campus activities, at which they were very effective.

The principal activities of the president's external role can be grouped as follows: government relations; community relations; profile and reputation; branding, marketing, and media relations; alumni affairs; and fundraising.

GOVERNMENT RELATIONS

Three major developments over the past four decades have dramatically increased the importance of the government relations role for university presidents in Canada. These are the explosion in demand for university places, the ever-increasing funding pressures and the growing importance of research. The first two issues concern primarily the provincial governments while the latter is more in the federal domain.

Explosion in Demand for University Places

Full-time Canadian university enrolments soared from about 4 per cent of the age cohort 20–24 in 1956 to almost 30 per cent by 2004.[1] They grew almost 4 per cent in 2010 alone and have more than doubled in the past fifteen years, totalling almost 900,000 full-time students.[2] The overall impact of this demand for places has been to change public interest in universities dramatically. Universities are no longer the private concerns of economic and social elites as they were in an earlier era; today there is a strong public political concern about the affordability and accessibility of the country's higher education institutions. This change, with a concomitant increase in the number and breadth of interested stakeholders, has significantly raised the public visibility of the university and its president.

Increasing Funding Pressures

A second consequence of the explosion in demand has been a decline in the resources available for each student. In recent years, after an initial increase during the economic expansion of the 1960s and 1970s, resources declined sharply as post-secondary education competed with health care, elementary and secondary education, and municipalities for taxpayers' dollars. Grants to institutional operating revenues were $21,000 per student in 1980 but had declined to $15,000 by 2006.[3]

Growing Importance of Research

The nature of the academic enterprise has changed substantively over the past few decades as research and scholarship have supplanted teaching as the first priority in most Canadian universities. This trend has been most manifest in the explosion of funding for research in Canada during the years of the Chrétien government in Ottawa (1993–2003). A number of major new competitive programs greatly enhanced the country's research productivity and helped to reverse previous "brain drains," notably to the United States. These included the Canada Foundation for Innovation, the Canada Research Chairs program, Genome Canada, a broadening of the mandate of the Canadian Institutes for Health Research (replacing the Medical Research Council), and the Canada Graduate Scholarships Program. Most significantly, in part because of the lobbying of leading Canadian university presidents (including many of those interviewed for this book), the federal government was persuaded of the importance of the links between investment in research and economic outcomes. While the focus has shifted somewhat under the Martin and Harper governments towards science and technology, investment in research has nevertheless had a huge impact on how much and in what way research is conducted on Canadian campuses. This has been well documented by Clark et al.: "The impact of the new federal government strategy can be seen in the four-fold increase in federal research funding to universities over the past decade – from $733 million in 1997–98 to $2,924 million in 2007–08. Of the 2007–08 total, 43 percent was associated with programs that simply did not exist at the beginning of this period."[4]

While politics continues to play an important role in how the new monies have been distributed, these investments have also significantly increased competition among the universities in several ways. First of all, Canada Research Chairs funds are allocated according to each institution's share of the federal granting agency awards, a direct measure of its research intensity. Secondly, the institution must put forward a highly qualified candidate for each chair for which it is eligible, a measure of its academic reputation and ability to attract the best researchers. Thirdly, the CFI requires matching funds from the private sector, again a measure of an institution's reputation and fundraising abilities.

Most recently, the 2010 announcements of nineteen new Canada Excellence Research Chairs in science and technology by the Harper government placed an even higher premium on competitive advantage. The successful institutions had to recruit leading researchers from other countries and persuade a blue ribbon international panel to award them a chair. While most of the chairs were awarded to G13 (research-intensive) institutions, four went to other universities, including the University of Prince Edward Island, one of the country's smallest.

All of these and related programs have changed the nature of university leadership. Not only are presidents expected to be comfortable in the corridors of Ottawa and the capital of their own province, but they have had to create new positions and new structures internally to enhance their institution's chances for success. These include new and expanded research offices, the strengthening of the position of vice-president, research even in smaller universities, and specific positions for government relations (at the vice-presidential level in the largest institutions).

A related development has been the evolution of the collective voice that speaks on behalf of Canadian universities. The national umbrella organization, the Association of Universities and Colleges of Canada (AUCC), has been around in one form or another for one hundred years but was formally incorporated in 1965 by the Parliament of Canada. While AUCC is not a formal accrediting agency, membership in it is viewed as critical to acceptance as a credible degree-granting institution. While AUCC is a valuable communications, research, and information agency, its primary role is as an advocacy group for university education in the country. Its focus is federal, which means that funding for research, international outreach, and student assistance are paramount among its activities.

Provincial associations of universities are also critical to a president's advocacy agenda. Among the key provincial associations across the country are the Association of Atlantic Universities (seventeen member institutions in four provinces); Conférence des recteurs et des principaux des universités de Québec (CREPUQ, nineteen members and affiliates from seven universities in Quebec); the Council of Ontario Universities[5] (COU, twenty member and one associate member institutions in Ontario); the Research Universities' Council of British Columbia (RUCBC, four university members), and the newly created British Columbia Association of Institutes and Universities (BCAIU, eight member institutions).

Both COU and CREPUQ are long-standing bodies, having been respectively formed in 1962 and 1963. Their missions and mandates evolved considerably as universities came more and more into the public eye, increasingly being seen as instruments of economic and social development for their respective provinces. In the largest provinces of Quebec and Ontario, these associations are vital to member presidents' ability to develop closer relations with key political and public service leaders.[6] While it is their aim to increase funding for the university sector as a whole and to pursue public policy objectives on behalf of all members, these associations are also extremely useful to executive heads individually.

While I was involved extensively in the former Universities Coordinating Council (UCC) of Alberta in the 1980s, I gained my primary experience with a provincial agency with COU from 1991

to 2008, serving on or chairing most of its key committees and acting as its chair from 2005 to 2007. As president of two institutions
significantly outside the "Golden Horseshoe,"[7] I found COU membership particularly valuable. It gave me an opportunity to raise the
profile of my institution in the corridors of power and helped me
meet the key players at Queen's Park, not only top civil servants
and cabinet ministers but also influential business, labour, and other
public sector leaders with strong interests in higher education and
research. The president of Ryerson or Toronto can walk across the
street to meet the premier or a key minister, whereas such visits are
a major undertaking for the president of Lakehead University, more
than 1,400 kilometres away. It is not just the travel distance but
the time required to develop relationships that gives local GTA presidents such an advantage; they frequently meet movers and shakers
at all sorts of public events, whereas the out-of-town presidents have
to make special, time-consuming trips and must often stay overnight
for even a single function.

COMMUNITY RELATIONS

With the burgeoning recognition of the critical role universities
increasingly play in local and regional economic development has
come much stronger community interest in and involvement with
Canadian universities. This is most evident in the smaller centres where the single local university is not only one of the largest
employers in town but is also seen as a critical asset both to the community's economic development and the future of its young people.

   It is difficult to imagine smaller cities like St John's, Charlottetown,
Moncton, Fredericton, Chicoutimi, Quebec, Sherbrooke, Kingston,
Peterborough, St Catharines, Hamilton, Kitchener/Waterloo, Wind-
sor, Sudbury, North Bay, Thunder Bay, Brandon, Regina, Prince
George, or Victoria without their local university. The impact is even
greater in smaller towns and villages like Sackville (Mount Allison
University), Antigonish (St Francis Xavier), Lennoxville (Bishop's)
or Wolfville (Acadia) where the university dominates the town.

   The increasing recognition of the importance of the university has had a significant impact on expectations for its president.
Relationships with mayors and city councillors have become much
more important, both in terms of the positive aspects of job creation, research opportunities, social programming, and institutional/

community profile and in terms of more negative concerns surrounding town-gown relationships, student behaviour, and poor
institutional or city reputations. Most presidents participate actively
in their local communities, sitting on various committees and boards
(hospitals, economic development commissions, chambers of commerce, arts organizations). They lead United Way campaigns, speak
regularly to service clubs, and attend a great variety of community
events, from charity and arts gala dinners and auctions to sporting
events, political fundraisers, and state-of-the-city addresses. They
entertain local leaders regularly at home, on campus, and in local
restaurants, not only to promote and raise funds for the university
but also to participate actively in municipal issues and opportunities.
Indeed, most university presidents are engaged in such activities on
many weekday evenings and almost every weekend throughout
the year.

Notwithstanding whatever tangible contributions the individual
makes through all this activity, there is a very important symbolic
aspect to the president's role. Presidents personify the institution
and people expect to see and get to know them personally. In my
experience, this involvement is overwhelming pleasurable and positive, both for the incumbent and for the institution. Universities are
highly respected in Canada, and the vast majority of interchanges
with the community are positive ones. As the face of the institution,
however, the president is also the first person to whom others turn
with problems or concerns. These can range from damages done by
student parties (for years, the principal of Queen's had to put a disproportionate amount of time into dealing with the negative public
relations resulting from the annual homecoming, which attracted
many young people not even attached to the university) to special
requests for the admission of students whose academic qualifications were suspect. The latter gave me some anxiety at first, but I
soon learned that the direct approach of upholding the admissions
standards was usually more effective than engaging in lengthy discussions that would almost always end up in disappointment.

PROFILE AND REPUTATION

As universities have become of greater public interest and demands
on them have grown, their profile and reputation are increasingly
important. No one feels this more than the president. My first full

year as president of Laurentian University was 1992, the same year that *Maclean's* magazine launched its annual university ratings issue; for the next seventeen years, I lived with relatively low rankings at both Laurentian and Windsor. I never had difficulty with the principle of such a survey and, in fact, congratulated *Maclean's* for taking the initiative. However, along with many of my colleagues, including several whose institutions fared much better than mine, I had serious reservations about the magazine's methodology and the way it linked a lot of independent variables into a composite score to produce a rank-order table.

For the first five years or so, I lobbied *Maclean's* to adopt the methodology of Australia's *Good Universities Guide*,[8] which rated institutions more like a hotel survey, assigning from one to five stars in a number of categories. Australia's guide also included special sections on which institutions were best for specified groups of students, such as women or adult learners. What I liked about the guide was its recognition that there was no "one best" institution, rather the best university for the individual, given his or her particular interests and needs. Needless to say, I did not persuade *Maclean's*. The *Maclean's* rank-order approach sells more magazines. I also learned subsequently that Australian presidents were just as upset with the *Good Universities Guide* as Canadian institutional leaders were with *Maclean's*!

Nevertheless, the *Maclean's* survey helped to usher in an era of much greater focus on university performance: it raised the profile of key performance indicators (KPIs) and stimulated families to take a greater interest in the university their son or daughter would attend. Boards of governors, seeking ways to evaluate the performance of their president and other senior administrators, latched on to KPIs and quality-assurance programs, although not to the same degree as in other Western jurisdictions such as Britain, Australia, and New Zealand.

The Australian comparison is a useful one. In December 2008, a government study on the future of higher education (the Bradley Report)[9] recommended the establishment of a national approach to quality assurance through the creation of the Tertiary Education Quality and Standards Agency (TEQSA). The agency was established in July 2009 but has since become so controversial that the Australian vice-chancellors pushed the government to appoint the highly credible Denise Bradley, a former vice-chancellor and the principal author of the report, as the leader of the regulatory body.[10] Her task is a daunting one.

The principal concern is that the government will be too heavy-handed in its regulation of the universities. No one can dispute the importance of quality assurance, but it is only effective to the extent that it is integrated into the academic culture of each institution. While Australia seems to be far ahead of Canada in establishing national performance indicators, it is not yet clear whether or not such indicators actually contribute to the improvement of the quality of teaching and learning in Australian universities. It is possible that too centralized a system is more of an exercise in public relations and politics than anything else, especially if a preoccupation with the bureaucracy around quality assurance becomes a make-work exercise that deflects faculty and administrators from their primary functions. Canadians will watch developments down under with much interest.

After a decade or so of tolerating the *Maclean's* survey and others, Canadian university presidents have taken the initiative in recent years to develop their own performance criteria. Notable examples are the Canadian modifications incorporated into the American instrument, the National Survey of Student Engagement (NSSE), and the Canadian Undergraduate Survey Consortium (CUSC), also known as the Manitoba Survey. Both of these surveys assess the extent to which students are engaged in and satisfied with various academic, social, and service parameters at their respective institutions, and thus they respond to the different missions and mandates of the institutions more than the *Maclean's* survey does.

The Government of Ontario, in close collaboration with COU, recently founded the Higher Education Quality Council of Ontario (HEQCO). Initially led by highly credible representatives (former Supreme Court justice and U of T provost and dean of law Frank Iacabucci as chair; Jim Downey as president; and former McMaster provost Ken Norrie as vice-president), the council is an arm's-length agency established to conduct research and provide objective advice on all aspects of higher education.

Efforts to assess quality in universities will always run into issues of subjectivity and ambiguity in terms of the aims and objectives of higher education. Nevertheless, credible evaluations of how Canadian universities are performing will continue to improve as governments and boards, on behalf of taxpayers and citizens, increasingly seek value for their investment. The role of the president in advancing this cause while protecting the academic integrity of the institution will be a significant preoccupation for years to come.

BRANDING, MARKETING, AND MEDIA RELATIONS

Another critical presidential concern in an increasingly competitive university environment is branding and marketing. While these terms are often antithetical to faculty, who worry about increasing corporate cultural influences, almost all universities regularly engage marketing consultants to help them "brand" the institution. While the results usually look rather similar, in the Canadian context at least,[11] well-prepared and consistent materials advance the profile and reputation of the institution and can help establish a stronger case for fundraising and government support.

I believe that the most important aspect of branding and marketing is the process itself. The exercises that go into defining the institution's strengths and attractions actively engage stakeholders in thinking about their institution, what it is and what they want it to be. Done well, a branding exercise can develop and reinforce pride in the university and challenge everyone to work more collaboratively for its advancement. Of course, there are risks. Some parties may react negatively to a particular catchphrase or logo, and there are always those who oppose such an exercise because of its cost. On balance, however, I believe that the branding process is not only valuable but essential in today's marketplace. To paraphrase Stephen Joel Trachtenberg, former president of George Washington University, unless your institution has endowments the size of Harvard's, enrolments are everything,[12] and therefore – put crassly – if a marketing campaign fails, the president can blame the public affairs department, but if enrolments decline and there has been no such publicity effort, the president will be the scapegoat.

An offshoot of branding is the sometimes difficult issue of media relations. Again, few presidents have training in this area, and almost all of us have been caught out by an interviewer or newspaper columnist who could have been much better handled with professional preparation. Over time, presidents develop their own style in dealing with the media, usually under the watchful eye of the staff in public affairs. My own approach was to be open and forthright. Even though this got me into trouble on occasion, it meant that I was often "good copy" and helped generate media attention when we wanted it. It is important not to overreact to negative publicity but to take the long-term view of media relations. Among the lessons that I have learned are the following:

- Nothing is "off the record." You should assume that anything you say may end up in print, on the radio, on television, or all three.
- The media want good stories and the university is a terrific source for them. Feed the media positive stories (research successes, exceptional students, and human interest anecdotes) and you will get excellent coverage.
- Deal quickly and openly with crises (this is one of the most important lessons). Books on this subject cite many instances when an institution's attempts to cover up or fudge a story led to much more extensive and detrimental coverage.[13]
- Do not take negative articles personally. Take immediate steps to refute incorrect information, but do not overreact to personal criticism. If you do, you may encourage further such criticism.
- Recognize the increasing impact of social networking media, especially on young people, the university's primary target group.

There are countless other lessons. One of the main objectives of media training is to get a president to stick to his or her message, to tirelessly repeat the same key points and refuse to be sidetracked. This is excellent advice but not one I was very good at following. In the end, despite moments when I was appalled at the coverage we got, I learned to take most of the negative publicity in stride. I also learned to appreciate how often a good-news story received prominent local coverage thanks to an enterprising reporter and a good media relations department.

ALUMNI AFFAIRS

One of the most pleasurable aspects of a president's role is interacting with the institution's alumni, both informally and through the alumni association. Active alumni are key among those most committed to the institution. They are a tremendous resource group, not only as advocates and donors, but also as boosters of the president's own morale and pride in the university.

Alumni represent all that is best about a university. Their success is the institution's success. They help celebrate its awards, its championships, and its most successful graduates, and they support all sorts of events, initiatives, and activities, both on and off campus. They serve on boards and committees, give generously to their favourite programs and activities, help recognize student and faculty leaders through awards and scholarships, and reach out to generations of graduates scattered all over the world and keep them in touch with their alma mater. Every Canadian university has stories of alumni who have gone on to great achievement or personal satisfaction but have never forgotten the role the university played in their development. No matter how many times I met alumni at various events, I always came away buoyed with the institution's impact on them and their gratitude for it.

Of course, alumni associations and individuals can also create problems for a president. This is most apparent when the latter makes a decision that runs counter to their views, such as to close a favourite academic program no longer as central as it once was or to drop a popular team sport for financial reasons. It is a serious mistake for a president to assume the automatic support of alumni. Establishing and supporting an alumni board that is independent of the university's alumni affairs office will help ensure valuable member services and unfettered and constructive input from alumni.

Alumni are key stakeholders, and it is perfectly appropriate that they be represented on boards and even senates and that their viewpoints be taken seriously in any significant decisions for the future of the institution. After all, the institution played a truly significant part in their lives. In fact, I have frequently found myself worrying that today's students aren't having the quality and intensity of university experience that those from an earlier era remembered. It is fair to wonder whether today's graduates will be as loyal to their institution as are those of the 1960s and 1970s.

FUNDRAISING

One of the most evident changes in the role of a university president lies in the area of fundraising. Here, the expectations held for the incumbent by the board, faculty, and staff have risen considerably. While fundraising has long been a dominant theme in American universities, wrapped especially around alumni and intercollegiate sports, it is a more recent phenomenon in Canada. While fundraising in this country has not yet reached the same prominence or visibility as in the United States, it has become a critical component of presidential success, sometimes misconstrued by search committees as a singular talent unrelated to the more traditional skills of academic leadership and good management.

In leading the University of Toronto to become the first to have its endowment exceed a billion dollars, Rob Prichard is arguably the most successful fundraiser in Canadian university history. He quickly put the issue in perspective by emphasizing that the money came because of the focus on academic change and not vice versa. Almost no part of the university was untouched academically during his ten years as president, and that is what has given him the most pride. He gives the rest of the credit to outstanding fundraiser Jon Delandria and the team he built for university development: "The pride is not that we got the money – that's just the proof that it worked. The pride is that we chose an academic mission, focused on it, and were unrelenting in pursuit of that mission and did everything necessary with government relations and fundraising to support that."

Another successful fundraiser, Peter George, has a similar story in that his success started more with vision and commitment than with any magic fundraising ability. His first public statement after his appointment in October 1994 was that the university was going to live up to its commitment to build a new students' centre. The students had been paying a levy for the previous five years to build up the half of the cost, but the university had not raised one cent for the centre. The breakthrough came when Dr George was approached by prominent Hamilton businessman Michael DeGroote, who had noticed the difficulties he was facing in raising money for the centre and asked how he could help. George replied that money would help. Michael promptly donated $4 million, with $2 million to follow "if needed." This success boosted the new president's confidence, and he later launched the "Changing Tomorrow Today" campaign in support of research and educational priorities: "The consultants said that $70 million was our maximum target but I said it had to be $100 million. We actually raised $130 million privately and leveraged another $250 million in matching and other gifts to research that made a huge difference." The Changing Tomorrow Today campaign was followed by a single-project campaign for McMaster's athletics and recreation centre. More recently, a second major initiative, "The Campaign for McMaster University," was launched with a $400-million target; as predicted by Dr George at the outset, the campaign more than exceeded its goal, raising some $473 million by the end of his presidency in the summer of 2010.

George regrets that it is much more difficult to raise money in the humanities, social sciences, and some of the core science areas than for medicine, business, and engineering. This concern led him and his wife, Allison, to direct their own gift for the campaign to the liberal arts, both to support the humanities and social sciences and to encourage others to do the same.

Notwithstanding that the biggest contribution presidents can make to fundraising is in the academic development of the institution, they can also play an important direct role as well. When the chips are down and the groundwork has been done, it is often the president who makes the final request. This can daunting for a newcomer to such activities, as very few first-time presidents have any training or experience in the area. Still, it is surprising how often individuals who initially dread making the call to a potential donor end up enjoying the activity.[14] Passion for a cause is infectious, which is why presidents and vice-presidents are frequently accompanied by faculty members when raising funds for a particular program or discipline. There is no one more persuasive than someone who is talking about a life's passion, whether it is a particular area of research, a community service, or the broader issue of access to and excellence in higher education.

Determining how much time to give to the external role is a constant challenge for the university president. It will vary considerably according to the individual's personality. Many are extroverts who like to be involved across a wide range of spectra, but even the more laid-back presidents are deeply involved in activities outside their institutions these days. More and more, it comes with the job.

Institutional Governance and Presidential Accountability

As the chief executive officer of the modern public university, the president is hired by the board of governors (in consultation with the senate) to, among other responsibilities,

- help the institution to define its mission, mandate, and priorities;
- ensure the effective management of the institution, its programs, and services;
- ensure the institution's fiscal health;
- ensure the quality of its academic endeavours – programs, teaching, research and scholarship, support services – primarily through the recruitment and management of faculty and staff;
- ensure a climate of academic freedom and support for the pursuit of knowledge and truth;
- ensure the reputation and effective marketing of the institution; and
- ensure accountability for all university operations to the respective authorities of the board, the senate, and various levels of government.

Institutional autonomy is sacrosanct in Canadian public universities. At its heart is the concept of academic freedom, the unfettered search for truth that must not be hindered or compromised by political or other interference. Academic freedom is ensconced in our universities through individual acts of Parliament (or legislature) for each institution. These assign authority and responsibility for the institution's conduct to a lay board of governors (or directors), in most cases in a bicameral arrangement with an academic senate. Academic freedom is further protected by specific clauses in collective agreements that define it in more detail, adding protection to faculty and others from discrimination on the basis of race, creed, gender, or sexual orientation. Boards, in turn, vest responsibility for ensuring academic freedom with the president, although it may be members of the board, ironically, who are most upset when the president supports a politically unpopular action precisely in the name of such freedom.

While presidents have always been directly accountable to their boards, the balance of power has shifted in recent years as universities have become much more in the public eye. In earlier days, when only a small percentage of the age cohort went to university, institutions were smaller and most of their activities fell below the public radar screen. The president's role was less onerous and simpler, for he or she needed only to preside over rather than manage the institution. Boards were smaller and often dominated by social elites, and most presidents had a pretty free ride, especially in the era before collective agreements, faculty and student activism, and the emergence of human rights issues to the forefront of our society. Today, the relationship is quite different. The president's role is complex, stakeholder groups (faculty, staff, students, alumni) are better organized and more active, and universities are more generally seen as engines of progress in the knowledge society. Boards and senates are larger and more broadly representative of all the interest groups around a university. As a result, the relationship between president and board has become both more complicated and more important than ever.

While the collegial governance model goes back hundreds of years, its particular manifestations among Canadian universities were largely defined by student and faculty activism in the late 1960s and early 1970s when many were united in the common purpose of promoting much broader participation in institutional governance. The critical importance of university leadership understanding organizational culture is particularly evident in the practice and effectiveness of governance in a given institution.

One must be careful in generalizing about university boards in Canada, since their makeup is different, not only in different provinces but among institutions in a given province. In general, however, a board is made up of a number of lay representatives of the external community (some appointed by the provincial government and some by the board itself), faculty representatives (usually appointed by the senate or constituent colleges), and staff, student, and alumni representatives (usually appointed by their respective constituencies). The president is the only voting member of the board from the senior management team.

Unlike the practice in most provinces, where boards make their own selection, in Alberta it is the Lieutenant-Governor-in-Council (provincial cabinet) who appoints university board chairs. This can raise the possibility of political interference in institutional governance, although the most recent such instance took place in Newfoundland around Memorial University's search for a new president. Citing supporting legislation, Education Minister Joan Burke summarily rejected the top two candidates identified by the university's search committee. In the ensuing national uproar, many blamed Premier Danny Williams for the intervention, but the minister's right to approve or reject nominees for president was built right into the Memorial University Act. Despite past practice to accept the university's recommendation, the minister's intervention led to the withdrawal of the leading candidate, Dr Eddy Campbell, who subsequently accepted the position of president of the University of New Brunswick. Many at Memorial and academics across Canada have expressed concerns about the university's ability to recruit and retain strong presidential and faculty candidates in a climate where there are perceived threats to the institution's academic freedom and autonomy. According to the Canadian Association of University Teachers (CAUT), the Memorial Board of Regents is now recommending that the legislation be amended to reflect the autonomy of the university in appointment practices as more in line with that on other Canadian campuses.[1]

The relationship with the board chair is obviously crucial for the president. Most boards only meet five or six times a year, although their key standing committees (executive, finance, human resources) usually meet monthly. It is thus the board chair (who normally chairs the executive committee as well), vice-chair, and perhaps the chair of the finance committee who are the most important regular contacts for the president.

An important factor in the president-chair relationship is the term of the chair. Most institutions operate on a revolving basis, with the executive of the board (second vice-chair, vice-chair, chair) serving two years in each position. In Alberta, however, the term is at the discretion of the provincial government. Myer Horowitz, for example, spent his ten years as president of the University of Alberta with the same board chair, John Schlosser. Given their strong working relationship, this worked extremely well. There is a lot to be said for a longer term of office for board chairs. In my own years at Laurentian and Windsor, I served under eleven board chairs in seventeen years. While some board members may be concerned if the president and board chair develop too close a personal relationship over a long time period, the kind of turnover I experienced (which is more typical in Canada) means that a lot of time and effort goes into establishing new relationships on the part of both parties.

Any discussion of the relationship between a president and a board chair should begin with the acknowledgment that the chair must have and must demonstrate full confidence in the president. The corollary is that the president must reciprocate. The nature of interpersonal relationships means that some chairs will be much more effective than others, but mutual respect is essential if the chair and the president are to serve the best interests of the institution.

Both the president and the chair (and, by extension, the board) must understand the difference between governance and management. The board has ultimate responsibility for the institution, but it delegates managerial authority for its performance to the president and holds him or her accountable. Bill Leggett observed, "Board relations are extremely important. You don't have to look very far to find examples of what happens when the president is offside with the board. A lot depends on the chair of the board. The worst thing that can happen to any president is to have a board that thinks they know how to run the university and want to. Boards are about governance and management is about management."

As previously noted, there have been several recent instances where a president who had been successful in one university left a subsequent post fairly early in his or her first term, apparently because of real difficulties with the board of governors. This has been most publicly evident at Concordia University in Montreal, where the last two presidents, both of whom had had successful presidencies elsewhere, had very truncated first terms.[2] While the details of each case are not publicly known, the departures at least raise the issue not only of presidential performance but of board accountability as well. This is especially the case where, as at Concordia, the presidents who "have resigned" receive very large severance payments. Not only do such expensive buyouts so soon after a new hiring raise questions of the board's fiscal accountability, they presumably make it more difficult to recruit a successor, given that potential candidates are apt to shy away from an institution with a reputation for poor board-president relations.

Of course, many university presidents have experienced difficult moments with their boards, even to the point of seeing their appointment in jeopardy. These are the times when the relationship with the board chair is most crucial, and this applies even to our most successful leaders. For example, Paul Davenport had problems with a board chair at the University of Alberta but went on to have a very strong relationship with his several chairs at the University of Western Ontario.

A chair who understands the academic milieu and appreciates the challenges of dealing with so many interest groups from a relatively limited power base can do much to help a new president through difficult times. The search process for a president is a long and expensive one, and the success of an appointment is in the interests of both parties. Of course, if it is subsequently clear that a new president is a poor fit for the institution, the chair has a responsibility to ensure that the board takes the necessary steps to find a replacement.

In underlining the importance of a supportive board chair, I do not mean to suggest that he or she is there merely to uphold whatever the president wants to do. Support is important, but blind support is not very useful and can even be dangerous. If the board chair is not well aware of the issues and the institutional politics, his or her support may not count for much at times of crisis. Most board chairs have considerable management and/or leadership experience and they can provide valuable support, not only by backing the president in difficult times but also by sharing their expertise and perspectives and by challenging the incumbent to reach higher and perform better. I know that I was most effective when serving under board chairs who were supportive and challenging at the same time. I benefited directly from their advice, expertise, and active engagement in the affairs of the institution and the community.

Some issues test the president-chair relationship very publicly. Almost every institution has outspoken professors whose controversial research or statements to the media lead to demands for their dismissal by members of the public, and such matters may eventually reach the board level, usually *in camera*. It is the role of the president to weigh the case objectively on its own merits, to take disciplinary action where warranted, but also to be prepared to defend an academic with controversial opinions in the name of academic freedom. Members of the board may not always see the individual cases the same way, but when the chips are down, the practice in Canada has been to support the president's actions in such cases.[3]

Of course, academic freedom is not a totally objective concept, and it can be used as licence to abuse human rights. The potential misapplication of academic freedom is most likely when voice is given to highly volatile political or religious issues on university campuses and verbal and even physical abuse may result. A university president must defend freedom of speech but not to the point of allowing it to degenerate into hate mongering. The line is not always clear.

In recent years, the leadership of Fred Lowy at Concordia University in Montreal epitomized both the challenges of the president's role and the dignity and sensitivity with which they can be handled. He faced extremely difficult issues concerning the Israeli-Palestinian conflict in the Middle East, a particular catalyst being a scheduled appearance by Israeli prime minister Benjamin Netanyahu on the Concordia campus in 2002. In the face of riotous behaviour, the talk was cancelled, and after that a controversial moratorium on Middle East-related activities on campus was imposed. Concordia's board subsequently granted its president the right to impose summary suspensions and to initiate expulsions for students ignoring the ban on such activities. In the words of Concordia historian Frank Chalk, Dr Lowy was put in an impossible position, "trapped between the twin goals of honouring the right to freedom of speech and avoiding the disaster that would result from riotous confrontation in the streets over Netanyahu's right to speak here."[4]

It is easy to say that a president's first responsibility is to preserve academic freedom, but that must be weighed against individual rights and personal safety. This dilemma is especially challenging when such wrenching decisions must be made in the heat of the moment, when one is getting conflicting advice but has little time to consider all possible consequences. Still, the best rule of thumb is to err on the side of academic freedom. The University of Ottawa did not fare well in the popular press for the way it dealt with controversial American self-described polemicist Ann Coulter, who had been scheduled to speak at the university in early 2010. In a letter to Ms Coulter, the university provost had cautioned her to watch her words lest she face criminal charges for promoting hatred in Canada.[5] This led to the cancellation of her speech, and publicity from the cancellation simply raised her public profile and enhanced interest in her subsequent speech at the University of Calgary (she had also spoken at Western without significant incident).

One of the most public events on the university calendar is convocation, and the awarding of honorary degrees can often be contentious and may put the president in a very difficult position in the middle of swirling media interest. I was never so grateful for a strong board chair than when I was forced to deal with a provocative incident at a convocation at Laurentian University in 1995.[6] On that occasion, I was to present two individuals, Michael Sopko, then president of Inco Limited, and Joan Kuyek, a local social worker, with honorary degrees. Unbeknownst to me, through last-minute discussions with my assistant, Ms Kuyek had arranged to have the speaking order reversed so that she followed Mr Sopko. Hence, to my surprise on stage, Mr Sopko was presented first. In his speech to the assembled throng, he announced Inco's decision to invest in the Voisey's Bay nickel deposits, a national news story that attracted considerable media interest. Ms Kuyek then followed and, speaking for at least double the allocated time, attacked Inco for its alleged rape of the environment, to which she attributed the illness and even death of employees and citizens. Whatever the merits of her arguments, it was ungracious in the extreme and a flagrant abuse of the convocation platform, which was there to recognize her own leadership in the Sudbury community. To attack Inco, and by extension Mr Sopko in front of his family and friends on an occasion that was to be a celebration of his leadership, was rude and inappropriate. The tension around the affair was heightened when many in the audience and the majority of faculty members on stage rose to give Ms Kuyek a standing ovation.

The aftermath was predictable. Not only had Mr Sopko been a past member of the board of governors of Laurentian, but Inco was the university's largest corporate benefactor and the major employer in the city of Sudbury. The chair of the board, Jamie Wallace, was president of Pioneer Construction, a major contractor to Inco, and the chair of the executive committee was Jim Ashcroft, president of the Ontario division of Inco. Each was terribly embarrassed by Mr Sopko's treatment. There were calls for my resignation, with some prominent board members and community citizens suggesting that

I had somehow orchestrated the whole thing. It never seemed to occur to them to question why a university president would set up the head of the institution's biggest benefactor for public attack. The board's executive committee held an emergency meeting, without my presence, to discuss what should be done. On campus, there was a lot of finger pointing at the faculty who had stood to applaud Ms Kuyek's remarks, and some people wanting me to fire the supposed instigators.

Under Jamie Wallace's strong and calm leadership, the issue was diffused, and I ultimately received the full support of the board in the case. As a result of this unfortunate incident, I introduced amendments to the senate bylaws that made one honorary degree per ceremony the norm unless there was a very strong case for recognizing more than one person on the same occasion (a policy I also took with me to Windsor). Notwithstanding his strong business ties to Inco, Mr Wallace was incredibly supportive of me throughout this difficult period, and I will always appreciate his leadership and his clear understanding of the difference between management and governance in the conduct of his duties as board chair.

Paul Davenport faced a highly publicized maelstrom at Western when the senate voted to award an honorary degree to Henry Morgentaler, noted Canadian abortionist. Notwithstanding the public opposition of his board chair, Dr Davenport upheld the honorary degree selection process, emphasizing the importance of academic freedom, yet he allowed those opposed to the selection to protest quietly without disrupting the ceremony. He won kudos across the country for his calm but firm handling of the affair, although he admitted that it was not an easy matter for anyone.

> I could have communicated it better to my board. I took it as business as usual, another set of honorary degree recipients. Some of my board members thought that I should have advised the board in advance. It was a tough time for Western but I judged this to be an issue of academic freedom and was quite firm in my defence of the decision of the senate committee which names the honorary degree recipients. I received tremendous support from the faculty at Western and from the Canadian Association of University Teachers. Three years later, Dr Morgenthaler received the Order of Canada and I received a flurry of emails and letters; most were positive.

Such incidents are not reserved for recent times. One of my favourite all-time stories about honorary degrees involved the University of Alberta in 1941. The saga is well described in Walter Johns's *History of the University of Alberta*.[7] The distinguished selection committee, which included the chancellor, A.C. Rutherford, first premier of Alberta, proposed that the recipient that year be none other than the current premier, William Aberhart. As was the practice, the president of the university, William Kerr, contacted the premier in February to tell him of the award, noting that it was subject to the formality of approval by the university's senate.[8] The premier was delighted and spent a considerable amount of time writing his convocation speech.

In those days, honorary degrees were officially confirmed the week before convocation by the senate following its annual dinner, and until then, this had been a mere formality. The senate met on 12 May 1941 to consider all the academic awards. Two Calgary lawyers who were opposed to the Aberhart award led a heated debate, and then there was, unusually, a secret ballot. The result of the vote was 17 for and 18 against. This was conveyed to the premier, who became very angry. Efforts were made to have the matter reconsidered that afternoon, but the result was a second negative vote, 15 to 16. The president and board chair resigned over the issue the next day, and a devastated Rutherford died less than a month later. In a way, history repeated itself almost fifty years later when the Oxford Union voted publicly against awarding an honorary degree to Margaret Thatcher, then prime minister of the country.

The presidents interviewed for this book were very clear on the importance of ensuring effective accountability to the board and its chair. On the premise that there will always be dissent and that a president must learn to work effectively with a board, Martha Piper resisted suggestions by some that she try to have several difficult people on the UBC board removed. Instead, she placed the highest priority on preparation for board meetings and she followed up every issue raised at a given meeting. Much of her energy would go into the details, even though she admits that most other presidents would delegate this sort of thing to an executive assistant. Her approach demonstrates the importance she attached to the relationship she and her senior team had with the board.

Dave Marshall has lunch at least once a year with every board member and strongly recommends this practice to new presidents. It gives the incumbent a chance to understand each individual's point of view and to solicit their ideas and support while also conveying perspectives and information that don't lend themselves as readily to formal board meetings. In Marshall's view, nothing is more import-ant to a president than good relations with board members: "If you don't have the board with you, it doesn't matter what else you do."

An advantage of informal meetings with individual members is that it discourages the domination of the board by a small in-group. It is sometimes tempting for presidents to spend most of their time with just the members of the executive committee, for instance, but it may be counterproductive if other board members feel neglected or left out. This applies as much to student, staff, and faculty repre-sentatives as it does to the lay members of the board. Treating each and every board member with respect and interest will pay dividends when key decisions later require voters who are strongly committed to the institution and knowledgeable about the pros and cons of a particular course of action. It also ensures that the president is well aware of the range of opinions and perspectives represented and hence that much better prepared for meetings.

Paul Davenport stressed the importance of relations with the chair and reflected on both his negative and positive experiences. He started well at Alberta with long-serving board chair John Schlosser, but faced greater challenges when Stanley Milner took over that post in 1991. Even though a government appointee, Schlosser had been seen by some in government as being too closely tied to the admin-istration. Hence, Milner, who had no previous experience on the board, was, according to university historian Rod Macleod, deliber-ately appointed as "someone without close ties to the university who could redefine the relationship and vigorously assert the govern-ment's position."[9] Davenport's last two years at Alberta were much more difficult as a result, and when the board, by a narrow margin, opted to establish a search committee for the presidency, he made it clear that he would not be a candidate for a second term under such conditions. Later, in response to strong reactions on campus, the board reconsidered its position, but before a final decision could be taken, Dr Davenport had accepted his appointment as president of the University of Western Ontario. He took up the position in 1994 and was twice renewed for his strong and effective leadership.

I think I swim pretty well in this collegial ocean – I like collegial relations but, to me, there's a framework around collegiality that does have a hierarchy to it – the board, the president, the vice-presidents, the deans, the senior administrators. I need that relationship – looking up at a board where I am able to work with them, agree on priorities, they assign priorities to me, and so on – exactly what I have had at Western for fifteen years and which I had when I arrived at Alberta with John Schlosser. After John left, things just didn't work out that way.

When he arrived at Western, Davenport experienced a series of chairs, all of whom helped him build up a board culture where members understood the board's role in governance, helped with strategic planning and setting priorities, and held him accountable for achieving those priorities and keeping them informed on all issues. He commented, "I would like to say that I have had the best job in Canada for the past fifteen years, in large part because I have had a series of great boards and board chairs to work with."

Davenport believes that when the chips are down, the board wants to hear from the president on the key issues of the day. This does not minimize importance of developing good relationships between vice-presidents or deans and the board, but it does underline the "buck stops here" accountability of the president and the board's expectations for the position.

You tend to underestimate the time you should give to board relations because you are the link between the board and the entire administration. That's not something you can delegate – you can seek to establish good relations, as I have, with particular board members and particular vice-presidents. I'm not one of those presidents who insists that everything should go through me, but I know that when push comes to shove, the board wants to hear me talk.

Peter George added another perspective when he noted the need, on occasion, to be nimble and quick to grab an opportunity for the university. He cited the example of having to secure approval for the expansion of McMaster's aquatic centre on short notice as part of a bid for the Pan-American Games in Ontario. In that case, with no time to go through all the hoops of the university's committee structure prior to declaring the university's interest in the centre, he got the support of the board executive committee and the *ex post facto* approval of the board in return for his commitment to take the project through normal institutional approval processes after the Ontario bid was approved.

Trust and confidence in the president are important prerequisites to that ability to move quickly, a fact underlined by Dave Marshall: "Boards say that the most important thing they do is choose the president." If effective relationships with the board are crucial to a president's survival, his or her relationship to the senate may be much more variable, reflecting the particular style and orientations of the incumbent and the institution's academic culture.

INSTITUTIONAL GOVERNANCE AND THE SENATE

Almost all Canadian universities function with a bicameral system, with the senate responsible for academic matters and the board for overall direction and fiscal responsibility. This relationship has evolved considerably over the past few decades, given that a complete bifurcation of academic and fiscal matters is artificial and even unworkable.[10] For example, the senate's authority to set admission standards has significant implications for enrolments, and hence for the financial position of the institution, and there is little point in approving an academic program if there is not a good market case for it and the requisite funding. It is thus imperative that boards and senates function effectively together with good communications and mutual respect.

While there was near consensus among the presidents interviewed on many issues, the role and effectiveness of the senate was not one of them. Some see the senate as an important instrument of governance and academic leadership in the university, while others are more skeptical of its power and impact. Jim Downey believes it critical that the president be truly engaged in the academic life of the institution, including through chairing the senate. For Downey, how a president stands vis-à-vis the senate is key to his or her academic leadership: "I think it is always a mistake for the president not to chair senate. There's no other way that you can stay truly engaged and to be seen by faculty to be so."

Bill Leggett concurred: "In my first year, a dialogue about whether or not the principal should really chair the senate took hold. After listening to the debate for some time, I made it very clear that I had come to Queen's to be its senior academic officer, not the CEO. Given

that reality, I intended to chair senate, which is, at Queen's, the ultimate academic decision-making body. The conversation stopped very
quickly." However, Leggett still wonders about the effectiveness of
the senate. He concluded that its most important role is to reinforce
and give substance to the reality that faculty input is central to the
academic life and direction of any university. He also acknowledged
the senate's utility as a sounding board and the value of its support
on key policy issues or when the principal/president is attempting
to achieve difficult but essential academic change. Whether or not
the senate is the most effective vehicle to identify and achieve these
end points, given its characteristically conservative nature, remains
a question for him.

Martha Piper put a lot of time into board matters but confessed
that she paid less attention to the senate. She was more cynical about
its affairs and saw people running for senate as much to resist as to
facilitate institutional change. This reminded me of what I'd experienced at the Open University when I was on sabbatical in England
in 1989. I learned that all full-time faculty members belonged to the
senate but that few attended its meetings in Milton Keynes because
it was a long way to travel for members disbursed all over England, Scotland, and Northern Ireland. Too often, the only ones who
came to a given meeting from afar were those passionately opposed
to something on the agenda. This certainly did not make academic
leadership any easier!

The role and impact of senates in Canadian universities have been
both reinforced and challenged by the growing importance of faculty
associations and collective bargaining since the mid-1970s. While
collective agreements have strengthened faculty roles in such areas as
the protection of academic freedom and the formalization of issues
of equity and standards and procedures for promotion and tenure,
the significant differences between the traditional collegial culture of
the senate and the negotiating culture of collective bargaining have
confused and complicated the board-senate relationship.

Even where it is seen to be less effective than desired, the senate may still play important roles in the university. In his classic
analysis, Birnbaum makes a useful distinction between the manifest and latent functions of senates.[11] He cites three major areas of
senate responsibility in most universities – effectively dealing with
institutional problems through rational processes, formulating and
clarifying goals and policies, and developing shared values leading

to consensus – and concludes that senates are not usually very effective in dealing with any of them.[12] Given this assessment, he asks
why senates are so persistent and concludes that this is because they
have a number of latent functions that are very useful to universities. These include being a symbol that contributes to the professional status of the institution with its focus on quality, standards,
and integrity; representing administrative acceptance of the role of
faculty in university governance; being a status provider; serving as
a garbage can and deep freeze for campus issues; alerting leaders to
issues brewing on campus; acting as a personnel screening device to
help identify future campus leaders; being an organizational con-
servator that protects the status quo and avoids disruptive change;
providing rituals and pastimes that add stability to the organization;
and serving as a scapegoat for things that go wrong in the institution.

   My own experience has been, on balance, more positive than Birnbaum suggests. This may not be surprising, as Mortimer and Sathre
found that administrators tend to attribute more influence to senates
than faculty do.[13] They suggest that widespread faculty participation is not the norm, thus undermining the perceived legitimacy and
effectiveness of senates. It would be easy to conclude that procedures
and practices in university governance are hopelessly outdated and
that presidents are powerless to do much about it. On the contrary,
I would argue that a president with a strong and genuine commitment to the senate as the senior academic governance body in the
institution can have a significant impact on its real and perceived
effectiveness.

TOWARDS MORE EFFECTIVE GOVERNANCE IN A UNIVERSITY

In preparing for several presentations on governance in the fall
of 2010, I realized that most of what I had to say about governance came back to the issue of institutional culture. This perspective is strongly evident in the work of Cynthia Hardy.[14] In looking
at retrenchment strategies in six Canadian universities during the
1980s, she found significant differences in the ways that an institution and its leadership reacted to very similar financial challenges, an
observation that reinforced the importance of the local institutional
culture. There was no one best approach, but the distinct character
of each institution came out strongly in the ways that it dealt with

retrenchment – formally or informally, in a centralized or decentralized manner, relying on a small group or encouraging broad participation. In her concluding chapter, Hardy argued for the use of collegiality as a strategic weapon, using power to create consensus around common goals: "[I]nstitutional collegiality must be created by individuals capable of using power to substitute a common vision for parochial interests. Thus collegiality is part of a political process whereby power is mobilized to prevent conflict."[15]

Similarly, in a comprehensive analysis of academic governance, Mortimer and Sathre emphasize the critical importance of developing a consensus around where the institution is going and how it is going to get there. This is a considerable challenge for a president. Many aspects of the traditional collegial style of governance are ill-suited to today's market and accountability pressures and to the need for universities to be nimble and responsive to opportunities and challenges alike. In this context of change and challenges to an institution's prevailing culture, the president has to be unusually savvy. As Mortimer and Sathre write, "The faculty's control of the curriculum, the board's responsibility for program oversight, and the administration's responsibility to account for the wise use of resources can all come into conflict and lead to some of the most wicked problems and long-lasting and corrosive relationships."[16]

While the formal roles and powers of boards and senates are remarkably similar across Canada, there are very significant differences in their effectiveness among institutions. As Hardy has shown, how an institution and its leadership react to the same financial challenges varies considerably according to its organizational culture. The key factors determining governance effectiveness in an institution are primarily cultural – the extent to which there is consensus on institutional direction and a relationship of trust among administration and faculty. The organization's culture is a product of its past – its mission and mandate; its history; its leadership, both former and current – and nothing is more important to a new institutional leader than to learn and understand that culture before making any effort to change it.

In the face of much pessimism in universities about their governance models, the president is the pivotal individual who can best do something about them. Consistent with Hardy's notion of collegiality,[17] Mortimer and Sathre see governance as an art form requiring considerable political skills on the part of its leaders:

It involves the capacity to deal with staggering levels of complexity – competing interests, and agendas, an extraordinary range of participants/actors, and negotiations and trade-offs that lead to progress and very often setbacks.

Politically savvy leaders operate within an environment that gives great deference to process, but are aware and responsive to the larger community's impatience with this legendary characteristic of the academy.[18]

The key to any system of effective governance, whatever its details, is trust among the key players. Like Mortimer and Sathre, I believe that the answer lies in an open system of governance. For them, openness is "a natural opponent of arbitrariness and a natural ally in the struggle to build trust and legitimacy in academic governance."[19] This point of view supports my own approach of using open processes to try to get all the key constituencies to buy in, especially faculty. A strategic plan that builds a strong community and aspires to improve the reputation and financial position of the institution will be in everyone's interest. At the same time, the plan must involve making clear choices that best serve the institution in the long term. Such decisions will make it more difficult for some to support the plan, and a president has to work hard to steer through this minefield by

- learning the institutional culture and how to work effectively within it;
- building a trusting relationship with the board and especially its chair;
- articulating a clear mission, mandate, and strategic plan, each developed, as much as possible, through broad consultation and consensus among the key stakeholder groups; and
- forging an institution in which the administration, faculty, staff, and students work together to address some of the key concerns identified above (academic standards and integrity, class sizes, alternative learning approaches, campus climate, institutional size, and mandate).

Notwithstanding their genuine differences in mandates and priorities, administrations, boards, senates, and faculty associations can collaborate effectively in many areas:

- Defining a unique institutional mission and mandate and establishing strategic directions for the university
- Increasing the role of quality as a criterion for funding allocations and lobbying government for the same
- Combatting grade inflation, promoting academic integrity, and upholding high standards while providing strong student support
- Ensuring a campus climate that promotes debate and dissent but also encourages all parties to put the institution's interests first. For example, the respective university presidents, student groups, and faculty and staff associations can seek common ground on key public issues so that the universities present a united front to government wherever possible.

The minefields are many and even the most well-meaning and talented leaders find it difficult to manoeuvre through all of them. This is hardly reason, though, to back off. Leadership requires ambition and courage, and the university presidents who approach such challenges with openness and integrity will develop the kind of respect and support that can help them achieve unprecedented levels of change in their institution.

Institutional Autonomy and System Diversity

The nearly universal high standard of Canadian universities is a matter of considerable pride within the academic community, but it comes at the expense of system diversity relative to most post-secondary education systems. The Canadian university is an excellent institution, but as set out in chapter 6, it may not be the most appropriate choice for every one of the students (who represent a much wider spectrum) now attending it. Many young Canadians might be better served by an entity more suited to their individual needs and capabilities.

At the university level, other choices might take the form of a polytechnic, an exclusively undergraduate university, a residential liberal arts institution, an open university, or a dedicated professional institution. Other post-secondary options that might be best for a given individual include a community college, a top-level trade school, or a private vocational college. Such options are not readily available in many parts of Canada, and even where they are, they may not enjoy the same prestige and name recognition of comparable institutions in other countries. In recent years, some provinces, notably Alberta and British Columbia, have taken significant steps to develop more differentiated post-secondary systems. These can serve as models for Ontario, which is seeking more creative responses to the high enrolment pressures in the Greater Toronto Area than are typically offered by its relatively homogeneous system of colleges and universities.

Among the presidents interviewed, there was widespread agreement about the need for more system diversity but less of a consensus about how this could be achieved and who holds primary responsibility for its achievement. The challenges begin with the whole notion of a university "system," not only across Canada but in each individual province. The network of universities across the country was not designed by any central or even regional authority, but has evolved as a patchwork of independently governed institutions under the loose jurisdiction of the appropriate provincial government. Almost every Canadian university has its own charter, its own act, and its own independence under a board of governors or trustees, usually in a bicameral arrangement with senates or academic councils. It is hardly possible to claim there is a system at all, let alone a coherent one.

Ironically, the universities' independence, together with the relative lack of a system, has bred institutions that are remarkably similar, probably as a result of the influence of the prevailing national academic culture, institutional leaders with similar orientations and backgrounds, and considerable collaboration across the country by faculty associations through CAUT. The university's status and prestige are tightly attached to having graduate programs and professors with impressive research dossiers and top funding. There have been few cases to date of Canadian universities receiving public recognition and high praise for the attention they have given to teaching, job preparation, or innovative delivery methods.

Even though provincial governments have significant financial control over the institutions (through funding formuli for operating and capital grants, and the regulation of tuition fees), politicians have been wary of intervening too directly in the governance of the universities. Even where there is a will to intervene, it is often frustrated by the complexities of transfer payments and federal-provincial jurisdictional disputes. For the most part, provincial governments have left questions of institutional priority and governance to local boards and senates.

An integral part of the Canadian ethos has played an important role in the development of the Canadian university. As much as there have been aspirations for world status among the country's best-known institutions, there have always been equally strong pressures for fairness and equity in the distribution of resources. Many Canadian universities are located in smaller centres and rural areas, and members of Parliament and provincial legislatures expect to be able to deliver resources to their home institution. As a result, almost all of the institutions in Canada have grown and developed significantly and in similar directions in recent years.

The very similar backgrounds and aspirations of most Canadian university presidents have also contributed to the homogeneity of university development in important ways. Overwhelmingly products of top Canadian, American, and British universities and almost universally experienced in Canadian academic administration, they share very similar notions of what a university should be and how it should be run, with relatively little variation in their academic programming at both the undergraduate and graduate levels (with research intensity being a dominant characteristic). These tendencies are strengthened by prominent national surveys like that initiated by *Maclean's* (which gives greatest weight to traditional academic inputs) and by faculty and boards anxious to enhance the status and prestige of their institution. For some institutional leaders, the motivation might even be to make their personal case for promotion to the helm of one of the larger universities in Canada; in the past decade, no fewer than eleven presidents came to their most recent institution from the presidency of a smaller Canadian university.

None of these orientations encourage a new president to take an institution in dramatically different directions. Central to a university's success is its academic reputation, which is almost always defined in terms of tough entrance requirements; generous endowments, scholarships, research grants, and awards; and the number and quality of graduate programs it offers. Research trumps teaching effectiveness when it comes to academic reputation; it is easier to measure and is at the core of faculty culture. This is why our universities are so much alike in their structures and aspirations.

There is far less reward for being different or innovative. One might expect the market to encourage institutions to define themselves uniquely to cater to particular clientele, both in teaching and research, but such an impulse is usually overridden by conservative academic values. We have seen some innovation, but institutions confront tremendous social pressures to conform to the fairly narrowly defined notion of what a university is. In the end, then, institutional prestige still counts most when it comes to an individual's choice of university.

THE ONTARIO CHALLENGE

Ontario offers an interesting case study for a number of reasons. It has the most universities in the most competitive market for student places, and there is a greater differentiation between its university and college systems than is the case in most other provinces. The last decade has seen enrolment expansion that tracks well ahead of expectations, primarily because of annual increases in the cohort participation rate well beyond projections.[1]

Recent decades have been characterized by what Jones and Skolnik term "academic drift," a tendency for all the universities to gravitate towards a common research-intensive model, the most expensive form of undergraduate education.[2] This is to emulate the predominant established research institutions (Toronto, Queen's, McMaster, Western Ontario, and Ottawa), which compete with the best international universities.

York and Carleton are comprehensive universities in the major centres of Toronto and Ottawa respectively, offering a broad range of programs and courses to serve those communities. The "regional" universities (Lakehead in Thunder Bay, Laurentian/Laurentienne in Sudbury, Brock in St Catharines, the University of Windsor) have grown rapidly over the past decade, introducing new graduate programs and greatly strengthening their research support and productivity. These institutions either have or aspire to "comprehensive" status.[3] Several former primarily undergraduate institutions (including Trent and Laurier) have also sought comprehensiveness, passing up opportunities to be best known as top undergraduate teaching institutions (like Amherst, Swarthmore, or Dartmouth in the United States) in favour of expanding enrolments, graduate studies, and research.

A few universities have developed stronger individual identities as a result of their history and past leadership. Waterloo stuck to its knitting in the earlier days of its commitment to cooperative education and high technology and has been phenomenally successful in forging a strong international reputation in those areas. Guelph evolved from being primarily an agricultural institute to being a notable research university in all areas of agriculture and biotechnology, at the same time developing a reputation for innovative teaching and student support.

Even the newest Ontario universities have not been immune to these pressures for conformity, although Nipissing, until very recently the smallest,[4] retains a dedication to teaching and undergraduate education. Ryerson Polytechnic Institute became Ryerson University in 1993 and quickly developed like any other downtown university, albeit with more applied programs than, say, York. The newest entry, the University of Ontario Institute of Technology (UOIT), was deliberately created to be different from the others, focusing on job preparation and applied research. However, its more radical edges have been softened by the socio-political pressures for academic prestige, and it appears to be growing much more like the other institutions than would have been originally envisioned by its proponents.

The very Canadian practice of relatively egalitarian government funding schemes sometimes frustrated the aspirations of the top institutions, as everyone shares in the increased resources, regardless of performance. However, the climate may be changing. For example, Clark et al. have noted that the great majority of Canada Research Chairs have been awarded to the country's largest universities. In Ontario, the six largest universities accounted for 80 per cent of the chairs allocated to the eighteen Ontario universities by the end of 2008.[5] More recently, the Canada Excellence Research Chairs Program, designed to attract top international scientists to the country, distributed $200 million for only nineteen positions in thirteen Canadian universities on the basis of a cutthroat competition.[6] These examples augur well for a more competitive era in which institutional quality and market forces would encourage universities to work harder to differentiate themselves from their sister institutions.

Nine of the eleven presidents interviewed for this book have served or are serving in Ontario, and the issue of institutional differentiation was a hot topic for each. The great majority favoured an evolution to a more differentiated system, and while each had ideas as to how this could be brought about, none had any illusions about how difficult that would be.

As former president of HEQCO, Jim Downey has a particular interest in the subject, although he is not persuaded that the Ontario system is as homogeneous as some depict it: "It may look on the surface from their mission statements that universities are all alike, but they are often quite different in the constituencies they serve, the programs they offer, and the response they make to their communities. The same is true of the college system, where there is probably even more distinction among the institutions." Still, he does believe there needs to be more diversification, not for its own sake, but to give undergraduate students more choice, especially as enrolment pressures increase over the next few years. The previously mentioned HEQCO-commissioned book, *Academic Transformation* by Ian Clark et al.,[7] argues that the standard model of undergraduate education in Canada is no longer sustainable. The authors propose a number of alternatives that seem likely to provoke debate in Ontario and in Canada as a whole, one that Jim Downey believes is overdue. Clark et al. pay particular attention to another HEQCO-commissioned work, a paper by Glen Jones and Michael Skolnik of the Ontario Institute for Studies in Education (OISE) that considers how to broaden student access by increasing institutional differentiation in Ontario.[8] The authors identify three primary gaps in the province's post-secondary sector and suggest the need for

a) free-standing, degree-granting, primarily teaching-oriented institutions that concentrate on undergraduate education;
b) an open university; and
c) effective pathways for students to move from a college to a university and even to graduate study.[9]

In response to projections for an additional 25,000 students for Ontario over the next few years, Jones and Skolnik consider a variety of options, outlining the pros and cons of each.[10] These writings are almost certain to be front and centre in the ongoing debates about the need for reform in post-secondary education in the province.

Not surprisingly, institutional leaders advocating a more differentiated system are talking about how institutions other than their own need to change, and their actions as president are remarkably similar regardless of institutional type. I was no exception. As one directly implicated in strategic planning for two regional universities, I was very much a part of efforts to enhance their reputation and status through improved and extended graduate programming, enhanced research in areas of potential and strength, and a stronger community focus. I saw these as critical components of the university's strategy for several reasons: they would encourage on-campus and regional pride; they would enhance the profile and reputation of the institution; and they would ensure that the research and scholarly activities would suit the needs and concerns of the institution's primary communities.

INSTITUTIONAL TIERING

Rob Prichard suggested that a number of Ontario universities could have forged quite different profiles to their own benefit and to the benefit of the province as a whole. For example, he could envision a Ryerson evolving into Canada's first internationally prominent polytechnic, with programs operating all around the province in collaboration with several regional universities.[11] He would have liked a Trent, a Laurier, or a Brock to focus primarily on undergraduate education and the quality of teaching and learning, developing the sort of reputation enjoyed by the best American small liberal arts colleges. He wonders why the Lakeheads, Laurentians, and Windsors have emphasized research and graduate expansion, believing that they could be leaders in teaching and learning were they to capitalize on their smaller size to place the undergraduate more in the forefront.

Peter George is also a strong advocate of more diversity, regretting that recommendations to that effect in the 1984 Bovey Commission report were never implemented.[12] He favours more tiering and, like Prichard, felt that opportunities were missed when the new universities were allowed to pursue graduate study rather than build themselves exclusively into four-year undergraduate universities. For both Leggett and George, the response to today's homogeneity is to facilitate a dramatic restructuring of the Ontario system so that a large percentage of undergraduate students in the province will be taught on a cheaper model in order to make possible a greater investment in the more expensive model necessary for effective graduate education.

Although none of the presidents was saying that the faculty at a dedicated undergraduate university shouldn't also do research, many expressed concern about the implications of the kind of tiering envisioned by Prichard and George. Perhaps influenced by her American experience, Carleton president Roseann Runte believes that competition and cooperation are the lynchpins of academic excellence:

If differentiation means stratification, then I am totally opposed to it. If differentiation means that one institution is, by character, more of a technological institution and another is a social science institution, that's fine. That's great differentiation – it's differentiation by field, it's differentiation by vocation, but not differentiation by quality or by level of research. I believe that a Nobel Prize could be won by a professor at Carleton or a patent that makes millions of dollars could be developed here.

She worries that labelling an institution as "tier two" is the kiss of death, making it very hard to recruit and keep the best faculty. She doesn't see how it would save money if the tier-two institution had to compensate its faculty better in order to compete. She also favours more collaboration among post-secondary institutions, but she points out that this is far less likely to happen in an overtly tiered system where the "better" institution has little incentive to share with the "lesser" one.

Uniquely placed to respond to the comments about Ryerson and Trent by Prichard and George (cited above), Bonnie Patterson was a dean at the first and a president of the second. She defended Ryerson's development track: "To be a world-class polytechnic, you still need high-quality master's and doctoral programs and you still have a hugely strong research agenda but focused to the strength of the polytechnical side with niche programs like journalism and television arts. I think in some ways that that's exactly what Ryerson has been doing."

Patterson noted the challenges inherent in trying to attract the best faculty to institutions whose mandates differ from the traditional, and she emphasized how critical strong funding was to competing successfully. She believes that a lot more time is needed before one can fairly assess the progress of these relatively young institutions, perhaps even fifty years. Like Roseann Runte, she stressed the importance of research to teaching and said that this is the best argument against tiering institutions: "If one accepts that the best teaching is informed by some level of research, then a lot of the angst around differentiation goes away. If, on the other hand, one follows a Carnegie system of ranking and defines a university as a 'research' institution or a 'teaching' institution, we are not going to get there as a system, whether formally or informally."

When Dave Marshall assumed the presidency of Mount Royal College, he encountered a prevailing notion that a dedicated teaching university is a cheaper alternative. He is proud that he and others were able to persuade the minister and the Campus Alberta Quality Council of the value of investing in a new kind of undergraduate university, one where research and scholarship were still central but with teaching, learning, and the student experience as the primary focus. Their vision led to an effectively diversified environment defined by six categories of post-secondary institution, two of which are at the university level – the comprehensive research university and the baccalaureate institution (Mount Royal and Grant MacEwan), with the latter differentiated in a positive way.

This development was given impetus by the results of a cost analysis that showed that the larger universities skimmed resources from undergraduate programs to subsidize graduate study. The ministry accepted that the new university should get a similar per-undergraduate-student grant as the established institutions, with the result that Mount Royal may invest more per capita at the undergraduate level than do the province's comprehensive universities.

It was the performance of Nipissing on the National Survey of Student Engagement (NSSE) that truly validated Marshall's commitment to the concept of an undergraduate university. He is confident that Mount Royal will develop into a first-class learning institution, ultimately standing up in status terms to the top research-intensive universities, if in a different way.[13] He stressed the importance of hiring faculty who are attracted by the undergraduate mandate and are not simply competing in the same pool as the others.

Notwithstanding that there are many small universities in Canada (Marshall noted that, in over half of the AUCC member institutions, less than 5 per cent of the students are in graduate programs), very few have aspired, like Mount Allison and Bishop's, to be known as first-rate undergraduate institutions. This is a very different matter from simply being, by virtue of size and geography, a university with mainly undergraduate enrolments.

If diversification means that Canada would be in a stronger position to compete internationally, having research-intensive universities at one end of the spectrum and student-oriented teaching institutions at the other, there is a large group in between that might have a more difficult time competing in a tougher fiscal environment. These are the regional and comprehensive universities that are spread fairly thinly across teaching and research programs. They would have difficulty narrowing their focus, particularly since their primary communities have grown accustomed to their accessibility and expect the range of programming and research they have developed.

In my own Ontario presidencies, I worked to focus the institutions more on their areas of strength (mining and environmental studies at Laurentian; the auto industry, the environment, and social justice at Windsor). Especially in the latter case, budget decisions were driven by the identification of such institutional pinnacles to strengthen significantly research and scholarship in these priority areas. For Marshall, however, this sort of differentiation would be insufficient: "I have said for a long time that the comprehensive university is a dead duck. Standing from the outside, they are the ones that need to make some strategic decisions about what they are going to be good at. I recognize the value of initiatives like your pinnacles at Windsor, but that is not institutional differentiation other than being good at a few program areas."

As an observer of Ontario from the outside, with experience in Quebec, Alberta, and British Columbia, Myer Horowitz has interesting perspectives on the issue. He recognizes the tension between institutional autonomy and system diversity but sees it as a kind of dynamic and even creative tension. He sees considerable differences across institutions within what he calls "a zone of acceptability." While Horowitz appreciates the value of a university that focuses on undergraduate teaching, he agrees with Dave Marshall that this model only works well if its faculty are also actively involved in research and scholarship. He cited his early experiences at Sir George Williams College (which later joined Loyola to form Concordia University), where faculty were not expected to do research but many did, in fact, through collaboration with McGill.

For Rob Prichard, a powerful instrument for differentiation is deregulated tuition supported by guarantees of financial aid. While there was a short-lived effort at some deregulation during the Harris era in Ontario, notably in a few professional areas such as medicine and law (where tuition soared as a result), tuition fees in Ontario and most other provinces are fairly strictly regulated. Prichard depicted such regulation as an anti-differentiation force of real power. However compelling the arguments for deregulation, the politics have contradicted them, and there has been little change in recent years despite ongoing interest in the topic.

THE NEED FOR GOVERNMENT LEADERSHIP

George and Prichard readily understand why the institutions have evolved as they have and why no president could go into a given community with a radical recipe for change without the strong support of the provincial government. Prichard put it as follows:

> I think it's incredibly hard for the presidents of any individual universities to chart a new course to this area because the paradigm is pretty fixed. I think it is incumbent upon the government to act because, if you understand the political economy of each university and the pressures on each president, it is simply the reality of the political context in which they work that only the people who control the chequebook can really change the system.
>
> The rhetoric here, every once in a while, talks about the need for more tiering, but I don't sense any government willingness to act on it ... we have a system where the squeaky wheel, often small institutions with unrealistic ambitions, gets oiled.

Prichard cited the contentious case of the attempt to merge OISE with the University of Toronto. The process took almost three decades, but in 1996 the merger was finally achieved. In his view, it would not have been achieved without the unambiguous message from the Rae government that the status quo was unacceptable. Prichard believes that the same sort of leadership is required to deal with the present challenges.

Prichard and George envision giving institutions financial incentives to limit their graduate work to highly selected areas and to reward them for re-intensifying their undergraduate experience, a position supported by Jones and Skolnik.[14] George mused about a "University of Ontario" with a chancellor and board that could determine the roles and mandates of various institutions but concedes that it is much easier to build something from scratch than to change the missions of well-established institutions. Any of the options for government are politically complex, and neither he nor Prichard senses any real appetite for major change in the system.

Paul Davenport, too, believes that the lead has to come from government, which could use the "enormous power of the public purse to differentiate the system." To this end, he advocated three specific actions:

1 The government needs to allocate funded graduate spaces to each university on the basis of such performance criteria as its research record and scholarships won by former students.

2 The minister should duplicate this at the undergraduate level,
   allocating funded spaces to assure smaller universities of a student population that keeps them financially stable.
3 Differentiation grants should offer additional funding to institutions that could demonstrate how they would use the money to
   develop into an outstanding undergraduate university.

At the time of the interviews, Ontario had just followed through
on the first action, allocating funding disproportionately to a
few universities on the basis of specific performance criteria. The
response of the less successful institutions was predictably negative,
but Davenport strongly supported the minister's decisions (while
conceding that his own university did well by the process). It showed
that the minister could take strong action when there was the will to
do it. Davenport hoped that the minister would be able to stand up
to the inevitable political responses and continue to allocate graduate spots on the basis of the strength of research and graduate programs at the various universities. Davenport, like Marshall, sees the
value of developing dedicated undergraduate universities: "I think it
is possible through the allocation of undergraduate spaces to work
with some of the universities to say that they should have basically
an undergraduate mandate – your professors should do research but
we want them focused on their students."
Another form of diversity is the sort of program that is delivered
on the various campuses within a system. Marshall advocates more
vertical integration, the creation of specialized institutions more like
the Dublin Institute of Technology.

We need to break the strict college/university grouping and recognize a spectrum of institutions. I think every province should
have what Alberta is developing. Ontario is speaking of the need
for greater undergraduate access in the GTA, so what about a
new market university, teaching focused, undergraduate only,
well funded? That would be my answer. On the east coast, and
in British Columbia, they already have this sort of development.
Ontario is the only one that really needs to consciously get out of
the closet.

For Waterloo's David Johnston, achieving greater diversity, which
he strongly favours, is a leadership issue:

We should try to have a more diversified system because I think "a hundred flowers bloom" is a better way of providing both equality of opportunity and excellence in public education. It comes down to leadership – from the premier, the minister of education, and from university presidents. I think Waterloo has been a good marker in that, at the age of fifty-one, it has been more unusual than most institutions. One of my greatest concerns in my first year here was that we not become too conventional and my greatest concern in leaving is that [Waterloo] not revert to being a conventional place.

Bill Leggett believes that Canada's relative lack of institutional diversity can be explained to a large degree by there being too many institutional leaders who simply want to emulate the University of Toronto when they should be taking stands that better define the uniqueness of their own institution: "My view on differentiation is that it shouldn't be imposed from the top; it should be decided at the local site. Each institution should decide on what it wants to be good at and focus intensively on achieving that. For example, I think Queen's has the sense now that it cannot be what it is if it gets too big."

In general, most of the presidents interviewed did not seem particularly concerned about government intervention threatening institutional autonomy. On the contrary, they saw intervention as the lynchpin to greater university differentiation in Canada.

The issue of a more diverse and better coordinated post-secondary education system is an important one in most provinces today. Canada has neither the wide-open market approach that so characterizes the United States nor the strong central government interventionist history of the United Kingdom, Australia, and New Zealand. To date, there has been more talk than action, notwithstanding the relative opening up of the system in Alberta and British Columbia. For the moment at least, Ontario remains the focal point for change. There appears to be support among some presidents for stronger government leadership on this issue, although one can imagine a very different tune coming from a president whose institution is being told to change in ways that he or she believes are inconsistent with its established mission and mandate. Perhaps the better chance for significant change is to create several new institutions in response to the enrolment pressures in the GTA – undergraduate universities as defined by Marshall, a polytechnic university like the one Ryerson might have been, and an open learning initiative.

PRIVATE UNIVERSITIES

As noted earlier, Canada has very few established private universities and none with the prestige of America's finest. There are several that compete for students on the basis of their innovative delivery systems or accelerated programs, but they struggle to attract sufficient student numbers to build the sort of prestige and reputation that is essential to their long-term success. It is a bit of a "catch-22" situation for these fledgling institutions. Until they build a sufficient enrolment base, they are hard pressed to hire the quality and number of faculty members who would help build their reputation, and yet, without the reputation, they have difficulty attracting the student numbers they would require to pay for them.

The prestigious private universities in the United States have long histories and have built strong alumni bases that feed their huge endowments. The only way that such an institution could be established in Canada, short of a miraculous multi-million-dollar investment, would be to convert an established Canadian public university to private status. At first glance, a good candidate would be a highly regarded university like Queen's in Kingston. It has the academic profile, strong alumni base, and relatively compact and personal campus atmosphere essential to success as a private institution. However, after removing provincial operating grants from the equation (these make up almost half of the institution's operating revenues), one does not have to be a sophisticated financial analysis to see that the cost of such a transition would be prohibitive. Tuition fees would have to be at levels that almost certainly would not sustain the requisite enrolments, at least without a multiple expansion of Queen's current endowments, which were reported at $624 million for 2008.[15]

Given the close proximity of most Canadians to the American border and the broad array of highly regarded American private universities, it is likely that those with the wherewithal to afford high tuition fees or the academic standing to cover them with scholarships will continue the present practice of going to the best American or other international institutions.

In short, while Canada would benefit from a greater array of innovative and niche-based private universities, there are few signs of significant change on the horizon and it can be safely assumed that the country will continue to be dominated by its public system for many years to come.

THE COLLEGES

We have already seen how community colleges in Alberta and British Columbia have been turned into various types of degree-granting institutions. The challenge is greater in Ontario where the traditional colleges of applied arts and technology (CAATs) were set up in 1966 to be different from, rather than feeder institutions to, the universities. Unlike the CEGEPs in Quebec and the colleges of Alberta and British Columbia, the CAATs did not offer the first years of university on their campuses and their faculty were significantly different in their orientations and training from university professors.

Given that at two or more Ontario universities less than 50 per cent of the classes are taught by full-time faculty,[16] it is increasingly difficult for presidents to argue against awarding further degree-granting status to colleges. Moreover, faculty members at the latter may be at least as involved in scholarship in their fields as the sessional instructors or teaching assistants are at universities. Nevertheless, Canadian universities retain a significant status advantage for many students and their parents.

Jim Downey recognizes the social challenges that the colleges have in the Canadian context:

There is, of course, a certain hierarchy of value and opinion about credentials. I don't know how you escape that because it's inherent in our society, often recognized by pay rates that people get for the work they do. There's no doubt it's something our community colleges struggle with because they believe that there is as much inherent value in being a plumber as there is in being a philosopher (and they're right). Why should society value one so highly and the other not so much, even though, these days, the plumber is likely to be making a lot more money than the philosopher?

Downey points to the cachet associated with the word *university*, citing, for example, the Guelph-Humber collaboration that likely would not have been successful without that name. Even in Florida, where there has been a concerted push for community college degree offerings, a 2007 study showed that only 1 per cent of 300,000 undergraduate students were pursuing their degree in a college environment.[17] Nevertheless, the Ontario system may be poised for a significant breakthrough in its development of a more integrated system in which colleges play a larger role in degree granting. The case has been building for some time, starting with the growing collaboration among colleges and universities that was symbolized in the Port Hope Accord in 1999.[18] I was part of the original group that developed this agreement, which anticipated most of the recent developments in college-university collaboration, including a stronger provincial government role in developing the system, at least one university-college conglomerate under a single governing board (Guelph-Humber), the development of more applied degrees in the colleges, and a proliferation of more generous transfer arrangements from college to university and vice versa.[19]

OPEN AND DISTANCE LEARNING

Open and distance learning (ODL) is one piece of the solution to the challenges now facing Ontario, as it can capitalize on the nearly universal availability of interactive communications technologies to respond to the diverse needs of today's learners. ODL readily lends itself to the virtual culture subscribed to by so many students and has greatly extended educational accessibility around the world. The demand for knowledge and expertise in distance education is insatiable, as attested to by the success of the Vancouver-based Commonwealth of Learning, which provides expert advice and free online materials to universities, colleges, and schools in all fifty-four countries of the Commonwealth. Enrolments worldwide are already in the tens of millions and growing exponentially.[20] While a strong case can be made for a much greater investment in open and distance learning in Canada, certain factors have restricted the extent to which ODL has been embraced by established universities. While the early Athabasca University and its international counterparts attracted adult learners back to formal studies and firmly established the credibility of open admissions, the rapid growth of ODL in Canada has been spurred primarily by the practice of campus-based students taking distance courses for convenience or to enhance their course selection. Many believe that the time has come for a more concerted and systematic approach.

Some, such as Clark et al., advocate creating a brand new institution, an open university for Ontario.[21] While this could be an exciting project, the economies of scale suggest that Canada would be better off capitalizing on its existing institutions. Independent of any bias I might have in favour of Athabasca University,[22] it seems to me that it would make more sense from a national perspective for Athabasca, in collaboration with the Téléq in Quebec for French-language instruction, to be acknowledged formally as Canada's open university, a claim it already makes. Athabasca collaborates with most of Ontario's colleges and serves many of its university students. Expanding this kind of collaboration has also been suggested by Jones and Skolnik.[23]

Unfortunately, it is highly unlikely that an Alberta- or Quebec-based (and -funded) institution would be thus designated in a country where authority for education is so jealously guarded by each province. Nevertheless, the Ontario government has identified distance education as an important component of its response to burgeoning enrolment pressures, and it has an opportunity to forge partnerships with its sister governments to their mutual benefit. The province would be better off to consider how partnerships like these could work with an expanded version of its own extensive Contact North/Contact Nord network instead of trying to establish an expensive new institution in the province.[24]

In fact, Ontario's most recent response takes heed of the latter concern but, predictably, on a "made in Ontario" basis. The 2010 throne speech announced the province's plans to establish an online institute "to bring the best professors from Ontario's postsecondary institutions into the homes of those who want to pursue higher learning."[25] Details were sketchy, leading the Council of Ontario Universities (COU) to produce its own position paper in August envisioning the development of a collaborative body to encourage, support, and coordinate e-learning initiatives among its member institutions.[26] Significantly, COU's approach is to have the initial process unfold separately for the university and college sectors. The latter group was still preparing its response at the time of writing, but a joint response from Ontario student, faculty, and staff associations also expressed concern about the creation of a new entity, preferring better funding of Contact North/elearnnetwork.ca, targeted investment in institutional e-learning infrastructure, greater broadband access to underserviced areas, and more student financial support.[27] They might also have mentioned more generous and more transparent credit transfer arrangements.

Given sufficient sustained funding, an online learning initiative could lead to a much more inclusive and collaborative post-secondary system in Ontario. Conversely, it could serve mainly to protect institutional autonomy and the status quo or, even worse, be a costly white elephant. In his seminal report on the future of higher education in Ontario in 2003, Bob Rae considered such an option and rejected it:

> While I have received some suggestions for a bold, new, Ontario-based institution that would be dedicated to distance and online education, I am not making such a proposal. It would be expensive and duplicative of what is already starting. The better way is to encourage competition in this area, insist on best practices, and find practical ways to fund innovation and collaboration.[28]

The Government of Ontario would do well to pay heed to his advice. Ultimately, as Skolnik has pointed out, the crucial variable is the extent to which faculty members oppose or embrace new technologies.[29] It will be fascinating to track the progress of the online institute concept over the next few years.

MORE RADICAL ALTERNATIVES

It can certainly be imagined that the exponential changes in communications technologies and their dramatic impact on the cultures of our youth are going to force universities to change much more dramatically than is suggested by the above analysis. In this scenario, giant private conglomerates will beat universities at their own game, offering high-quality online courses and support and catering to the learning needs of not only the traditional university age cohort but also adults throughout their working lives and even into retirement. Notwithstanding that it clashes with traditional academic cultures, this approach has been given added impetus by its compatibility with the learning and living styles that characterize today's young people. Duderstadt et al. suggest that we may be on the cusp of significant changes:

The university has survived other periods of technology-driven social change with its basic structure and activities intact, but the changes driven by evolving information technology are different, since they affect the very nature of the fundamental activities of the university: creating, preserving, integrating, transmitting, and applying knowledge. More fundamentally, because information technology changes the relationship between people and knowledge, it is likely to reshape in profound ways knowledge-based institutions such as the university.[30]

Without denying the possibility of such a tsunami, one that epitomizes Bergquist and Pawlak's virtual culture, I would never underestimate the power and strength of the traditional university culture that has sustained the institution for more than a thousand years.[31] The tension between these forces may yield interesting and even spectacular changes, but the more likely probability is a more diverse system that retains much of our traditional academic culture.

CONCLUSION

The growing demand for university places, the dramatic changes in communications technologies, and the different approaches to learning of the new generations of students will combine to put enormous pressure on Canada's post-secondary institutions to change – and to change dramatically. At the same time, Canada's well-established, traditional academic values, the natural resistance to change in the academy, and even our national character will conspire to moderate and temper the pace and degree of that change. It is not just a question of persuading institutional leaders to be more innovative, but also a public education challenge to convince students and their parents of the value of institutions that do not resemble traditional universities.

There is clear need for reform, notably in Ontario. The real pressure for change will probably come from the fiscal side as the constant increases in class size finally undermine the whole system and make necessary the kind of change that Clark et al. are advocating. It will not come easily, however, and provincial government leaders will have to demonstrate courage, fortitude, and creativity if they are to prevail. They cannot afford to underestimate the strength of the prevailing academic culture or the pride that individual communities have in their local university.

The most likely and, I would argue, desirable scenario is a more differentiated system, with institutions individually identified by one or two of the six cultures of the academy presented by Bergquist and Pawlak. The collegial culture will continue to thrive in the country's smaller, primarily undergraduate universities, with some of them building a national reputation for teaching excellence. The most selective and research-intensive universities will continue to manifest the tangible culture, building on strengths in graduate studies and research to raise their profiles on a world scale. Some of the more innovative and newer institutions and perhaps a private university or two will represent the virtual culture in offering online learning and support services geared to the convenience of students in a more corporate, consumerist approach to teaching and learning.

Almost all of the institutions, and especially the comprehensive and regional universities, will continue to struggle with the complexities and contradictions of these cultural mixes. The collegial and tangible cultures will run up against the virtual and managerial, the latter being strengthened in times of fiscal constraint. Financial problems will also exacerbate conflicts between the managerial and the advocacy sides, putting great pressure on presidents to find ways to implement cutbacks and layoffs while retaining labour relations that are not disruptive to the academic mission of the institution. Change will be accelerated by financial pressures if the whole system shows signs of collapsing, for the country will not be able to subsidize public education to the extent that it has and politicians will wrestle with the limits on tuition fee levels.

The time is ripe for significant diversification. While there will continue to be strong resistance to change in universities that have spent the past couple of decades building their research and graduate study profiles, there is still much room for innovation, especially where it is supported by financial incentives from the government. It will take determined leadership from government, university, and college leaders over the next few years if Canada, through each of its provinces, is to develop a system that both meets the growing demand for student places in degree-granting institutions and reverses the current trend towards a lower-quality experience for too many students on university campuses.

Whatever the degree and pace of change, one thing is clear. University presidents will have to play a much stronger role in guiding their institutions through the maze of tradition and change, the subject of the two concluding chapters.

PART FOUR
The Way Forward

13

How Much Difference Does a President Make?
The Case for Open Management

As I stated at the outset of this book and have emphasized throughout, the role of university president in Canada is both more important and more difficult than ever. While university presidents might not make as much difference as they often think they do, they are in a position to play a pivotal role at a time when Canada needs both to reaffirm the importance of its universities and to reform them.

Writing in the American context, where the president usually has more ascribed authority than his or her counterpart in Canada, Cohen and March do not paint a very encouraging picture about a president's ability to lead an institution they depict as an organized anarchy: "The president is resented because he is more powerful than he should be. He is scorned and frustrated because he is weaker than he is believed capable of being. If he acts as a 'strong' president, he exposes his weakness. If he acts as a 'democratic' president, people consider him timid. For the most part, his behavior has only modest impact on beliefs about presidential legitimacy or power."[1]

There is much about Cohen and March's work that is compelling, and any experienced president will recognize the institutional political environment and appreciate the sardonic presentation of its complexities and frustrations for would-be leaders. Their claim that the university "doesn't know what it is doing"[2] is glib in the extreme but not always easily refuted. It is not so much that institutional leaders don't know where the organization is heading, but more that universities typically play so many parts at the same time that, like Stephen Leacock's horseman, they may be seen to be riding "madly off in all directions."[3]

Echoing Cohen and March, Peter George pointed out how it is difficult to get an objective assessment of a president's impact because the metrics are primarily subjective. The words of Harold Shapiro, quoted in the preface to this volume, speak to the juggling act that must be played by today's university president. The job is so large, complex, and wide reaching that even the most energetic office-holder cannot do justice to all of its components at the same time. Consequently, the incumbent must decide which objectives are most important and then delegate responsibility and authority for their realization, reserving only the parts that are most appropriately done by the president and/or that suit his or her particular talents and interests.

This underlines the importance of institutional fit. The successful presidents interviewed for this book were appointed to the right position in the right university at the right time. There are other presidents, equally capable and equally well qualified, who have been less successful in a given institution because the fit was not as tight or timely.

This puts a high premium on the presidential selection process. Given the importance of understanding the local culture, I would hope that more institutions would give their best vice-presidents or deans the opportunity to perform the role of president. The four internal appointees among the presidents interviewed (Peter George, Myer Horowitz, Dave Marshall at Nipissing, Rob Prichard) are proof positive that it can work well.

The question of how much difference a university president can actually make to an institution is bound up in the unique aspects of the academic culture and in the ways that the culture can limit the incumbent's power. The position is often contrasted with the role of chief executive officer of a private corporation or even that of college president, which has traditionally had more direct decision-making authority.

There is some disagreement among the presidents interviewed about the impact of a given president. Martha Piper's immediate response to the question was "not much." She believes that leaders in general can make a significant difference but that it is much harder in universities, given their long history and resilience. For Bill Leggett, leadership in any successful institution is a team sport. He is also realistic about the ephemeral quality of many achievements:

I watched several people whom I admire do wonderful things at their institution, only to have them reversed or de-emphasized by their successor. Each new leader must change something, if only to put her or his mark on the institution. This is a reality you have to accept. The most lasting thing a president can do is set a clear standard of excellence and drive hard to achieve it. Strategic directions are likely to be more fleeting.

A number of respondents decried the tendency of institutions to overreact to the weaknesses of the incumbent in searching for successors. Rob Prichard observed that, too frequently, a search committee initially seeking a clone of a successful incumbent increasingly focuses on the incumbent's imperfections and ends up selecting a candidate who is the diametric opposite.

Roseann Runte sees value in the rhythm of change that results from a new appointment. Sometimes an institution needs a bold change agent, while at other times it can best benefit from someone who focuses more on the human side of the equation. "When a new person comes in, they will always move the furniture a bit, and there is also a tendency to pick almost the opposite of the previous president. If the previous incumbent moves things ahead quickly, the next person will be a stay-in-place president, which gives the change time to sink in. You push and then you run in place."

As in politics, timing is crucial. Runte describes a time at Ste-Anne when there were bitter faculty complaints about the lack of space. It seemed to her that there was enough space but that it was poorly organized. So, she consulted a space expert who drew up a plan that she thought was superb. She triumphantly presented it at the next senate meeting and was taken aback when a number of faculty members came out "with guns a-blazing" and shot the plan down. Consequently, she shelved it, thinking she had made a mistake. Three months later, someone asked at senate what had happened to the plan. She brought it back to the next meeting; it was adopted and made a tangible difference on campus. She learned her lesson: "You have to wait sometimes until people are ready for change – you have to slow down and back up a bit. It's not just the change but the readiness of people for that change. Timing is everything and you have to pay attention to that."

Dave Marshall disputes the notion that university presidents lack real power. He concedes that they may not always have the ability to make instant decisions without consultation, but even there he sees it as a matter of effective leadership:

We have huge power to change lives, change people, change institutions. People in an organization need to feel that someone's in charge whom they trust, whose principles and values are the right ones for the institution. It's a tremendous sense of comfort and allows them to get about their business without worrying about mine. No president can single-handedly change an institution, but the president can create an environment where the institution will comfortably change.

In his usual effusive way, Rob Prichard agreed: "I think the president makes a profound difference and the job continues to attract excellent people who work incredibly hard at relatively modest wages, give every ounce of themselves in hard jobs; I salute them."

Jim Downey also believes that presidents can make quite a difference, although probably not as much as many American texts suggest. He sees the issue especially in terms of setting a tone for an institution, of identifying its capabilities and helping it achieve its potential. This is what builds morale and helps an institution reach higher. He cited the impact on their respective institutions of the presidencies of Rob Prichard at Toronto, Paul Davenport at Western, and David Johnston at both McGill and Waterloo:

I think a president who can mobilize the resources of the institution and get people working together can make an enormous difference. Nobody has as many levers to affect the course of a university's development as the president. The art and science of leadership is knowing when and how to use them. The other part is maintaining the confidence of three groups whose support matters most: the faculty, the board, and the management team. To lose any one of those is to run the risk of a failed presidency. To lose any two is to ensure failure.

With experience in both large and smaller universities, Roseann Runte noted that the way presidents make a difference varies by institution. In fact, one of her mentors, recognizing that her strength was in interpersonal relations, tried to discourage her from going to Old Dominion University on the grounds that beyond a certain size, say 12,000 students, one personality could not change an institution. She disagreed and took the job:

How you achieve change differs with institutional size. In a small institution, you can almost talk to everybody every day. In a big institution, there are people in other buildings who aren't going to see you for three months, so you have to find the ways to tell them what it is that you are trying to do and persuade them to be part of the plan. It is an interesting challenge. Because you don't see them every day and speak to them every day, they are going to get second-hand information, so it really is important to be sure what it is that you want everybody to share and to be active in communicating this message.

Others were more circumspect. While he believes the presidency is an important position, Myer Horowitz thinks the more important consideration is that the individual in the job recognize its limitations. Because decision making is shared, which he considers a very positive attribute in universities, the most important contribution that a president can make is to foster an institutional climate that makes it possible for talented people to do what they do best: "You make your major contribution by making it possible for other people to do their thing. The climate of the place is important. We don't have the power – the authority – to reverse things dramatically. If I'm honest with myself, on some things it would have been nice to have control, but when you reflect on it, it's a good thing that decisions have to be shared."

Paul Davenport cited an email exchange he had with management guru Peter Drucker, the subject of which was the latter's opinion that the job of university president was the hardest leadership job in modern society given the responsibility to so many stakeholders in a place so decentralized. He had written back, agreeing that this was generally true but that Drucker was underestimating the power of voice that a university president had.

The one thing the president has, and it does seem in contradiction of the normal view of who we are, is that we have our voice … and people listen to it. I didn't realize until I was president that people would take down what I said and spout it back to me. I then realized that if I could have a simple and clear message and repeat it over and over again, I would have a real effect on how people behaved. It became my mantra at Western – "the best student experience at a leading research-intensive university in Canada."

Bonnie Patterson would like to think that a president's influence is considerable but is ultimately measured by the strength of the academic and administrative leadership team rather than by the individual who is the president: "I don't know how to measure how much difference a president makes, but without the leadership and vision and the will to get implementation, I think you would have either a petrified campus where nothing would change or you would have a floundering one, all over the place."

Does a strong president have a greater impact on an institution than a weak one? As much as the achievements of a successful president may be undermined or changed by a successor, so, too, can a university survive or at least outlast an unsuccessful leader. Noting some specific recent cases where an institution has withstood a weak presidency and bounced back under a successor, Dave Marshall pointed to the resilience of universities: "I do believe that every institution can endure for a short period of time even a total absence of leadership. The fact is that I could be gone for six months and this place would tick along just tickety-boo. I think it could go on for five years without much damage to the enduring components of the institution."

Jim Downey and Peter George are less convinced. While giving a seminar on presidential search processes at UPEI recently, Downey was asked about the recent high incidence of failed presidencies where incumbents left their posts well before the end of their first term: "I responded that it was not necessarily a failure for the institution to actually act [to remove] a weak president. It may be a greater failure to let a weak presidency go through a full term rather than deal with it as soon as it is evident that there is a problem."

Peter George took it one step further:

I think a bad president hurts more than a good president helps. Like most things, someone who is really bad at a job brings a lot of defence mechanisms into place. Our history has been that we will put up with someone to the end of their term rather than get rid of them early because we don't want the risk of embarrassment to the institution. The defences shore up a weak performer. It amazes me how many poor performers even get renewed.

In considering the impact of strong or weak presidents, Bonnie Patterson emphasized the strength of the academic culture in a university:

> Institutions outlive individuals. The academy is a really strong culture with a very clear mandate. My sense is that an institution will outlive weak administrators, for sure – how much collateral damage has to then be repaired is then the issue. On the other hand, if it's a good administrator, some of what is left won't be sustainable because the next person will come in and want to take it in a different direction or maybe it has run its course and it's time for change anyway. But I think, by and large, stronger leadership gives more sustaining capacity in the long term.

As already observed, assessing presidential performance in an institution with such diffuse goals is problematic. As with teaching, the true measure of someone's effectiveness might be better taken years after the completion of his or her term of office. Nevertheless, the term of office itself is one measure of success. For example, in a significant number of recent cases, an incumbent left the post before completing his or her term because, for one reason or another, the presidency was not working out. While the focus of this book is on successful leadership, important lessons can be learned from failed presidencies. Of the 114 most recent past presidents in the forty-seven universities in the presidential survey (see Appendix B), about a dozen left before the completion of their term of office (in all but one, it was during their first term) and a similar number were not renewed for a second term.[4]

While an external observer can never be sure about the reasons for a premature departure, almost all the cases cited involved at least one of two factors – a poor institutional fit and conflict with the board chair, the latter often emanating from the first. The impact of institutional culture was most evident in three cases where the incumbent had been a successful president at his or her first university but not the second. In many of the other instances of early departure, it was evident from early on that the individual's style did not fit well with the new institution and thus the truncated term was less surprising to knowledgeable observers. Similar factors played a role in many of the non-renewals or in cases where an individual decided not to seek a second term (the individual might have been disappointed with the post or fear that they might not be reappointed for reasons of performance).

All this is not to suggest that completion of one or even two terms is necessarily a measure of success. An incumbent can fit into the institutional culture without achieving very much, and perpetuating the status quo is probably an easier survival strategy than helping an institution to change.

THE PRESIDENTIAL EGO

Dave Marshall observed that it is amazing, for such a high profile position as the presidency, how important it is for the presidential ego to be submerged. An accomplished harmonica player in a blues band, he used a musical analogy: "It's like playing in a blues band – you need to play your instrument very well but your greatest pride is not how you play but how the combo as a whole does ... the band sound and the grooving. You get free licks but only eight bars, sixteen if you're lucky!"

I, too, have often thought of a university president as the lead player in a jazz combo. In the conversation with Marshall, I recounted my own reaction to an AUCC presentation by conductor Boris Brott, who likened university management to conducting an orchestra. While I found the talk stimulating, there was no way I could imagine the collection of independent entrepreneurs who make up any faculty following my lead and sticking as closely to the script as musicians do in following a conductor.

University leadership is frequently referred to as "herding cats" (in fact, I used the expression earlier), reflecting the independent-mindedness of faculty that is prerequisite for an unfettered search for truth. Perhaps it is not an accident that jazz players are also often called "cats." In the combo, success breeds success and the participants play off the strength of each other. A particularly good riff inspires others to do better as well. Similarly, a strong university researcher, teacher, or president can help boost colleagues to greater heights, leading by example but also by encouraging and thriving on the success of others.

In neither academia nor jazz do the breakthroughs come easily. They depend on hours of work or rehearsal, and the leader must demonstrate both confidence in the players and patience and persistence in the quest to constantly improve performance. This kind of leadership makes extra demands on the persons in charge, but the ultimate focus is on the performance, not the players, and the performance is best served by what Marshall described as emotional intelligence.

> Anyone who wanted to be a university president too badly either never made it or bombed out quickly. The common element in all great presidents is that they have a high level of emotional intelligence. They have the understanding of themselves, good feelings about themselves so they don't need to get the strokes – it goes back to Loevinger's work.[5] I can think of a few who didn't have this but they all disappeared very quickly.

There is support for Marshall's view in a study by Fullan and Scott, who surveyed 513 academic administrators on fifty-seven leadership attributes. They found that seven of the top ten characteristics of successful leaders concerned emotional intelligence (personal or interpersonal), two involved cognitive ability, and one involved competence in time management.[6]

While those who take on management positions may have a natural propensity to want to please others, they quickly discover that you cannot please everyone in an environment where freedom of expression and independent-mindedness are such critical values. Some people avoid administration because they are uncomfortable with having to make choices among competing options, while others may relish the power that comes with being the final arbiter. The most effective leaders retain an appropriate balance between listening carefully to all sides of an issue and having the courage and confidence to make decisions when they are clearly needed.

INNOVATION AND INSTITUTIONAL CULTURE

There is a remarkable consistency in the reflections of the above presidents. It is hardly surprising that people who have performed successfully in the role would believe that a president's success can make a significant difference to an institution's performance, but all of the presidents interviewed agree that the most effective leadership is achieved in much more circumspect ways than would be the case in most organizations.

Each university has its own particular culture, but it is one that is embedded in centuries of academic tradition that is, for good reason, notoriously resilient. While strong leadership is critical when tough choices must be made, the independence and autonomy of faculty must ultimately be reaffirmed in an institution whose basis for legitimacy is the search for truth.

One of the ironies of the university is that while it is an institution of ideas and forward thinking, it can also be a rigid bureaucracy strongly resistant to change. No one should underestimate the ability of faculty to carry on as they always have regardless of who is in the president's office. This issue concerns David Johnston, who sees ensuring an innovative and agile institution as central to the leader's role: "When I step down here [Waterloo], my hope would be that the institution has reinforced a culture of innovation and aspiration and is quite robust in it. These institutions are so much larger than any individual, but the individuals help to establish the culture and the atmosphere in which quality prevails."

Ultimately, I am not sure that there could be a better conclusion to a discussion about the difference a president can make. No change is permanent, but a presidency that takes full account of the prevailing institutional culture and, where necessary, modifies it, has the best chance of achieving long-term success.

ADVICE TO NEW PRESIDENTS

Notwithstanding the significant differences in the size, mandate, and profile of their institutions and the variations in their personal styles, the presidents interviewed share many common attributes and values and the advice they would offer to new presidents is very consistent. Indeed, some have developed presentations that offer such advice, based on their own experiences and value systems. Paul Davenport is a notable case in point.

> I have a little speech called "Seven Guidelines to Collegial Leadership," and one of them is to have a message that is clear and simple and to say it again and again and again. The context is that you are surrounded, as president, by these enormously bright faculty members, many of whom have much more raw intelligence than you do, but they are very busy and focused, as they should be, on their research areas and teaching, and they're not going to listen to a complicated speech with forty different objectives.

Dave Marshall has a similar presentation. He offers eleven pieces of advice to new presidents, each of which is accompanied by a supporting anecdote. These anecdotes may well form the basis for a book or for the world speaking/musical tour he dreams of, but they strongly parallel the approach to management of his successful colleagues. They paint a picture of a value-driven, highly active, and highly visible president who is nevertheless strategic in selecting and implementing priorities, who communicates these endlessly, and who focuses on assembling a team of the very best people and ensuring that they always get the credit for any achievement.

Taking the lead from the group interviewed, I offer here the following seven key pieces of advice central to a president's ability to make a significant difference to an institution:

1 Take the time and trouble to learn the institution's history and to appreciate its particular culture, but use that knowledge to change that culture in ways that would best serve the long-term interests of the university.
2 Insist on the highest standards throughout the institution, and do not compromise. This applies especially to hiring and tenure decisions and to academic standards for students.
3 Take a lot of time and trouble to recruit and support the very best people as part of your top team. Be careful to complement your own strengths and compensate for your weaknesses. Seek talent, diversity, and a variety of experience.
4 Work actively to develop a climate that thrives on debate and dissent. Lead by example, openly inviting dissenting opinions. Don't get trapped in your office, but regularly get around the campus.
5 Be very clear on institutional direction and strategic priorities, and never miss an opportunity to communicate your vision and planned actions clearly and simply.
6 Have the patience to ensure that those most involved understand and take ownership of the vision and associated actions.
7 Do not seek or expect personal credit for particular successes, but make sure that others are publicly recognized for and encouraged in all of their achievements.

Notwithstanding the cross-national differences between Canada and the United States identified at the outset in this volume, this advice jibes closely with the conclusions of a 2003 American forum on effective university leadership. Ponder and McCauley identified eight core competencies for successful college and university leadership:[7]

- Understanding and navigating the organization
- Building and maintaining relationships
- Valuing diversity and difference
- Managing yourself
- Managing politics and influencing others
- Demonstrating ethics and purpose
- Self-awareness
- Developing others[8]

Most of this discussion can be summed up in what I call *open management*,[9] the notion of managing an organization according to the values that define it. Open management builds on the work of Chris Duke (2002), which looks at the university as a learning organization, and that of Joseph Badarraco and Richard Ellsworth (1989), which focuses on the concept of value-driven leadership. In the case of a university, the defining values include openness, curiosity, the joy of discovery, discipline, and integrity. A true university must not only tolerate but also celebrate dissent, always in the search for truth. In this context, a president may often lead from behind, nurturing rather than directing, challenging rather than telling, and encouraging rather than criticizing.

Of course, the indirect approach will not work on all occasions. As Peter George noted, there are times when a quick decision is critical and the president has to act without going through the usual channels that are so much a part of university's culture. There are other times when a president has to have the courage to stand alone, even when all advice is to the contrary. This is what Nelson Mandela did when he embraced the Springboks rugby team when South Africa hosted the World Cup, even though the team had always symbolized white domination in the South African culture.[10] His stand paid off handsomely, for he had recognized that reconciliation between the white and black cultures was essential to his country's future; many others had been unable to see that far ahead. While Mandela ultimately succeeded primarily because he had the courage of his convictions to persevere, it also helped that he acted early in his presidency while people were still watching to see what kind of leader he would be and that he won the admiration and credibility of others by avoiding presenting the face of bitterness and recrimination that one would expect from someone who had spent twenty-six years as a political prisoner.

Of such stories is transformative leadership made, but as discussed in chapter 3, most Canadian university leadership is transactional most of the time. Through making incremental improvements in quality, focusing on specific strategic objectives, and exercising strong interpersonal skills, the best university presidents build institutional cultures that encourage faculty, staff, and students always to strive for the highest standards. In this way, they demonstrate that Canadian university presidents can make a significant difference to the day-to-day experience of everyone on campus and to the long-term benefit of the country as a whole.

14

Leadership under Fire: Seven Major Issues for Today's Presidents

This book makes the case that, given an appropriate institutional fit, a good president can make a significant difference to his or her institution, especially if there is some continuity of purpose and direction under successive incumbents. It contrasts the challenges of managing in earlier times with the more complex, public, and multifaceted role of the president in the twenty-first century, and emphasizes that both the context and the role are continually changing, especially since long-standing traditions of university governance are subject to public scrutiny and accountability as never before.

Canadian universities and their leaders are increasingly under fire from a broad range of stakeholders who believe that our institutions are in deep trouble and can only be saved by a radical transformation of our whole approach to post-secondary education. Others point to the university's long history of surviving doomsday scenarios and suggest that the threats to its mission and autonomy are exaggerated and overblown.

The position taken here accepts neither extreme. I suggest that the academic culture defining our universities is very strong and that the best of it must be preserved at all costs, but I also recognize that significant and major change is essential if Canada is to regain its position as a world leader in university education and research. Our challenge is both to reform the institution and to preserve its best characteristics at the same time.

I have focused throughout this book on the role of the president, not to exaggerate it but to underline its fundamental importance and responsibility. Canadian university leaders are under fire, but they are more than able to rise to the occasion. Good presidents can make important differences and never more so than when they embrace the following seven challenges, each one fundamental to institutional success over the next decade or two.

ENSURING INSTITUTIONAL QUALITY

Make quality the defining issue for funding teaching, learning, and research.

While much lip service is given to quality issues in Canadian higher education, the political pressures for more university places have led governments in every province to tie funding to accessibility. While university presidents have frequently protested the lack of money for "quality," they have consistently undermined their own case by relying on enrolment growth to meet their fiscal challenges. The marginal funding gains from increased tuition revenues emanating from higher enrolments may help balance the budget in a given year, but a consistent dependency on such incremental funding can dig the institution into a considerable financial hole in the longer term. The resulting decline in quality is thus as much the responsibility of the presidents as of the governments they tend to blame for the situation.

Bill Leggett demonstrated exemplary leadership at Queen's when, during the double-cohort period, he resisted tremendous governmental pressure to take in more students. It was his conviction that a larger Queen's would undermine the strengths of its close-knit academic community. He stood up for institutional quality despite widespread criticism that Queen's was not accepting its share of the additional students. This took courage and fortitude.

It is even harder for presidents of institutions less well endowed and less in demand to sacrifice enrolments in order to put the quality agenda first. As long as university grants are primarily enrolment based and tuition fees tightly regulated, institutional leaders will have little choice but to expand enrolments to cope with ever-increasing costs. The danger, if nothing changes, is that the quality of undergraduate instruction will continue to deteriorate until it reaches unacceptable levels and the standing of Canadian graduates will no longer be a source of national pride. Furthermore, some of the smaller and weaker institutions may already be in serious jeopardy, with the communities they serve suffering a significant negative impact. Given that most Canadians have access to only one university in their community or local region, we cannot afford the American luxury of letting institutions proliferate and market forces predominate, with the result that some institutions have to close for insufficient enrolments.

We have seen that it is easier for university presidents to raise issues of overall system decline than it is for an individual to speak publicly about the particular shortcomings of his or her own institution. Indeed, there have been a number of occasions, notably in Ontario, when presidents talked seriously of a collective "drawing a line in the sand" on the enrolment issue. To force the government to provide full funding for each new place, the universities together would state their unwillingness to accept more students than they had in the previous year. Each time such a suggestion was made, however, the minister of the day would call the institutions' bluff and almost none of them would hold the line; they would instead accept additional students above their quota, finding the marginal extra revenues too enticing to pass up.[1] Consequently, the revenue per student continued to decline, class sizes grew larger each year, and the complaints persisted without resolution. In effect, the government got its additional accessibility and the institutions paid for it in terms of declining quality in the learning environment and in student support services.

It is hard to see this scenario changing without university funding being significantly overhauled. As it now stands, parents are much more concerned with whether or not their children get a university place than with whether the particular institution really is the best option for their son or daughter. People are generally far less familiar with higher education than with, say, an elementary school, and thus issues of university quality are far less in the public eye. So, following Bates,[2] the pattern will probably continue: institutions will remain dependent on enrolment growth to balance their budgets and will thus offer ever-larger classes taught by increasing numbers of part-time instructors and teaching assistants.

The situation is approaching crisis proportions. While some would argue that a full-scale crisis might be healthy in that it could force institutions to change in ways they would not otherwise consider, waiting for a crisis to resolve a situation is time-consuming, energy draining, and often ineffective. University presidents and the respective government leaders have a critical responsibility to act before this happens.

Student activism is one catalyst that might assist presidents in making their public case. The student power movement of the late 1960s and early 1970s had a direct impact on university management and governance, significantly broadening the base of institutional governance and challenging the narrowness of curricula and admissions. For a couple of decades now, university students have been paying ever-higher tuition fees for larger classes and less personal attention on campus. While the age of sit-ins and protests may have passed, students could still have inordinate influence if they decided to boycott a given institution or otherwise raise the public profile of concerns about the quality of their education. While I do not envision such a student movement in the near future, I do believe that institutions that seriously address legitimate student concerns about quality and service may thereby enhance their own reputation and profile in ways that branding and marketing campaigns could never achieve by themselves. This may be of particular interest to presidents attempting to distinguish their university from the competition in the public eye.

Of course, "quality" is a term that is easily bandied about, and it is important for presidents to be clear about what they mean by it. While it most fundamentally concerns academic standards for both student and faculty performance, the most important task for the president is to ensure that issues of quality in all areas are constantly in the forefront so that a common notion of what it is gradually emerges on campus.

INCREASING INSTITUTIONAL DIFFERENTIATION

*Work to encourage the development of a more diversified
post-secondary educational system.*

Rather than expect all universities to improve quality across the board, a more promising reform would be to bring about more institutional differentiation. The country cannot afford to continue to allow most institutions to aspire to the same comprehensive status, and Canadians would be better served by a system that provided more alternatives to students with different aspirations and talents. In this scenario, some universities would take on a greater share of undergraduate teaching, while the more research-intensive institutions would focus increasingly on graduate studies. Achieving this objective is much more realistic than expecting all universities to recalibrate their respective emphases on teaching and research in the same way.

Reform such as this is unlikely to go very far without significant leadership from politicians, leadership that may be controversial and even risky to an individual's political future. It is much more likely to happen after a serious crisis of program cuts and layoffs is experienced across a number of institutions or as a result of major inquiries into post-secondary education at both the provincial and federal levels. Change like this presumes that political leaders will have better understood the impact of a university education on the economy, on social policy, and on the quality of the work force.

This is an uphill battle, given the predominance of health care issues, provincial deficits, and the shrinking tax base that demographic trends foretell. Until the general public see the importance not only of accessibility to, but also of the quality of our universities, as they do for health care, post-secondary education will continue to lag behind many other priorities in most provincial budgets. The new generation of presidents will have to marshal all the arguments and as many influential spokespersons from outside the academy as possible to drive home the vital importance of investment in post-secondary education to Canada's future.

Canadian post-secondary education would benefit enormously from more differentiation of the sort being spearheaded in Alberta and British Columbia. This need not be at the expense of the uniformity of quality at the undergraduate level that is a hallmark of the country's public university system. Moreover, the changes would be relatively minor, and the result would in no way mirror the American system of a plethora of institutions of all sorts and levels of quality. It is time for a more system-based approach, one that divides responsibility for the many facets of higher education among distinctly different types of institution. At the university level, these can be divided among four major categories.

SMALLER, UNDERGRADUATE-FOCUSED UNIVERSITIES

As outlined in chapters 1 and 12, Canada already has a number of small universities that offer excellent undergraduate teaching and a personal and supportive campus life. These institutions tend to do very well on student surveys such as the National Survey of Student Engagement (NSSE) and the *Globe and Mail's Canadian University*

Report because classes are smaller, professors know their students and involve undergraduates in their own research more than is the normal practice on larger campuses with extensive graduate programs. The same can be said for some of the constituent colleges at the larger universities; they offer their students the best of both worlds – a personalized educational environment in a large and prestigious research university.

The majority of the small universities are in more rural areas, notably in the three Maritime provinces, Quebec, and, more recently with the evolution of university colleges to university status, Alberta and British Columbia. These institutions should be encouraged to focus on undergraduate teaching and discouraged from seeking to grow to comprehensive status by adding graduate studies.

It should be acknowledged that a number of very good primarily undergraduate institutions aspire to more and stronger graduate programming and that it may be difficult, politically, to persuade or require them to focus exclusively on an undergraduate mandate. It may be easier in some cases to create new institutions or to award university status to some community colleges.[3] However, as Rob Prichard, Paul Davenport, Dave Marshall, and others have suggested, a great deal is possible with different funding schemes that encourage a high quality of undergraduate teaching and learning. The exposure of far more students to strong undergraduate teaching will pay rich long-term dividends for both the individuals and Canadian society.

COMPREHENSIVE UNIVERSITIES

The challenges of institutional differentiation are greatest for the significant number of "comprehensive" universities in Canada, those mid-sized to large institutions that offer a broad spectrum of both undergraduate and graduate programs. Most of these universities individually serve a sizable geographic area, and in their effort to cater to local needs, they have grown rapidly in size and complexity. The result has been that a number of them are now too large to be as personal and supportive of undergraduate students as they once were and yet are insufficiently resourced to play so many concurrent roles successfully.

Universities must be responsive to their local communities but not to the extent of stretching themselves too thin, of trying to be all things to all people and risking the concomitant danger that they won't do anything very well. The community and the country will ultimately be better served if the university offers fewer but stronger programs that clearly distinguish it and attract the best students from all over the country. Research and scholarship are as important to comprehensive universities as they are to medical-doctoral institutions, but the profile and reputation of these universities can best be raised if they focus on fewer and more concentrated areas, especially those that enhance the universities' value to the region in which they are located. As well, encouraging more student mobility across Canada and internationally would make it easier for such institutions to narrow and improve their courses; it would relieve some of the pressure to offer everything that those in its primary catchment area expect.

Presidents of comprehensive universities will have to move ahead carefully and very strategically as long as government funding rewards size over quality. I was always conscious at Windsor that my notion of "the best of both worlds" (lots of program choice in a more personal environment) could very easily deteriorate into "the worst of both worlds" if the institution tried to cover all the bases and grew so large that it lost the personal touch of a more compact campus.

MEDICAL-DOCTORAL UNIVERSITIES

As proposed by the G5 presidents (Montréal, McGill, Toronto, Alberta, and UBC), the best contribution that the medical-doctoral institutions could make to the improvement of undergraduate education would be to reduce their intakes at that level and focus more on building graduate programs, raising their national and international reputations for quality, research, and scholarship in the process. This would leave more of the undergraduate field open to the institutions in the other three categories. Of course, graduate education is more expensive than undergraduate and such an approach would thus need additional government financial support, but it could go a long way towards helping establish a more differentiated and purposeful system of post-secondary education in Canada. It would also be more effective than the current practice of some of the largest institutions of subsidizing graduate studies with revenues from the undergraduate level. The one exception to this approach would be that affiliated colleges and suburban campuses of the largest universities where undergraduate teaching is the primary concern would be recognized and allowed to be funded much like the smaller undergraduate universities.

SPECIALIZED INSTITUTIONS

The fourth group of institutions were far less evident in Canadian higher education in the past. These are the specialized institutions designed to respond to the needs of particular niches of the population. The category includes new universities with purposefully different mandates (UOIT, OCAD, Emily Carr University of Art and Design); collaborative arrangements across sectors (Guelph/Humber); colleges that have evolved to university status with government support, although these are quickly evolving to a category "a" status (Mount Royal, Kwantlen Polytechnic University); specialized institutes that address the needs of particular professional groups (HEC Montréal, École polytechnique de Montréal); or those that have embraced new delivery mechanisms and open admissions (Athabasca University, Royal Roads, La Télé-université). There are also some private universities, most of which are small and confessional in nature, and a few secular ones that have tried to establish themselves as innovative and student responsive in the struggle for recognition and enrolments.

Canada needs to encourage more innovation in institutional mandates, structures, programming, and teaching and learning, giving students more genuine choices across distinctive institutions in a more concerted and differentiated system. Change like this is much more readily achieved through dedicated institutions within which there is a convergence of the prevailing culture, mission, and mandate, but it requires strong institutional and government leadership, including unprecedented federal-provincial collaboration, and the patience of all parties to give fledgling or changing institutions sufficient time to succeed. To undertake these innovations is to recognize the value of encouraging the development of different institutional cultures as defined in chapter 3 – some more collegial and others more virtual or tangible. This is a much more promising approach than expecting a given institution to embrace the entire range of needs and cultures.

These suggestions are made with the key assumption that faculty will be encouraged to do – and will be rewarded for doing – research and scholarship in their field at any Canadian university, so that, as much as possible, the country will avoid the worst aspects of tiering – that is, labelling some institutions as second-rate or so blurring the distinction between universities and colleges that the integrity of each is seriously compromised.

FACILITATING STUDENT MOBILITY

Enhance student mobility, both within Canada and internationally.

University leaders should use Bill Leggett's advocacy for much greater student mobility across Canada as the lynchpin in several parallel agendas – encouraging universities to focus more on specific areas of expertise, combatting parochialism, and encouraging young people to develop a much stronger sense of Canada. If anything, the current post-secondary education system discourages such mobility. Not only is there very little coordination among the provinces, but some of their policies actively discourage student exchanges by requiring higher fees for out-of-province students or making them ineligible for scholarships, even where the money for them originated federally or outside the province.

Both individual students and the country as a whole would benefit enormously if more young Canadians criss-crossed the country to go to university. This may be a hard sell to politicians in governments strapped for money or jealously guarding their provincial jurisdiction over education, but presidents should promote this sort of mobility as yet another way that universities can contribute to national unity and understanding and produce more outward-looking and knowledgeable graduates.

As Bill Leggett has suggested, one way of paying for student mobility would be to forego creating new universities, or expanding existing ones, in regions of high demand (such as the GTA); the monies saved could fund student travel to the universities of their choice elsewhere in the country. Ontario, for example, benefited significantly from not having to provide places for students who attended universities in Nova Scotia and New Brunswick during the double-cohort period. Unfortunately, Canada seems to lack the formal mechanisms to even contemplate such a student mobility scheme, let alone manage it through the inevitable quagmire of federal-provincial jurisdictional disputes.

RESPONDING MORE CREATIVELY TO FINANCIAL
PRESSURES

Work within the ever-deepening financial challenges to find innovative, cost-efficient ways to ensure a better quality of undergraduate student experience.

With institutional costs driven upward by faculty salaries in a sellers' market, increasing well beyond inflation levels, and almost all provincial governments struggling with significant deficits and spiralling demands for more funding, especially in health care, universities across the country are facing financial challenges of crisis proportion. There are two ways of coping with these: finding additional revenue from new or current sources or using existing resources more effectively to improve the quality of student learning.

While I support more flexibility in tuition fees (apart from easing financial problems, flexibility might also facilitate greater institutional differentiation through market forces), I believe it highly unlikely that politicians would agree to the complete deregulation of fees, especially in the core areas of undergraduate arts and sciences. Nevertheless, presidents must continue to press for more liberal tuition regimes while taking on the concomitant responsibility to ensure, through generous scholarship and other financial support schemes (such as the income-contingency repayment plans employed or contemplated in Australia and the United Kingdom), that no qualified students are denied university entrance because of affordability. Presidents also need to work to ensure, in consultation with student leaders, that any additional tuition revenues are allocated to areas of teaching or support services that demonstrably improve the quality of undergraduate education on campus. In my experience, student leaders who get past a knee-jerk negative reaction to tuition increases become primarily interested in seeing tangible improvements on campus as a consequence of their increased investment. Conversely, it has been easy to empathize with the frustration felt by student leaders who have recently had to watch tuition fees rise without any apparent impact on the quality of programs and services.

The new generation of presidents should also be more aggressive in forging collaborative agreements across universities, between universities and colleges, and with the private sector to address the crucial components of fiscal responsibility – accessibility, quality, and cost-efficiency. Such agreements have been made on the administrative side (collaborative purchasing, joint insurance schemes), but much more could be done academically. For instance, it is ironic that Canadian institutions are more apt to have joint degree programs with universities outside the country than within it when the advantages to both quality and cost savings of in-Canada collaborative programming are obvious, as demonstrated in Carleton and Ottawa's collaboration in some areas of graduate study.

Online technology greatly facilitates collaboration through open educational resources (OERs) that include shared course materials and learning management systems. The 2002 MIT OpenCourseWare initiative, for example, raised the international profile of educational sharing and has encouraged other prestigious universities to emulate this approach.[4] Providing wide access to a broad range of learning materials without charge can make a huge difference to educational accessibility and success, not only in Canada but internationally as well. Athabasca University's Rory McGreal was named the UNESCO/COL chair in open educational resources early in 2011 with a particular emphasis on the importance of OERs in the developing world.[5] Creative use of resources like these can greatly enhance an institution's ability to make better use of its existing faculty members by avoiding unnecessary duplication of effort and freeing professors to concentrate on their own teaching and research.

The stark realities of financial management are that the need to balance the annual budget comes first and foremost and that even the most innovative and outward-looking presidents have to deal with immediate challenges that can't always be addressed by longer-term tactics. Since governments and most university boards no longer permit long-term deficits, presidents have no choice but to find creative ways to do more with the same or less. While this kind of challenge is cyclical, it gets more difficult with each new era of economic belt-tightening. The very difficult fiscal pressures in the 1990s and again recently have forced universities to become much more efficient in their operating procedures. No longer can they afford to allow facilities to be significantly underused in the summer, on evenings, and on weekends as was common a couple of decades ago. Today there are far fewer areas that can be shaved or cut, an increasingly higher price is paid for deferred maintenance, and the whole process is too often carried out under the shadow of what seems to be a decline in the quality of the undergraduate experience.

While better funding for both undergraduate and graduate education across the country would address many of these concerns, sustained higher investment in universities seems unlikely in the current environment. Even with more financial support, universities must be more innovative on their academic side, whether using the combination of much larger classes and small group seminars that I experienced at the University of London, a more integrated and planned investment in online learning and student support, or better collaboration between and among universities in teaching and research than has been attempted to date.

Most Canadian universities have not changed very much over the past few decades in their delivery of undergraduate teaching (except in the rather negative ways described above). Presidents would be much more effective if they could raise and discuss these issues collectively and take a more collaborative approach in the overall interests of the quality of the university student experience across the country. There is much they can do to raise the profile of this issue on campus and to challenge provosts, deans, and departmental chairs to respond. Every institution has professors with innovative ideas, but they need mentorship and support if these are to reach fruition in programs and approaches that really make a difference. Financial support is essential, but an appropriate reward system is also crucial. Release time, expert advice, and a supportive organizational climate are all components of an effective support strategy. No matter how difficult the times, there must always be room in the budget process for incentives for new approaches and their implementation. I always found it ironic that institutions tended to cut the most innovative projects and ideas in the toughest times, just when they were needed the most.

Notwithstanding all of the above, the biggest challenge on most campuses for university presidents is to find ways to work with faculty, staff associations, and unions to ensure effective labour relations that result in budgets that provide both competitive wages and benefits and appropriate levels of operating support. The president has primary responsibility for developing an open climate that, through effective communications and consultation processes, brings the whole community on board, but he or she must be prepared, at the same time, to take a tough and principled stand when the fiscal integrity of the institution is threatened.

CHAMPIONING THE CASE FOR CANADIAN UNIVERSITIES

Raise the profile and coordination of universities right across Canada, and speak up on issues of major national concern.

Canada's universities operate in one of the world's most decentralized educational systems and thereby have significant institutional autonomy. While this offers them protection from undue government interference, it also frustrates change, especially on the national level.

In spite of the sensitivity of the constitutional jurisdictions around education, it is incumbent upon university leaders to be much bolder in seeking to establish a more integrated, diversified, and coordinated higher education system across the country. Bill Leggett observed that Canadian university presidents are far less likely to speak out on important national issues than they once were: "It's quite frankly shameful how seldom university presidents stand up on the big provincial or national issues confronting our society, too often cowering behind political expediency or a fear of negative consequences for their institution at the hand of increasingly interventionist governments."

In many ways, it is understandable that today's leaders are more reticent about speaking out publicly. Universities are more dependent upon public money than they were in more elitist times, and there are risks in being publicly critical of the government of the day. Still, nothing is more important to the country's long-term future than investment in and assurance of the highest quality of post-secondary education. Even if this is seen as self-serving on occasion, university leaders cannot miss any opportunity to engage the general public and its leaders in this issue.

When the presidents of the G5 universities spoke frankly to Paul Wells of *Maclean's* magazine in 2009,[6] they got a lot of attention, much of it negative. They repeated a long-standing argument that the country's egalitarian approach to higher education inhibits the ability of our most research-intensive institutions to compete with the best internationally. Canada needs more graduate students, and they wanted to focus their institutions on master's and doctoral studies and research, leaving more of the responsibility for undergraduate education to others. They advocated greater differentiation in the system, with each institution focusing on its core mission and mandate. To this end, they suggested a first ministers' conference on the innovation economy. By including corporate leaders in the conference, they hoped to broach the long-standing concern about the poor performance of Canadian industry in commercializing research, and by broadening the purpose of the conference, they hoped to avoid some of the pitfalls of Canada's jurisdictional disputes over education.[7]

The response to Wells's *Maclean's* article was disappointing but all too familiar. Rather than welcoming a healthy debate on a critical national issue, too many respondents accused the presidents of being self-serving and elitist. In fact, they should have been commended for provoking debate and asking for a national platform for their concerns. The five presidents are paid to be institutional advocates, so they can hardly be criticized for partisanship, but they also recognize the quality concerns associated with institutions that are expected to be too many things to too many people. As argued above, the country would benefit greatly from a range of more focused institutions, from superb liberal arts colleges to research-intensive graduate schools. A national summit on these issues is long overdue, but is unlikely to happen until more Canadians and their political representatives become aware that the country is gradually losing its international competitiveness. Today's presidents must not only speak up but also ensure that leaders from all facets of Canadian society become actively engaged in debating the sorts of issue raised by the G5 heads.

University presidents also have a responsibility to forge a common front among the various stakeholders within their institutions. The very different perspectives of administration, faculty, support staff, and student leaders on some issues tend to blunt the impact of their respective representations and frequently allow politicians to play one off against another. All campus groups must work more openly together to find consensus on how best to advance their common cause.

A key way to advance the common cause is to speak out much more forcibly about what a university is and must be. In his thoughtful and often provocative book *Zero Tolerance: Hot Button Politics in Canada's Universities*, Peter Emberley calls for a robust public relations campaign to stimulate public understanding and tolerance of the university's "mysterious processes": "The campaign must profile what universities do best: form individuals who exhibit thoughtful reflection, cultivated imagination and informed criticism; produce citizens who look upon politics as a noble enterprise on behalf of the public good, not simply interest; and stimulate intellectual and spiritual journeys that offer meaning and purpose."[8]

If institutional leaders are fearful of undermining their cause by being too critical of their political masters or by publicly favouring traditional concepts about university that are no longer in vogue, they must recognize that not speaking out on such a crucial issue will do even more damage to their public credibility in the long term. Healthy debate is what universities stand for – if it does not emanate from their leaders, from whence will it come?!

PROVIDING MORAL LEADERSHIP

Recognize the importance of the moral authority of the role of president for social reform and ensuring that graduates are effectively prepared to deal with the important ethical issues of the day.

Given Western society's recent history of blatant abuses of power by those in leadership positions, notably politicians and corporate leaders, one of the most important characteristics of an effective leader is integrity. This is nowhere more important than at a university. Following from the earlier discussion of open management and value-driven leadership, it is critical that the leader of an institution dedicated to academic freedom and the search for truth actively and openly demonstrates these values. This is a viewpoint strongly endorsed by Shore: "If a university is to retain its unique position in society as a place where new ideas can be expressed, discussed, challenged, and refined, it must be something more than merely a credential-granting institution that aids individuals in increasing their earning power and position in society. This will only be possible if the university once again examines its historic roots, and recognizes its role as a center of moral education."[9]

This does not mean that a university president should become a crusader for selected moral values or wear them on his or her sleeve. Indeed, nothing would more quickly undermine the authority of an individual who is beholden to so many stakeholder groups and who works in a culture in which the most effective leadership is low-key and self-effacing. The need is, rather, for each president to demonstrate these values in his or her day-to-day work, encouraging debate, challenging myths, emphasizing the importance of widespread consultation and institutional research, but also not being afraid to take a strong stand on an issue once the appropriate consultation and research have been completed.

Harold Shapiro has been a notable advocate for university presidents' providing stronger moral leadership.[10] Through presidential leadership by example, a curriculum that is constantly updated to deal with the never-ending moral issues raised by technological development, and the requirement that students take greater responsibility for their own education, the university is perhaps our most important instrument for ensuring the development of a just and ethical society.

Functioning both as a servant and critic of society, the university must be a place that not only recognizes but celebrates dissent. While I prided myself on writing a different speech for each of the more than one hundred convocations at which I gave an address, I did repeat one theme quite regularly. This was to question whether or not Galileo would be granted tenure in a modern university. My conclusion was that he might be just as ostracized today as he was in the seventeenth century, although not for the same reason. My fear is that while we highly value academic freedom, we too often take it for granted and tend to promote and support those with views similar to our own. In fact, I worry that someone with views that were considered as radical today as those of Galileo were then would not even be hired by our universities! The ivory tower is designed to protect academic freedom, but its relative isolation can breed smugness, arrogance, prevailing ideologies, and political correctness.

Shapiro emphasizes the importance of the president's role in recognizing these dangers and sees educational reform as a "mini social protest movement" that can and must take us to a better place.[11] Perhaps, ultimately, open management is the most important single responsibility of a university president – to ensure, by aspiration and by practice, that the institution truly lives up to the ideals by which it is defined.

ENSURING THE QUALITY OF GRADUATES

Never lose sight of the university's core function of producing graduates who are independent learners and creative thinkers, the kind of citizens that the complexities of today's world demand.

Nothing is more important to the future of the country and its higher education system than the quality of its graduates. Presidents must embrace the challenges of improving the core activities of teaching and learning so that universities develop curious, confident, creative, thoughtful, and independent learners. This is a question of recognizing the contributions of all the disciplines and their interrelationship and, especially, of understanding that today, when knowledge is more readily available than ever, the most important thing a student learns is how to access, analyse, and apply that knowledge in the best interests of society. This point is vital and obvious, but it can all too easily be lost among the many other functions our institutions take on. It is the president's role to ensure that the institution never loses sight of this defining endeavour.

More than anything else, fulfilling this responsibility means protecting the scholarly culture that lies at the heart of what a university is and must be, even though it does not always readily lend itself to simple performance indicators or to direct returns on investment. Just as the most spectacular results of research may be serendipitous rather than lockstep, so the process of learning is often haphazard and unpredictable. The president's primary job is to help develop and preserve a campus environment that fosters an accountable but essentially unfettered scholarly culture.

Emberley reminds us that the university at its best needs protection from the outside interference it increasingly faces:

The singleminded desire to re-engineer the university adopts the unwarranted assumption that the West's process of technological and social development are an unmitigated blessing. With its continued commitment to soul-leading conversation, the world of imagination, critical judgment and the unalloyed intellectual and spiritual journey, the scholarly culture of the university is the only true antidote to the anomie of our times and the locus of our hope for the renewal of our world. The university can serve these functions only if it can continue to enjoy the detachment from society's urgencies and certainties, and if it is permitted to continue the leisurely examination of intellectual and spiritual possibilities that provide us with a higher idea of ourselves.[12]

Emberley's exhortation lies at the heart of the challenges of university leadership today. It explains why presidents must speak up regularly about the critical role of the social sciences and humanities, disciplines that too often take a back seat to science and technology in discussions about the importance of universities. It is no accident that so many corporate and public sector leaders have liberal arts degrees, given the critical importance of communications, human relations, and creativity to institutional leadership. Martha Piper's widely cited 2002 Killam Lecture set the gold standard for this topic:

If we are going to achieve this goal, the building of a civil society, I would like to suggest that we need to build our understanding along three lines of inquiry in the human sciences: first, we must encourage knowledge and scholarship that will enable individuals to better understand themselves, their values, and the roles they play as citizens; second, we must pursue knowledge and scholarship that will assist us to define our Canadian identity and our role as global citizens; and third, we must advance knowledge and scholarship in those areas that bear on legislation, public policy, and social programming.[13]

Dr Piper thus addresses the last three topics in this section simultaneously – speaking up on a crucial national issue, providing moral leadership, and emphasizing the importance of the quality of graduates. Canada will ignore her advice at its peril.

THE ROLE OF PRESIDENT: A PERSONAL PERSPECTIVE

It would be wrong to conclude from the foregoing that a university president's job is more challenging than rewarding. Nothing could be further from the truth. There is great joy in leading a group of highly skilled faculty members in an enterprise so central to modern society and its future. Writing in the Australian context, Ramsden addresses the universal characteristics of academics that make leading a university so ultimately exciting and enjoyable: "These include their high levels of intrinsic motivation and love of academic challenge; the fact that they are self-starting, self-regulating, independent professionals; their willingness to discuss and debate issues openly; their lifelong learning skills and commitment to constant enlargement of their knowledge; their excellent communication skills; and their talent for imaginative thinking."[14]

For the incumbent, most of the time, nothing could be a more rewarding endeavour than being a university president. The institution is increasingly central to the challenges and opportunities of the modern world, it is comprised of talented faculty and staff with innovative ideas, and it thrives with the energy, the optimism, and the enthusiasm of young people. It offers tremendous rewards to its leaders, from watching students grow in confidence and aspiration to sharing in the joys of discovery at the cutting edge of research and scholarship. It offers great opportunities for mentorship,[15] but it is also a superb learning environment for even the most experienced president. At its best, it is an open community for the free exchange of ideas and, whatever its flaws and shortcomings, is our best hope for a better world, economically, socially, and politically.

Presidents have to be particularly courageous in confronting two opposing forces – powerful pressures for accountability and change that emanate from sources not always sensitive to the core nature and function of universities and the resistance to change that is too often found on our campuses. They have to be reflective and strategic in this regard, picking issues carefully and working hard to bring boards and faculty and staff along with them. The challenges are larger and more urgent than ever, and the uncertain power base of the president does not make the job any easier. It requires strong but sensitive leadership that is not afraid to articulate significantly different and innovative roles and processes for a given institution while always working within its academic culture to achieve change that is real and deep, not short term and artificial.

Presidents will continue to come primarily from within the ranks of the Canadian academy without significant external management experience or training. The breadth and complexity of our institutions and the issues they confront require all the leadership skills they can muster, however, and they really have to do better than just accept that they will learn "on the job." This is a central issue for Fullan and Scott:

> The shift in university cultures to take leadership identification, selection, and learning seriously will not be an easy one. It involves developing our leaders as models, teachers, and learners; starting succession planning early; using relevant, online leadership learning systems for staff to self-assess and develop against; making professional development role-specific and valid; and shaping an environment that gives people not only room to lead but also room to learn. In a word, leadership selection and learning must become the new priorities for universities and colleges.[16]

The research for this book and the interviews with some of Canada's most effective presidents have reinforced my notion that there is no one best profile, one best style, or one best approach to the job of president. Consider their very different orientations, styles, and talents. I could, for example, attach one admittedly subjective outstanding characteristic to each: Paul Davenport (communicator), Jim Downey (thoughtful commentator), Peter George (institutional promoter), Myer Horowitz (mentor), David Johnston (role model), Bill Leggett (crusader), Dave Marshall (change agent), Bonnie Patterson (strategist), Martha Piper (advocate), Rob Prichard (visionary), and Roseanne Runte (nurturer). These leaders have been equally effective in very different contexts and in very different ways. Each president has made an important contribution to the future of Canada. Given the challenges facing the country and its universities, we will need many more leaders like them in the years ahead.

Canadian university presidents must, can, and will make a significant difference.

Presidential Profiles: Eleven Who Have Really Made a Difference

Each of the following was interviewed in person by the author at the place and date specified. Each interview was recorded, and the specific excerpts were subsequently verified by the individual in question. Most of the interviews were two hours in length with a couple going on longer and one, that with Paul Davenport, restricted to one hour.

PRESIDENT	LOCATION	DATE
Martha Piper	Vancouver, BC	22 January 2009
Jim Downey	Toronto, ON	19 March 2009
Paul Davenport	London, ON	24 March 2009
Peter George	Hamilton, ON	25 March 2009
David Johnston	Waterloo, ON	26 March 2009
Rob Prichard	Toronto, ON	28 March 2009
Myer Horowitz	Vancouver, BC	24 April 2009
David Marshall	Calgary, AB	18 June 2009
Roseann Runte	Ottawa, ON	13 August 2009
Bill Leggett	Kingston, ON	22 September 2009
Bonnie Patterson	Toronto, ON	8 December 2009

The following profiles are based on the interviews with each president, augmented by details from their *curriculum vitae*.

PAUL DAVENPORT
President, The University of Alberta (1989–1994)
President, The University of Western Ontario (1994–2009)
Paul Davenport grew up in Summit, New Jersey, and credits both of his parents for instilling in him a real love of learning. He went to

Stanford, initially to study mathematics, but quickly gravitated to economics after taking an elective course in second year. He credits the Stanford approach, with its emphasis on a broad liberal education, with giving him the opportunity to discover what was to become his favourite discipline.

> I was taking courses from all over the place – philosophy, political science, and economics, which I just loved. Here was a course where I could use my mathematics but I could also use economics when I was reading the morning paper and understand why interest rates were going up or down.
>
> So I switched to economics in year three, which was easy to do because you only had to take a quarter of your courses in your major. I had some great teachers in economics – I think of Edward Shaw, the great monetary economist who taught us macro and was very inspiring. He was certainly an early role model.

Davenport graduated in 1969 with great distinction and honours in economics, and he was a Phi Beta Kappan. He was widely recruited by American graduate schools and was on the point of going to one of them to study economic history when he was offered the largest single scholarship then available at the University of Toronto. He met his future wife, Josette, a French citizen, and a few years later, they were both Canadian citizens and he was a professor of economics at McGill University.

Paul was dedicated to his discipline and paid little attention to the management side of universities until asked to prepare a paper for FAPUQ (La fédération des associations de professeurs d'université du Québec) on university funding in Quebec. He made representations – which were later to be his hallmark – for more government funding, higher tuition fees, and income contingency loan-repayment schemes. After some arm twisting, he agreed to be vice-president for external relations for the McGill Association of University Teachers (MAUT) and was soon representing it at an all-day meeting in Quebec. This raised his profile at McGill, and he was then asked to be associate dean of graduate studies, a position that exposed him to all parts of the university. He performed the role from 1982 to 1986 and, in the last year, was appointed to the Conseil des universités, an advisory group to the minister of education.

Dr Davenport gave up a sabbatical to France in 1986 to become vice-principal for planning and computer services under McGill principal David Johnston. (One result of having to cancel his sabbatical was a promise to Josette that they would spend every summer vacation in France, a commitment he lived up to for the next twenty-three years.) Only three years later, after turning down several approaches from presidential search firms, Dr Davenport accepted the presidency of the University of Alberta. He was described by a local newspaper as "an outsider," and he faced a steep learning curve in moving west. He had to learn on the job.

Dr Davenport did much to raise the profile of the university and especially to strengthen its graduate programming, but as already outlined in chapter 11, he was appointed president of Western before Alberta's review of his first term was completed. He took up the position in 1994 and was twice renewed for his strong and effective leadership.

Davenport moved very quickly when he started at Western to establish two clear priorities – to raise the entering grades of students (at the time, the university had fallen below the Ontario average) and to be much more successful in the competition for large, collaborative research grants (it was standing twenty-second in the country). He initiated a strategic planning process during his first week on the job and achieved impressive results. At the conclusion of his presidency, Western stood second only to Queen's in entering averages in Ontario (it would have stood higher if it had taken the same number of students as Queen's) and seventh in Canada for all CFI money.

In terms of disappointments, Davenport wonders if he could have better handled board relations at Alberta by responding more effectively to what he considered to be undue board interference in administration. He also spoke of the challenges of communicating the need for budget cuts effectively (which he had to do on several occasions at Alberta and Western).

Although he didn't mention it in our interview, Dr Davenport was an outstanding national spokesperson for the importance of investment in Canadian universities, serving with distinction as chair of both the Council of Ontario Universities (COU) and the Association of Universities and Colleges of Canada (AUCC) and tirelessly advocating the cause at meetings and conferences. His presentations were always marked by clarity, strong research, and good organization, and he is widely recognized as one of the best communicators among Canadian university presidents in recent decades.

JAMES DOWNEY
President, pro tempore, *Carleton University (1978–1979)*
President, The University of New Brunswick (1980–1990)
President, The University of Waterloo (1993–1999)
Jim Downey's start in life was hardly one suggesting he would become a university president. He grew up in a small Newfoundland outport of fewer than a thousand people. When he went to Memorial for the one-year teacher preparation course, it was the first time he had been to St John's, even though it was only a hundred miles from his home.

By the age of seventeen, Jim Downey was principal of a two-room school. "That sounds extraordinary now but it was not uncommon in those days in Newfoundland. So, I taught for a couple of years. There was a common expectation that young teachers in the denominational school system would take an interest in the church. In the second year, I was asked if I would take the services on Sunday, so, in addition to teaching, I became a student minister."

He found that he liked the ministry, and after saving money from two years of teaching, he went back to Memorial to complete his degree with the idea of entering the United Church ministry. In fact, halfway through his first year back at Memorial, he was called to replace a minister who had died suddenly. This led to the offer of a church in Portugal Cove, about ten miles outside St John's, where for four years he preached twice each Sunday (to the same congregation, which meant he wrote two sermons each week) and performed the usual functions of marrying, baptizing, and burying, all the while pursuing his degree at Memorial.

Downey's academic success led professors to persuade him to stay on at Memorial to do a master's degree in English, following which he received the very lucrative Rothermere Foundation scholarship, only available to Newfoundlanders pursuing a PhD in England. Ironically, it was in London that he discovered his identity as a true Canadian. He vividly remembers today, for example, the pride and identification he felt upon seeing works by such artists as Harold Town and Alex Colville in a show of contemporary Canadian painters at the Tate Gallery.

The discovery of his Canadian identity led him to choose Carleton University, situated in the nation's capital, to begin his academic life. He embarked on what he describes as a conventional career in English at Carleton, but he was soon drawn into the academic politics of the times.

> The student movement was highly voluble, but the real revolution, the more lasting one, was the young faculty revolution. It was very active at Carleton and I got caught up in it early. It was about getting the old guard out and the younger guard in. The way it was done was through an emphasis on the rights of the individual faculty member, getting rotating terms for chairs, deans, and presidents. I got caught up in it not because I was a radical – in fact, quite the opposite – I was skeptical. So I was trusted by the radicals because I was young and by the old guard because I was skeptical.

His rise through the ranks was rapid. He became one of the youngest-ever chairs of the English department, and Oxford University Press published his doctoral thesis on eighteenth-century English sermons, a manifestation of his interests in literature, theology, and public speaking. At thirty-five he was a full professor and dean of the faculty of arts.

Dr Downey's ascendancy to the presidency, however, was not as purposeful as it was for many of his colleagues. In the fall of 1978, an extraordinary sequence of events led to his having to face a career option he had not remotely contemplated. Carleton president Michael Oliver had resigned a year before the end of his term to take up the new position of director of international affairs for AUCC, and the presidential search committee recommended Bill Beckel of the University of Lethbridge as his successor. This was a surprise to many, including the presumed heir, vice-president, academic, John Porter, the eminent sociologist. Porter resigned immediately, leaving the two senior positions in the university simultaneously vacant.

Even though he was the newest and youngest dean ("and therefore the one who had made the fewest enemies"), Downey was asked to take on the duties of acting president until Beckel arrived – in addition to covering for the vice-president, academic. He recalled, "There was no process of understudying the president, there was no process of having been recruited to the presidency or even thinking that someday I might do that. I was thrown in – in fact, if I remember it correctly, for three weeks, I was dean of arts, acting vice-president, academic, and president *pro tem*. Hence, I first thought of being a university president the day I became one!"

When Bill Beckel came a few months later, Jim Downey reverted to the VPA role. Even though he had acted as president during a time of serious budget cuts, he had enjoyed the experience, especially appreciating the way his team came together to support him, and he and Beckel worked effectively together at Carleton for a year. "By then, however, I had the bug and so when the University of New Brunswick came to call, I was easy prey." Jim was appointed president of UNB in 1980.

Downey was brought in at a difficult period in the university's history. The UNB faculty had just voted for unionization after a period of strained relations with the administration, and a first contract was just being negotiated. Partly because of his experience at Carleton, where he had seen first-hand what bitter negotiations could do to the academic culture of an institution, he was able to persuade the board and union to accept binding arbitration to settle the tough salary dispute. He quickly established good working relations with the faculty and a much more positive work environment, one that carried through the next decade and beyond.

Jim Downey was an effective president of UNB for ten years, and his approach to leadership made him an attractive candidate to other institutions seeking to improve campus relations and morale. It was thus not surprising that, after completing his second term and serving as special advisor to the premier of New Brunswick and co-chair of the New Brunswick Commission on Excellence in Education for a couple of years, he was recruited to the presidency of the University of Waterloo in 1993, where he went on to serve a six-year term. He may have been hired in part because he was a humanist and thus his appointment would broaden public perceptions of Waterloo, generally known as an international leader in technological and applied education. He found a very different culture at Waterloo from UNB's, but was nevertheless successful in repairing some of the divisions in the place.

Perhaps more than most university presidents, Jim Downey is known as much for his external contributions to the role as for his performance on the job. In addition to his many speaking engagements, he has overseen AUCC's seminar for new presidents and was the first president of Ontario's Higher Education Quality Council of Ontario (HEQCO). He was also extremely active in the Association of Commonwealth Universities (ACU), serving as its chair in 1998–99.

PETER GEORGE
President, McMaster University, 1995–2010
Peter George grew up on Toronto Island. His grandfather had been lighthouse keeper at the Western Gap, his mother was born on the island, his father's family had a summer home there, and that's where his parents met. He started in the Island School, which only had three or four rooms, and he was allowed to keep his dog under the desk!

The push in the house was always education. He was expected to do well and to apply himself diligently. He skipped a couple of grades. After he'd completed grade 8, his options were city high schools in rough neighbourhoods and his parents were concerned, especially because he was two years younger than the norm. As a result, he ended up writing the entrance examinations for the University of Toronto Schools and commuted there from the island and later from Weston when his family moved into the city.

He took twelve grade 13 subjects and could have entered almost any university program. He chose social and philosophical studies at the University of Toronto, the program because it offered some new subjects that sounded interesting and the university at least in part because it was affordable and close by. He fell in with a crowd who both studied and played hard, so he did well academically but also had a lot of fun (he notes that having a good growth of beard helped him get served in bars when he was only sixteen). He completed his honours degree in economics and political science and then, not knowing what else to do, went on for an MA.

He met his future wife, Gwen, a nursing student at Toronto Western Hospital, on the night of his last exam for his first degree, and they eloped five months later without telling anyone. Within a few months, she was expecting their first child, and she dropped out of school. This led him to take a job as an economist with the Ontario government, but he found it boring because there was little work for him to do: "My taste of government was unfortunate – it was much more professional a few years later, but I just happened to get a poor branch at a poor time."

So, Gwen went back to nursing school, and he was awarded a good scholarship package to do his PhD at Toronto. They completed their respective programs, and when George was appointed as a lecturer at McMaster University in the summer of 1965, they moved to Hamilton with their new son. He liked McMaster from the beginning. During the second year of a two-year contract, he received a letter awarding him tenure even though he was still awaiting the oral examination for his PhD. George noted, "Now, you have to apply formally and put together a dossier and get external references, but at that time, it just seemed to come magically from above. When I think of what we put candidates through now, my own experience was as if tenure and promotion were gifts from a higher power!"

After a stint in Tanzania on a CIDA project and two more years teaching and chairing the departmental graduate studies committee, Dr George was contacted while on sabbatical in Cambridge, England, to see if he would stand for associate dean of graduate studies. He performed the role, his first administrative job, for five years and had very good relationships with the students. Then, in 1979, he received a wake-up call when he was denied promotion to full professor. He resigned his administrative post, took a sabbatical, completed two books, and was promoted to full professor before the end of his leave. He was also appointed dean of social sciences at this time, a position he enjoyed thoroughly and which helped him to recognize the value of an administrative career. However, when he lost out to another internal candidate for provost, he again reverted to academia, resigning the deanship and taking another sabbatical to focus on northern peoples and northern resources.

Through all this, his profile was high, and after several interviews for university presidencies, he was approached by Brian Segal, the chair of the Council of Ontario Universities, to consider being its president. His initial reaction was negative, for he saw COU as primarily a consensus-only, data-gathering institution. However, when Segal told him that the presidents wanted to change the job into an advocacy and government relations role, he was persuaded to stand and held the post for four years, from 1991 to 1995.

Not only did he help transform COU into a much more effective and proactive organization, but he also enhanced his own qualifications for a presidency. The position gave him valuable government relations experience that he never would have had as provost. When the incumbent was not offered another term, he was appointed president of McMaster in 1995, a position he held through three full terms to his retirement in 2010.

Having served as president in a time of major expansion for many Canadian universities, Peter George still stands out as someone who really made a tangible difference to his institution. He raised money for and oversaw the development of new buildings and facilities on campus, and McMaster increased its research and educational profile significantly.

A priority for George from the outset was for a more student-centred agenda in terms of facilities and programs. With great support from former Laidlaw president and philanthropist Michael DeGroote, he led a successful campaign to establish a long-promised student centre. This achievement boosted his confidence, and the rest of his career was punctuated by fundraising triumphs.

Physical expansion and successful fundraising are not the only legacies that Dr George has left McMaster. Like Rob Prichard at Toronto, he devoted almost his entire career to his institution, working tirelessly at the local, national, and international levels to raise its profile and reputation, with considerable success. On the other side of the ledger, however, he regrets what he believes to be a loss of the sense of family and community as a result of the rapid growth of our universities and the associated issues and conflicts.

Determining how to provide effective leadership in an institution with a strong culture of collegiality and resistance to change lies at the heart of the challenges facing today's presidents. While the presidents interviewed demonstrated a variety of perspectives, it was clear that each one of them cared passionately about the university as an institution and worried about finding the elusive balance between consultation and action. With an impressive track record over three terms and an openness and candour that stand out, Peter George is as qualified as any to find that balance.

MYER HOROWITZ
President, The University of Alberta, 1979–1989
When Myer Horowitz moved from McGill University, where he was an associate dean and head of educational administration, to the University of Alberta to take up the chair of elementary education in 1969, few would bet that he would be president of the university only ten years later. His rise was meteoric – from dean of education in 1972; to vice-president, academic, in 1975; to president in 1979.

Horowitz started out with modest means in Montreal. The only member of his parents' generation to go past high school was his uncle Nathan, who pursued an effective law career and whose only son was another prominent Canadian, Irwin Cotler. His uncle was an important influence, always playing word games with Myer and encouraging his development.

Horowitz was a very good student in high school, and a pivotal moment came when he was asked to "teach" geometry and history for a few weeks while the regular teacher was ill. This solidified his growing interest in teaching, an ambitious aspiration in a city where the Protestant School Board of Greater Montreal was said not to hire Jewish males, even though the city's Jewish children all went to its schools, not to mention that Jewish students regularly dominated the top places in the provincial matriculation examinations.

His route to teaching was not an easy one. After a disastrous year in commerce at McGill, he went to work for a couple of chartered accountant brothers before taking his teacher training at McGill's Macdonald College. After graduation, he alone among his friends did not get an immediate offer of a place in a school for the next fall. "My male friends and the Jewish girls all received letters of acceptance and I did not. I waited a week and told a few people and they were ready to march on my behalf. I asked them not to because I wanted a job."

The letter of appointment finally arrived. As angry and frustrated as he he'd been in the face of a form of discrimination all too prevalent in Montreal in that era, Myer Horowitz took many positive lessons from this experience, notably that he could count on behind-the-scenes support, in this case from some of his teachers and his principal and colleagues at Macdonald College. He started teaching at Victoria School and felt a strong need to perform well: "Yes, I felt pressure, but it was not as if it loomed large and constantly in my life in the sense that I had a responsibility not only to myself but to any Jewish male who came along to the school board. It was more a personal thing – I was going to prove to them that I merited having been hired."

He pursued his BA degree part-time at night at Sir George Williams College (later Concordia University). In his fourth year at Victoria School, he met Barbara, who was teaching at another elementary school. They were both transferred to Northmount High School for the 1956–57 school year, and they soon were married. Later that year, a notice came around about a Kellogg Foundation grant for a master's degree in educational administration at the University of Alberta. Barbara urged him to apply.

He ended up going to the University of Alberta a year later, even though he didn't win the scholarship. What's more, he originally didn't know where the university was located (Edmonton), a subsequent source of great amusement to his biographer, Gordon McIntosh. It happened again a year later when Art Reeves, dean of education at Alberta, urged his young graduate student to go to Stanford to do his doctorate and Horowitz had to ask where it was. There was family business to look after first, and he returned to Northmount High School for one year after completing his thesis on administrative practices for severely retarded children in Canada. He spent two years at Macdonald College as a lecturer in the School of Education before finally going to Stanford in 1962.

Myer Horowitz thrived at Stanford, where he enjoyed being treated as a colleague rather than a student. His doctoral thesis was on a teacher internship model, a model that he later brought, in modified form, to McGill. He returned to McGill as an assistant professor in 1963, was an associate two years later, and became a full professor in 1967 at the age of thirty-four, one of the youngest ever to have achieved that level.

While he might well have succeeded another of his mentors, Wayne Hall, as dean, Horowitz was recruited to Alberta as the chair of elementary education and never looked back. He quickly became dean of education and, only three years later, vice-president, academic. It was only then that he began to think seriously about the possibility of becoming president, especially because he was urged to think that way by the incumbent, Harry Gunning. He was named to the position four years later.

Horowitz was thus relatively well prepared for the presidency and had a clear notion of his priorities. Because of his experience as VPA, he was keen to give fresh thought to the undergraduate curriculum and particularly to the need for a core curriculum regardless of discipline. He was also very concerned about internal relationships and the way that decisions were made, concerns that reflected his natural interest in educational administration and the need for a collegial and productive working environment. He also wanted the institution to become more self-critical, believing it should put particular emphasis on benchmarking its performance against performance elsewhere. Finally, severe financial pressures and budget cuts during his tenure as president focused his attention on funding issues and government relations.

As one might expect of someone whose career success had been so dependent upon interpersonal skills, Dr Horowitz is proudest of the extent to which he succeeded in bringing the university community together, building a strong and coherent leadership team. He was highly respected by Alberta's political leaders as well, notably Premier Peter Lougheed, who publicly praised him on a number of occasions, notwithstanding that Myer was a well-known member of the New Democratic Party in a province dominated by Conservative politics. His personal touch extended to students, as well, and he is particularly appreciative that they voted to name their theatre after him.

Working through his first VPA, George Baldwin, he introduced one of the first comprehensive reviews of academic programs in Canada, one that he believes helped improve significantly a number of the university's academic offerings. However, Horowitz has two major disappointments as president: first, a very high profile attempt to redress inequitable payments for female support staff did not turn out quite the way he had intended it to; and second, on a completely different level, he regrets that more was not done on reforming the university curriculum.

Myer Horowitz was leader of the University of Alberta in the 1980s, an earlier era than that of most of the others interviewed for this book. This is reflected in his approach to leadership. He believes that the position of president needs to be firmly grounded internally as academic leader and that it is a mistake to increasingly define it as CEO and to create the position of provost to assume some of the previous internal leadership roles of the president. This is not to suggest that he believes that the role should be unchanged from what it was in his time, but simply that he is more comfortable with the earlier approach.

There is one other critical component of Myer Horowitz's contribution to Canadian education, and that is the huge network of leaders at all levels of education across the country for whom he has been an important mentor. Still, he would have made a wonderful high school principal!

DAVID JOHNSTON
Principal, McGill University, 1979–1994
President, The University of Waterloo, 1999–2010
While his appointment as governor general of Canada in 2010 has eclipsed his previous positions, David Johnston is recognized as having been one of Canada's longest-serving and best-known university presidents. A native of Sudbury, he grew up in nearby Sault Ste Marie, Ontario. His family circumstances were very modest and every penny counted. His mother was legally blind from her early forties. As a result, Johnston had to be quite self-sufficient, and he learned this quickly, aided by his outstanding athletic abilities. He was catcher on the fastball team that won the Ontario championship and excelled first at football and ultimately in hockey. He had part-time jobs from the age of nine and was always determined to go to university.

Johnston calls himself a "Bill Bender kid." Bill Bender had been Harvard University's dean of admissions before the Second World War, and he'd returned from it convinced that the university had to be much more open in its admissions and more in touch with the real world. Bender had seen Harvard graduates in the forces and believed that, as pampered members of the elite, many of them lacked leadership skills. He persuaded president James Conant and a group of wealthy benefactors that Harvard had to be much more open in its admissions policy, including to the extent of admitting women and graduates of public high schools. Thus Harvard opened its doors to students like David Johnston.

Johnston went on to have a brilliant career at Harvard, not only academically but as a star player on its hockey team. He was the role model for the character Davey, Harvard team captain, in Erich Segal's novel *Love Story*. In fact, he came close to a career in professional hockey after two years as an All-American at university, but because of his size (150 pounds) and a crippled left hand that hampered his stick-handling, he decided that the risk of injury was too great and so he went off to Cambridge, England, to pursue a career in law.

He found Cambridge a bigger adjustment than Harvard, notably because of the class system and the famous British "indifference." He persisted nevertheless and received his LLB degree in 1965 and the same degree from Queen's University, Kingston, Ontario, in 1966.

While at Queen's, he signed up to article with Osler Hoskin in Toronto, but Queen's asked him to come on the faculty as an assistant professor. He was reluctant to accept, given that he had already signed on with the law firm, but before making a decision, he appealed to his sponsor, Purdy Crawford, for advice. As he recalled, "So, I went back to Purdy, who asked me what I wanted to do. I said I'd like to be a professor for a year or two. So he said to go ahead and when I had the courage to face the real world, to come back and they would teach me how to practise law. So, I make a habit of going back to the firm annually and reminding them that when I get the courage, they will have to teach me how to practise law."

From that time forward, it was an academic career for David Johnston. Two years later, he moved to the faculty of law at the University of Toronto, where he was asked to assist the chief justice of Ontario in conducting a review of the law school at the University of Western Ontario. Within days of the publication of the resulting report, Western president Carl Williams asked Professor Johnston to be its next dean. Johnston was thirty-three years old.

Five years later, he was recruited by both the University of Alberta and McGill to be executive head. He was concerned that the McGill appointment might be too big a challenge because of his shortcomings in the French language, but the search committee moved very quickly and persuasively. He accepted the McGill position of principal in 1979 at the age of thirty-nine and served in the role for three five-year terms, dramatically improving his French in the process.

Professor Johnston was a whirlwind at McGill, both on and off campus. It was a difficult time, politically, for the university. Bill 101, the controversial language legislation dealing with French in the schools and the workplace, had just been passed. Its main proponent, Quebec's minister of cultural development, Camille Laurin, had been denied entry to the university's highly selective psychiatry program when he was a medical student at the University of Montreal and consequently refused to set foot on the McGill campus. Academic recruitment of Canadians was a major challenge for McGill, as potential faculty worried about the university's future in Quebec, but Johnston met that challenge by initiating further international searches in countries where McGill's cachet was still high. He also worked to make the institution much more a part of the new Quebec and less a part of the world of Montreal's anglophone elite.

When asked what he is most of proud of having accomplished during his tenure there, he says simply that he believes it was a better place in 1994 than it was in 1979. More than anything else, he believes that the role of principal is primarily about intangibles, about building belief in the institution and its quality and strengthening the esprit du corps.

Johnston returned to the academic ranks in the Centre for Medicine, Ethics and Law and churned out seven books in five years. When serving as chair of the board of Harvard (while still on faculty at McGill), he was approached to consider the presidency of another major American university. After some soul-searching with his wife, Sharon, he decided to remain in Canada, but he did recognize that he was happiest as an administrator and he took on the presidency of Waterloo when it came available in 1999. It is no accident that leaders like Research in Motion's Mike Laziridis and Jim Balsillie, the developers of the Blackberry, have thrived in Kitchener-Waterloo and worked closely with the university. The "can do" attitude that leaders like David Johnston have brought to the community is instrumental in the community's confidence and consequent economic and social development.

Even prior to being named governor general, David Johnston enjoyed a higher public profile than most of his academic colleagues. He has been a champion of technology-mediated learning, chairing several task forces, including the federal government's Smart Communities Advisory Panel. He has been prominent in the media, hosting *The Editors* and *The World in Review* television series and several Canadian parliamentary leadership debates.

Mentorship is important in Johnston's life, in both directions. He still remembers the impact his grade 2 teacher, Miss Stewart, had on him in quietly encouraging him to learn multiplication. Legendary Boston Bruins hockey player and subsequent Harvard hockey coach Cooney Weiland (the first Harvard coach not to have a university degree) was an inspiration to him and the subject of an essay he wrote for his own children titled "Lessons from a Coach." Its central theme is that a great teacher can challenge a group of individuals to jell as a team – that the whole is far better than the sum of its parts. It is a lesson that Professor Johnston applied to his leadership style and that lies behind his strong belief in the vital importance of teachers to the future of society.

On the other side of the ledger, David Johnston has played a significant role in the development of a number of Canada's best presidents,
including three interviewed for this book. Paul Davenport and Bill
Leggett served as his vice-presidents at McGill, while Rob Prichard
was his student at Toronto. All three pay tribute to his encouragement, his example, and his continuing support for their own careers.
Other protégés include the late François Tavernas at McGill, who
went on to be president of Laval University, and Waterloo's Amit
Chakma, who served as vice-president, academic and provost, under
David until he assumed the presidency at Western in 2009.

WILLIAM C. LEGGETT
Principal, Queen's University, 1994–2004
As already noted, Bill Leggett spent his first eight grades of school
in a one-room schoolhouse. This was in Mono Mills, Ontario, a tiny
village six miles east of Orangeville. Even more astonishingly, all
eight grades were taught by the same teacher, Miss "No Nonsense"
Parks. While an inauspicious beginning for someone who was to go
on to be one of Canada's most prominent academics, there was one
harbinger of things to come. While in primary school, Bill served
two years as school janitor, coming in early to light the wood fire,
clean the boards, pour water down the chemical toilets, scrub the
floors, and ensure that the place was ready for the school day. To
many faculty members, this sounds like the ideal presidential profile!

Leggett went on to high school in Orangeville, where his father
had a couple of small businesses – an autobody shop and a bowl-
ing alley. As he readily admits, there was not a lot to indicate that
he would one day be one of Canada's foremost academic leaders:
"I was a very good athlete and a very poor student. I didn't lack
intelligence, I guess, but I certainly lacked academic interest. So, I
was the master of the absolute minimal effort all the way through.
I never failed anything but seldom passed anything with more than
five marks to spare."

He still remembers a pivotal conversation he had with his father
when he was in about grade 12, about the only advice about his
future he ever received from him: "He said that there were two ways
to make a living – with your head and with your hands. He had
made his living with his hands and strongly suggested that I should
make mine with my head." The impact of these words, however, was
less than immediate. Bill's grade 13 performance was a superb piece

of minimal effort; he passed all nine requisite provincial courses with a 53 per cent overall average. The school principal, who had taken a particular interest in him, persuaded Bill to retake grade 13, imposing the requirement that if Bill's grade in any course dropped below 75, he must immediately cease his passionate involvement in team sports. The academic results were much better, and finally heeding his father's advice, he decided to embark on a career in teaching.

He ended up at Waterloo College (later Wilfrid Laurier University) to pursue a general BA in the humanities. Realizing how close he had come to not making it, he applied himself more rigorously and did well academically. The most transforming influence was a biology course he took as an elective in third year. The professor, Geoffrey Power, inspired him to pursue the subject as his life's work, starting as an MSc student at the University of Waterloo and subsequently doing his doctorate at McGill, with a view to eventually getting a teaching position there. Dr Leggett went on to become a prominent researcher, with over 170 peer-reviewed publications in the areas of fish ecology and fisheries oceanography, and one of the most distinguished academics to serve as president of any Canadian university.

The trademarks of his principalship at Queen's were formed by his early academic experiences and his forthright personality. He arrived at McGill for his doctoral program in biology only to discover a department in shambles. The result was a major housecleaning that denied tenure to less-productive faculty and brought on exciting new researchers. Leggett thrived in this challenging atmosphere, increasingly giving rein to his love of research and teaching with no thought whatsoever of doing administrative work. In a pattern that was to repeat itself several times, he at first refused and then reluctantly accepted the overtures of his colleagues to put his name forward for departmental chair when the position became vacant. Perhaps a bit to his surprise, once appointed, he truly enjoyed the position: "What I found was that, as department head, you could do small things for people who were making a difference that really made a difference to them. They weren't big things, but the results and the positive feedback were often quite immediate and very rewarding."

Like Rob Prichard at Toronto, he quickly established a style and priorities that were to be later replicated on a larger scale in his subsequent positions. He refused to sign any NSERC (Natural Sciences and Engineering Research Council of Canada) applications from faculty until he had vetted them personally. The already-established upward trajectory of the department and his insistence on an objective self-analysis of the quality and relevance of all teaching programs soon led to dramatic improvements in the department's reputation for quality, productivity, and research funding.

Not surprisingly, when David Johnston arrived as McGill's new principal and was searching for a dean of science, Bill Leggett was a leading candidate, notwithstanding his personal conviction that he needed to go back to the classroom and lab. He finally agreed to do the job but only after negotiating a day-a-week in his lab and a year's delay so that he could more firmly establish his research program.

At McGill, Leggett did much to clean up the mathematics department, refusing to accept an "old boys' external review" and submitting faculty CVs to his own hand-picked group of external experts. The results were immediate and demonstrable. The quality of graduate students, scholarships, and research productivity all went up, and Dean Leggett enjoyed strong support for his leadership among faculty who shared his aspirations for enhanced excellence. Again, it was hardly surprising that David Johnston came after him a second time when the position of vice-principal, academic, came up. The results were similar. Dr Leggett performed the role for five years, characteristically taking on the faculty of dentistry and coming close to shutting it down, but in the end helping to transform it into a much more effective academic unit.

At the end of his first term, he was determined to go back to the ranks. He did not envision himself succeeding Principal Johnston even though many tried to persuade him to do so. In a candid conversation with his close confidante and wife, Claire, he noted, almost in jest, that he would consider the top job in only one Canadian university and that was Queen's, believing, as he did, that this opportunity would never come because the university had been grooming its own internal leadership.

But it did come. After refusing its initial overtures, Leggett was eventually persuaded that Queen's genuinely wanted a principal who could bring fresh approaches to the institution, and accepted the position in 1994, once again with the provision that he could spend a day a week in his lab. He went on to become an outstanding principal. During his ten years at the helm, the university improved significantly in the four major areas he set out to address. First, Queen's became Canada's leading university in giving students international experience. Second, the quality of faculty scholarship improved markedly, as he again challenged the old boys' network, insisting that every position, from assistant professor to vice-president, be an open competition. Third, research productivity doubled. And fourth, the campus was transformed by an unprecedented number of capital renewal and expansion projects. It is a continuing source of pride to him that no mortgages were added for any of these projects, all of which were delivered on time and within budgets. He led the largest fundraising program in the institution's history.

His proudest achievement was the university's enhanced international outreach and the opportunities that created for his students. His cites as his biggest disappointment the unionization of the faculty, believing that academic unions are totally inconsistent with the idea of an environment of free inquiry and individual accomplishment, which he sees as the cornerstones of academia.

As much as any Canadian university president of the past two decades, Bill Leggett was dedicated to making a real difference in the quality of teaching and research at the institution he led. His other legacy is a host of graduate students, all of whom are working in their discipline and more than half of whom have appointments in leading universities across North America and in Europe.

DAVID MARSHALL
President, Nipissing University, 1990–2003
President, Mount Royal University, 2003–2011
Even though teaching was strongly represented in his family, Dave Marshall never expected to be an academic. His father was a farmer near Orangeville, Ontario, who went back to high school and then on to university in his thirties to become a professor. His mother was a teacher and his two brothers are outstanding researchers at Guelph and Trent respectively. Nevertheless, teaching was not his first choice. After getting his BSc in chemistry at Western in 1970, he looked to the private sector. "I never intended to go into teaching. My first choice job was to be a lab technician at Labatt's Brewery where I was told you got to drink as much beer as you want. I was about the 499th candidate for that so I didn't get it. I got a job and a letter of permission to teach in Collingwood, Ontario, because they needed a basketball coach. That's how it all got started."

Marshall believes to this day, and often advises young people, that if you just go with the flow, doing what you like, everything will fall into place and that's pretty much how it has been throughout his career. He was not qualified to be a teacher and had to do the Northern Ontario teacher training program (two summers at Lakehead University) in order to teach music with his chemistry degree. He taught in Sault Ste Marie for two years and then did his MEd in secondary education (educational technology) at the University of Alberta in 1973–74.

After stints on Baffin Island, where he worked as a regional educational consultant and technologist, and in St Lucia, where he directed a CIDA project to establish the curriculum branch of the Ministry of Education, he wasn't sure what to do next, so he pursued his doctorate in educational administration at the University of Alberta. He had a number of job offers subsequent to this but decided to try his hand at being a professor, working first as an assistant and later as an associate at the University of Manitoba between 1980 and 1985. He loved the academic life, especially the teaching, but wasn't sure he had the stick-to-it-iveness to be a top researcher.

He was briefly lured into the Manitoba government to start a new regional services branch in the Department of Education but decided that government work was not his calling: "I did that for a couple of years and realized that I would never survive as a bureaucrat. I have too much of an ADHD personality. I just could not do it – to *be* the bureaucracy was just not my style."

Then, in 1985, the opportunity came up to be dean of education at Nipissing University College in North Bay, Ontario. Dave applied, with only three years as a professor and two in government behind him, but he got the job at the age of thirty-six. He really enjoyed the post and found that he was good at it, especially in "creating the setting where others could be great academics." At the time, Nipissing was an affiliate of Laurentian University and not very well known, as Marshall found out when he put his name forward for dean of education at Western and did not even make the short list. When the incumbent Nipissing president completed his term, Marshall was an obvious internal candidate, given that the institution was best known for its faculty of education, and he was appointed to the position in the summer of 1990.

His immediate challenge was to attain full university status for Nipissing, which meant getting independence from Laurentian. There had always been a rivalry between North Bay and Sudbury, and the issue was fairly loaded, politically. However, Marshall threw himself into the task, lobbying not only government but also the presidents of the established universities, who tended to resist the idea of new players around the cou table. It was also important to get the support of Laurentian, especially given that Sudbury had three members in the Rae government, two of whom were cabinet ministers. As president of Laurentian at the time, I was impressed with his arguments and fully supported the case before the provincial government.

Marshall's single-minded determination paid off when Nipissing was given independent university status in 1992. He then set about to let the rest of the country know about Nipissing University and the quality of the graduates it was producing. He confesses that he did not know very much about being a university president at the outset, but threw himself passionately into the job and learned a lot from his colleagues in the process.

Under Marshall's leadership, Nipissing came to be recognized for the high quality of its undergraduate student experience, with its smaller classes and emphasis on teaching and learning. While it did not perform particularly well on the annual *Maclean's* rankings, it stood at the top of surveys that emphasized student perceptions, notably those conducted by the *Globe and Mail* and the National Survey of Student Engagement (NSSE).

When Mount Royal College in Alberta was looking for a president who could take it to university status, Dave Marshall was an obvious candidate, and in 2003 he assumed the post. By 2010, he had been in the position for seven years and Mount Royal had achieved full university status under new Alberta legislation that provides for uniquely undergraduate universities (and which Marshall played a key role in bringing about).

Dave Marshall has developed a national reputation for having built two primarily undergraduate universities almost from scratch. Yet, when he is asked what he is proudest of, his answer may surprise some: "It may sound hokey, but I am proudest of the accomplishments of faculty. I'm still happiest when I see faculty members beam about the work they are doing. I started a process at Nipissing and have continued it here whereby two faculty members present their research at each board meeting. I think I'm most proud of creating an environment where faculty and students can excel."

In an age when many presidents are challenged by faculty unionization, Dave is also proud of his achievements in faculty relations at both institutions, having learned about mutual-gains bargaining while at Nipissing and bringing that approach to Mount Royal.

His major disappointment has come with hindsight, as he has increasingly grown to appreciate the value of developing a strongly differentiated undergraduate institution.

> I think I missed the opportunity at Nipissing to change the reward structure to ensure that it was differentiated in a purposeful way rather than by default. It is different right now by size and geography. It's smoking everybody on various student satisfaction studies and I'm delighted. So, clearly it's doing what we wanted it to do. But I worry about the enduring nature of that without the conditions in place to ensure it endures, which is primarily in a combination of programming and reward structures for faculty.

David Marshall almost became president of the University of New Brunswick in 2002. He would have been an excellent choice, but Canadian higher education may be the ultimate beneficiary of his failure to get that appointment. Through his writings, his active participation on a number of committees and commissions, his strong advocacy in Alberta and elsewhere, and especially his demonstrated success at Mount Royal, Dr Marshall has made and is making invaluable contributions to more diversified and more strongly learner-centred university undergraduate education in Canada.

BONNIE PATTERSON
President, Trent University, 1998–2009

There were not a lot of early indications that Bonnie Patterson would become a university president. In fact, she left her working-class family at the early age of fifteen to board with a high school teacher's family and enrolled in a practical five-year business and commerce program. She went to Western and got married after a first year of less than distinguished marks and then took the next year and a half off to tour the world.

Travelling changed the way Patterson viewed her education, and she returned to Western with enthusiasm and dedication, quickly evolving from being an indifferent scholar to being one who made the dean's honour roll. After a social science degree, primarily in political science, she embarked on her master's degree part-time and was quickly identified by a couple of her mentors as an ideal candidate to join the faculty.

She started out as a maternity-leave replacement in the Ivey School of Business and continued as a faculty member there for five years, also managing what was then called the Indian Business and Small Business Consulting Services, which gave her some exposure to the world of management. Her success at teaching originally pointed her towards teachers' college, but her faculty colleagues persuaded her to continue her graduate work. She completed a master's degree in library sciences, focusing on information sciences, database development, and logic, the first relational databases. From there, she developed a new administrative studies program at Western, one more oriented towards the social sciences than the other business programs were.

A colleague at Ryerson (with whom she was writing a book on university and college training in administration) persuaded Bonnie to apply for a position there, and Ryerson became her home for the next fifteen years. She started as a faculty member but, with the strong encouragement of president Brian Segal, became a department head the next year, a position she held for five years, following which she went to the president's office as chief of staff for the new president, Terry Grier. Her Ryerson career culminated in her appointment as dean of the business faculty, in which capacity she served for another five years.

Bonnie Patterson had an interest in administration from an early age. Her people skills, together with her early practical education and her strong interest in consensus development as a model of leadership, made her an effective leader with a growing reputation outside her own institution. When Peter George resigned as president of cou to take the reins at McMaster, Bonnie was chosen as his successor.

All this experience made her an ideal candidate for a presidency, but her first real exposure to the position as chief of staff to the president of Ryerson did not instantly orient her towards such a career: "When I worked so closely with Terry Grier and saw how long and hard he worked seven days and seven nights a week, I thought 'who would want that job?!' And that continued for quite a long time."

The cou position afforded her opportunities to interact with government and exposed her to a great variety of institutions and people. While she didn't initially see this experience as preparation for a presidency, it did show her the value of relationship management. She came to see both the strengths and the frailties of the individual Ontario executive heads and increasingly realized that she was well positioned and prepared to consider a presidency herself.

Patterson was appointed president of Trent in 1998, after a period of some turmoil in the institution and with the good counsel of former Queen's principal David Smith, who had been interim president for the year before her arrival. Her challenges were significant, but she had the benefit of an explicit mandate from the board and a report on Trent's challenges and opportunities, prepared the year before by Harry Arthurs and Joyce Lorimer. So, it was pretty clear what she needed to do, although she did not realize at the outset how challenging it would be to carry out her mandate with an almost completely new senior team.

When asked to point to her most important achievements, Professor Patterson started with something less tangible – a much enhanced internal confidence in the university among its faculty and staff. She was seen as having allowed "Trent to dream again." She gave the university a sense of purpose; she helped it take responsibility for its own future rather than see itself as a victim.

There were important practical achievements as well – new partnerships with the city and county in the development of an innovation cluster, a new spirit of philanthropy, and a major broadening of the institution's mandate beyond the liberal arts, notably with the opening of new professional schools of education, nursing, and forensic sciences.

> Suddenly, there was more than a deconstructionist voice at senate (which had previously ruled the place). Deconstructionism is one thing, but building and implementing is another, and professional programs tend to be more pragmatic – they like closure and like to "get on with it." It created a new balance and a new conversation at Trent. I feel very proud of that – I think it set the institution up to accept an evolving culture instead of just its historical one.

Patterson's leadership can be seen, in this way, as transformational, and it is not surprising that she faced considerable opposition from those dedicated to the earlier Trent. This was particularly evident

in faculty and student resistance to her efforts to close the downtown colleges, which had been a hallmark of the original institution.
She felt their closure was an essential step in getting Trent back to
a healthy financial position and out of the unsustainable one she
had inherited.

Her major disappointment was with the way the whole debate
about "corporatization" heated up over the decade. She believes that
this debate was fuelled not only by what she did but also by her having had a business school background:

We had a very lively activist group in humanities and the social
sciences and I think the rhetoric became a little high at times.
The college issue was what they called their first clear example of
corporatization on their campus.

At the end of the day, it was about change and people's ability
to accept it. Did we do too much too quickly? Maybe, but my
own view is that, without it, we would not have been financially
sound, and so we won some things over that process. The angst
that exists within a small number of folks who are still there is
probably the unfortunate outcome of that period of change.

She had scarcely completed her two terms as president of Trent
when another opportunity came along, before she'd even had time
to think about what to do next. When COU president Paul Genest was appointed deputy minister of intergovernmental affairs and
associate secretary of the Cabinet of Ontario in August 2009, Patterson was an obvious selection as his temporary replacement until
a formal search could be concluded. The result of the latter was also
not a surprise – she was the best candidate and is now serving a
three-year term in the position. After that, it would not be surprising
to see Bonnie Patterson in another leadership position in Canadian
post-secondary education.

MARTHA PIPER
President, The University of British Columbia, 1997–2006
Martha Piper may have grown up in a small industrial steel town
(Lorain, Ohio), but she always knew that she would go to university.
Both of her parents and even her grandfather were university gradu-
ates, a rarity in those surroundings. Fewer than 10 per cent of her
graduating class of 250 went on to university.

She worked hard at school and wanted to be a doctor, not a nurse as would have been the expectation for women in health care at that time. After her strict father discouraged her aspirations, she settled on physical therapy. Coincidentally, there was a strong program in the field at Michigan, the university it was assumed she would attend, given that the above three relatives were alumni and the strong affiliations that the institution has always engendered.

Her next few moves were all part of following her husband to different communities. She married Bill Piper, a clinical psychologist who was doing his PhD at the University of Connecticut, and so she worked as a therapist there and did her master's degree in child development. When he was then accepted into the medical services corps, they moved to Washington, DC, where he interned at Bethseda Naval Hospital. She worked as a therapist at Georgetown University Hospital and had a child.

Her husband was then recruited to the psychology department at McGill University, and Piper found work at Hôpital Sainte-Justine in Montreal. In her own words, "I was still bending bones and having babies but it just wasn't enough for me." So, she went on to do her PhD at McGill and was ready for a life as a researcher when she was approached to be director of the school of physical and occupational therapy.

Ironically, I had tried to get a job there when we first came to Montreal, and they would have nothing to do with me. I was not British trained, I was American and I didn't have the pedigree to get a job there. I went and continued my PhD and was then appointed director to tremendous chagrin at the school. I was only thirty-two or thirty-three years old, a brand new PhD with no academic experience, and I was coming in to run the school, which was a mess. That probably seasoned me more than anything.

Piper still saw herself as a scholar and worked very hard at research, but she was also getting on the radar screen for administration. Again, Bill was being pursued, this time by the University of Alberta, and coincidentally there was an opening there for dean of rehabilitation medicine. Independent of his appointment, she applied and was successful. Again, she worked hard to revamp the faculty, finding Alberta a land of milk and honey after the tough financial times in Quebec, but was still intent on dropping administrative work and focusing on her academic career. It never happened.

Alberta president Paul Davenport first approached her about applying for provost, which she ultimately declined to do, but he did persuade her to stand for vice-president, research, and she was also encouraged in this direction by the head of the chairs of academic departments even though she was "just" a physical therapist. "I went up against a very well regarded biochemist, but Paul went to the wall for me. I will always owe my career to him." Paul Davenport went to Western shortly thereafter, and Dr Piper was left with huge responsibilities, made more complex with a new president and an acting vice-president, academic. It was the first time that she realized that she might consider a university presidency, although she did not accept any of the initial overtures from search consultants and still intended to return to the academic ranks.

Then, the UBC opportunity came along and she considered it seriously. She credits former Alberta cabinet minister and University of Alberta board member Don Mazinkowski for the pivotal advice that persuaded her to go for it. He told her: "Ninety-five per cent of the time, you get opportunities that will probably come again. If you're lucky, once or maybe twice in your life, you will get an opportunity that will never come again. This is not about being a president, it's about being president of the University of British Columbia. That is a chance that will never come again."

Dr Piper knew a lot about UBC because she had studied it carefully while vice-president, research, at Alberta. It was the competitor and the benchmark, but nothing could have prepared her for her first days on the job in 1997. The university hosted the APEC (Asia-Pacific Economic Cooperation) summit only two months after her installation, and it became an international story when the RCMP used pepper spray against protesters at the Museum of Anthropology. The new president took a hard line with protesters, and there were calls for her resignation from some quarters. "That APEC really tested me very early. I often looked back on those events and thought – after that, I could do anything!"

Piper went on to spend nine very high profile years at UBC, not only raising the stature and reputation of the university but also playing a prominent role in persuading politicians to give much more support to university research across Canada. The goals of profile raising and research funding were critical to her coming to

UBC. She saw UBC as a strong university but not nearly well enough known, nationally or internationally, and she strove to build on the legacy of her predecessor, David Strangway, in both of those areas. In the process, she considered it important to raise the profiles of Canada's western universities in general: "I'm always struck, having lived here [Vancouver] for quite a while, how ignorant people in Toronto are about the West. They give lip service to it. I'm not a negative westerner but ... the power is going to shift in the next decade or so, there's no question in my mind."

Two other areas of success stand out for Piper: the building of international linkages with prominent universities around the world and the vision of the university she introduced to the campus, putting students at the centre and preparing them to be "exceptional global citizens for a civil and sustainable society."

She had her disappointments, as well. Perhaps her biggest regret is that she and others were not able to build on the momentum she had had so much to do with starting towards increasing government support for the humanities. Her fall 2002 Killam Annual Lecture, "Building a Civil Society: A New Role for the Human Sciences," was extremely well received across the country, but she was ultimately disappointed in the aftermath.

> After I gave the Killam address, I thought we had an incredible opportunity but we were our own worst enemies. Some of my biggest critics were humanists worried about selling our souls, and so SSHRC [Social Sciences and Humanities Research Council of Canada] launched a massive consultation process that went nowhere. Had we seized the day, I believe that the Liberal government, with Eddie Goldenberg, Jean Chrétien, and Chaviva Husak in their respective roles, would have moved that as their last piece and we would be in a much different situation today.

Notwithstanding this frustration, Martha Piper is seen by her colleagues not only as a national leader in the promotion of university research but also as a successful champion of the humanities and the social sciences at a time when politicians were often sceptical and much more enamoured with science and technology.

Perhaps the best indication of Dr Piper's reputation in academic circles across the country was the reception she received from her fellow executive heads, an audience not easily moved to demonstrable response. As the keynote speaker at the AUCC meetings in Windsor in the spring of 2008, she received a suitable tribute to her effectiveness on the national level – a standing ovation.

J. ROBERT S. PRICHARD
President, The University of Toronto, 1990–2000

Perhaps more than any of his colleagues, Rob Prichard was born to lead his institution. His family came to Canada from Britain when he was a boy, and his father took up postings at the Hospital for Sick Children and the faculty of medicine at the University of Toronto. As already noted, he grew up in and around the U of T.

Rob Prichard was a good but not outstanding student, especially compared to his sisters, both of whom are university professors. He studied engineering at Swarthmore College near Philadelphia but soon moved into economics, art history, and political science. These were activist days and he was very involved in the politics of civil rights and the Vietnam War.

A Swarthmore professor suggested that he take advantage of a new program at the University of Chicago. Its academically oriented business school offered a summer semester to a student from a liberal arts college who wanted subsequently to do an MBA. The idea was to attend the summer session, return to complete the senior year at the home university, and then be in a position to go back to Chicago with a semester's credit for an MBA. However, Prichard made such an impression that he was asked to stay at Chicago and do the MBA in finance without returning to Swarthmore. He took an accelerated program and completed his degree at the age of twenty-two, only a couple of months later than he would have received his BA.

Prichard wanted to combine the business degree with law, but first he travelled the world, living and working in Hong Kong and China. He came back to the University of Toronto to do his law degree and quickly discovered that this was where his real talents lay. He was leading the class. Given the law school's tradition of inviting the top student to join the faculty and its need for someone with a background in economics, he was offered a faculty position after completing his degree and, after graduate school, a type of futures contract. "It had never crossed my mind to do it. I was going to go into practice, learn to be a good lawyer for a few years, and then decide on a career, whether in government or business or law."

With his unique background, Prichard went to the Yale Law School to study under the eminent Guido Calebresi, founder of the new combined field of law and economics. He then returned to U of T's faculty of law and was soon asked to work with noted scholar Michael Trebilcock to build a law and economics program to world-class standards. This they proceeded to do, which gave the young scholar the opportunity both to learn and to demonstrate skills that were later to serve him well as dean and then president. He thrived under Trebilcock and before long was invited to teach law and economics at Yale and then Harvard. "I got tenure and taught at the two best law schools in the world and got a reputation as a person who could make things happen administratively. A law school is a tiny little place, thirty faculty, fifteen staff or so, but in that little context, we got going. And because it was interdisciplinary, it connected me with the business school, the economics department, and other parts of the university."

Like Bill Leggett, Prichard sees serendipity in some of the opportunities he had in his career. In 1983, U of T law dean Frank Iacobucci was appointed by interim president David Strangway to be provost, leaving a vacancy in the deanship. Everyone's first choice for dean, Michael Trebilcock, made it clear that he had no interest in the position, and attention turned to his protégé. Rob Prichard was thirty-three years old and only an associate professor who had spent the last two years away from the institution.

He jumped into the deanship with confidence and enthusiasm. To this day, he sees his stints as chair and dean as microcosms of both the challenges he faced and the achievements he realized later as president – curriculum reform, better hiring, building the library, fundraising, and developing stronger relationships with alumni and the broader community. Thus, a young and dynamic Rob Prichard assumed the reins of Canada's largest university in September 1990 and quickly set about making a huge difference, building on the vision of his immediate predecessor, George Connell, to make the University of Toronto Canada's strongest performing entry in the world of public research universities and to organize its affairs around that principle.

While perhaps best known publicly for his success as a fundraiser and promoter of the university, Professor Prichard has a different view of his most important achievement. The University of Toronto had been perceived in many different ways over the years – as a research university, public university, metropolitan university, city university, multi-campus university, oversized university – and he set out to change that.

> My greatest pride was beginning to articulate the university in a single mission. We systematically went about changing everything in the direction of being a more research-intensive university. We marched through every part of the university doing that ... There was virtually no part of U of T that was not touched academically between 1990 and 2000 to make it more in accord with the overall vision.

He cites many examples, including the elimination of first-entry degree programs in a number of fields (forestry, occupational health, physiotherapy, nursing, and pharmacy), the integration of OISE into the University of Toronto (a controversial decision at the time that has since been strongly vindicated), and the systematic strengthening of weaker faculties such as the business school, none of which were achieved without difficulty.

For Prichard, the fundraising success was a natural product of this integrity of vision and action, not something separate from it. "Sure, I'm proud that we raised the money, but people think we raised the money because I'm a good fundraiser. I don't think I ever spent more than 5 per cent of my time on fundraising. I hired a superb fundraiser in Jon Delandria and supported him to build a fabulous group of professionals to raise money for the U of T."

Another achievement in which he takes special pride is Toronto's leadership in the field of student financial assistance, a development associated with Prichard's advocacy for higher tuition fees. Toronto was the first to put in a financial aid guarantee for undergraduates and then for graduate students, which demonstrated its commitment to accessibility and countered accusations of elitism.

Even Rob Prichard, one of the most consistently positive and enthusiastic leaders one could ever meet, had his disappointments. He candidly admitted that he found the sheer scope of the position overwhelming at the outset, and believes that he tried to do too much himself in his first year or two. He wondered aloud if he did enough to defend the University of Toronto's position in the province in those early days, although the university's subsequent performance in most areas of funding, provincial and federal, would prove his approach fruitful.

He deeply regrets having been unable, with his colleagues, to persuade governments to embrace its universities as other governments have done in other jurisdictions, such as California, but again, this disappointment is tempered by the changes he has seen in academic competitions, which today are much more driven by objective measures of quality than they were a decade earlier. A very tangible indication of this is that Toronto has been awarded more than 260 of the country's 1,800 Canada Research Chairs distributed to date.

ROSEANN RUNTE
President, Université Ste Anne, 1983–1988
President, Victoria University, The University of Toronto, 1994–2001
President, Old Dominion University, 2001–2008
President, Carleton University, 2008 to present
If her 1988–94 leadership of Glendon, a college of York University, is included, Roseann Runte is Canada's longest-serving president in terms of consecutive years of leadership, and she has only recently started her tenure at Carleton.

Roseann's mother was a teacher and her father a business person, so she sees academic administration as the perfect balance between the two vocations. However, while she had an early interest in administration, her ascendency to her first presidency at Université Ste-Anne was slightly unusual, with comical elements that would make a superb movie.

Her route to academia was through languages, perhaps because of a grandfather who spoke seven. An American, she was educated at the State University of New York (SUNY) at New Paltz (BA) and the University of Kansas (MA and PhD). She originally expected to major in mathematics but chose French when encouraged by faculty members at SUNY. She has believed in the power of people to influence others positively ever since.

Runte came to Canada in 1971 to be a lecturer in adult studies at Saint Mary's University in Halifax; a year later she joined the French department at Dalhousie in the same city. Her subsequent achievements, both academic and administrative, are many and impressive. She is a renowned creative writer, a champion of bilingualism, and an internationalist who was the first woman to be named president of the Canadian Commission for UNESCO. What is striking about her career, other than its long list of achievements, is her dedication to self-improvement.

This started when she began teaching in the university and decided to take graduate courses in education. With the express purpose of learning more about academic administration, she took courses in curriculum design, the history of higher education, educational finance and financial administration, and related courses in the law. She also took courses in computing that she felt would prepare her for future learning environments. I asked her if these were intellectual interests or a more systematic way of preparing herself for leadership positions. She answered, "There was a survey of women academic administrators who all said they didn't intend to go into administration but did when someone asked them to do so. I was the exception. From the beginning, I looked at the administration of higher education and thought to myself, there may be some ways to make a positive contribution." So, her preparation was focused and deliberate, a pattern that has continued throughout her career.

Soon after arriving at Dalhousie in 1972, Roseann was recruited by the faculty union to be on the bargaining team. She became very disillusioned when the team's priority, equal pay for women, of which she had been the key proponent, was sacrificed early on at the table because the union's leaders were concerned that the 600 male faculty members wouldn't favour sticking to a contract priority that would only affect the few women professors. So, when offered the opportunity to be assistant dean of arts and sciences, she accepted, believing that she could make more of a difference from the administrative side.

Not long afterwards, her name was put forward for the presidency of tiny Ste-Anne University in Nova Scotia. As an American, a woman, and an anglophone, she did not expect to be seriously considered, but she went for the interview anyway. When she had not heard anything back after three months, she logically assumed she would not get the position. One can imagine the shock she felt when she opened the local newspaper one day to read a front-page story about the new president of Université Ste-Anne – Dr Roseann Runte! She had not been contacted, and her contract, of course, hadn't been negotiated, but she accepted the position. The challenges had only just begun.

Her appointment was controversial. The current head of the Eur-
idiste fathers said in the paper that the founding father of Ste-Anne
would turn in his grave while the grass became brown because a
woman had been appointed president.

One of Runte's earliest initiatives was her attempt to make students and their families feel welcome on move-in day. When a father
responded by trying to get her to carry a small refrigerator up the
stairs to his daughter's room, she thought the plan needed reassess-
ment. She hit on the idea of handing out her prized butter cookies
instead. If she carried a cookie jar around, she could not as easily be
asked to carry things up the stairs. The practice proved a wonderful
way for students and families to meet their university president and
to see her as a warm and unpretentious leader on campus. It was so
successful that she has done this in every job since.

Then came the annual alumni-administration hockey game. The
alumni president assumed that this game, a major local event with
thousands of spectators, would be cancelled. How could a woman
be the leader of the administration team? Roseann, with a background in figure skating but no exposure to ice hockey, took it on
as a challenge, and so the game was scheduled as usual. In preparing
for it, she faced the facts that the players were bigger than she, the
sticks could be lethal, and she would probably look bad and might
even get hurt. Instead of cancelling or declaring sickness, both of
which would undermine her authority and credibility as president,
she took a more creative approach. If you can't play the game as
designed, change the game.

So, on game night, she skated out to the opening faceoff, dressed
in a top hat and tails and carrying a large bag. Before the referee
could drop the puck, she had skated over to the rival team's goal-
tender, hauled a bunch of scarves out of the bag, and wrapped them
around him and the net so that he was all tied up. In response to
this, the referee gave her a fifteen-minute penalty, which pleased her
because it meant she could sit on the bench for a while. After serving the penalty, she skated to the faceoff circle and took off her hat,
which happened to contain a neighbour's pet rabbit. The creature
jumped out and leapt all over the ice while the players made futile
efforts to catch it, much to the delight of the fans in attendance.

As with the cookies and the refrigerator, she had taken a difficult situation and turned it around. She often recounts this story to
women's groups, emphasizing that you don't have to accept what is

expected, that there is a solution to every problem and that there is going to be a better tomorrow. The message is strong and effective – and one that lies at the heart of what's good about higher education.

When I asked her to identify her proudest achievements during her many years of university leadership, Runte's response reflected her strong personal values: "The really important things are what you do for people – sometimes it's an individual and sometimes a group. They're the things that never get written up in annual reports – it's not the buildings or the new programs but the difference that one can make in people's lives."

She does not admit to any major disappointments over her many years of university leadership.

Roseann Runte epitomizes the "learning" executive, the leader who applies the concept of lifelong learning as much to herself as to the institutions with which she is associated. What better example to faculty, staff, and students could a university president provide?

Universities Included in the Presidential Recruitment Survey*

PROVINCE	UNIVERSITIES (47)
British Columbia	Royal Roads, Simon Fraser, UBC, UNBC, Victoria
Alberta	Alberta, Athabasca, Calgary, Lethbridge
Saskatchewan	Regina, Saskatchewan
Manitoba	Brandon, Manitoba, Winnipeg
Ontario	Brock, Carleton, Guelph, Lakehead, Laurentian, McMaster, Nipissing, Ottawa, Queen's, Ryerson, Toronto, Trent, UOIT, Waterloo, Western Ontario, Wilfrid Laurier, Windsor, York
Quebec	Bishop's, Concordia, McGill
New Brunswick	Mount Allison, St Thomas, UNB
Nova Scotia	Acadia, Cape Breton, Dalhousie, Mount Saint Vincent, Ste-Anne, St Francis Xavier, St Mary's
Prince Edward Island	UPEI
Newfoundland	Memorial

* Most francophone universities were not included because of their practice of electing presidents. See the brief discussion in chapter 1.

Notes

PREFACE

1 Quoted in Duderstadt 2007, xi.
2 Fullan and Scott 2009, 91.
3 Bowen and Shapiro 1998, 86–7.
4 Reported by Paul Davenport (see chapter 13, this volume).
5 Ponder and McCauley 2006, 211.
6 Bargh et al. 2000, 112.

CHAPTER ONE

1 British North America Act, sec. 93, 1867.
2 Clifton 2005, 302.
3 However, the Canadian federal government does have a significant impact on post-secondary education through transfer payments and, increasingly, targeted programs within its areas of jurisdiction. For an excellent review of the federal government's role in post-secondary education, see Fisher, Rubenson, et al. 2006.
4 Bargh et al. 2000, 31.
5 Well depicted by Harman 2005, 169–86.
6 "Canada's Universities Make the Grade Globally," *Globe and Mail*, 16 September 2010, A1.
7 CCL 2007, 22. Nevertheless, at the provincial level in Ontario, at least, there is some recognition of the value of a coordinated approach to quality assurance through the creation in July 2010 of the Ontario Universities Council on Quality Assurance.
8 Ibid., 158–61.
9 Ibid., 9.

10 Announced on the website of the Canadian Council on Learning (http://
www.ccl-cca.ca) by its president, Paul Cappon: "Message from President
and CEO," 8 January 2010.

11 Depending upon the various acts establishing each university, the provincial governments have the power to name at least some of the members
of the board of governors of each institution. This power is perhaps most
prominent in Alberta, where the board chair is named by the government,
but in the overwhelming number of cases, there is very little overt political
interference in university governance beyond the direct funding issues of
operating grants and tuition fee policies. A major recent exception was the
interference of the government of Newfoundland in the presidential selection process at Memorial University, which is discussed briefly in chapter
12.

12 Derived from scrutiny of the websites of these twenty-eight universities
identified from the AUCC list (http://www.aucc.ca).

13 Emery (2005, 2) notes that the percentage of full-time university students
in the twenty- to twenty-four-year-old population (the age group of largest
university attendance) rose from 4 per cent in 1956 to 29 per cent in 2004.

14 Owram, quoted in Emery 2005, 6.

15 AUCC, "The Value of a Degree in Canada's Labour Market," 25 October
2010, 1, http://aucc.ca/publications.

16 The term used by David Foot to describe the children of the baby boomers. See D. Foot, with D. Stoffman, *Boom, Bust and Echo* (Toronto: Foot-
work Consulting, 2004).

17 From respective campus websites.

18 CCL 2007, 54.

19 BNA Act 1867, sec. 91.

20 The winning slogan on Peter Gzowski's national radio program *This
Country in the Morning*, submitted by Ontario teenager Heather Scott
(attested to by R.W. Scott, Heather's father, 18 May 2004, in a letter to
onebag.com, a blog website written by Doug Dyment).

21 Padilla 2005.

22 Bargh et al. 2000, 149.

23 The term "president" is used generically throughout the book to describe
the head of a university in Canada, as it is by far the most common term
employed. McGill, Queen's, and a few others use "principal," while some
of the French and bilingual universities use "recteur."

24 For example, in 1966 student enrolment at McGill was 14,090 (*McGill
News*, Winter 1999–2000, 1), about the size of today's Brock or Windsor,
and smaller than the majority of Ontario universities today (as reported

on the Common University Data Ontario [cudo], the website of the
Council of Ontario Universities, http://www.cou.on.ca).

25 Among the positions and departments that didn't exist in most Canadian
universities in 1960 but that are now commonplace would be vice-
presidents for research, development or advancement, and even government relations; positions and offices for research services, copyright,
technology transfer, human rights, employment equity, ombudsperson,
government relations, and special needs; and positions in and/or much
greater investment in legal services.

26 Cohen and March 1986.

27 Roseann Runte was also principal of Glendon College of York University
from 1988 to 1994. Hence, she has been head of an institution for more
than twenty-five consecutive years, but Glendon is not included in the
chart, as it is not a free-standing university.

28 Jean-Paul Desbiens, *The Impertinences of Brother Anonymous* (Montreal:
Harvest House, 1962).

29 Magnuson, *A Brief History of Quebec Education: From New France to
Parti Québecois* (Montreal: Harvest House, 1980), 114.

30 *University Affairs,* 9 September 2008.

31 Statistics Canada, "University Tuition Fees," *Daily,* 16 September 2010, 1.

32 One should not make too much of this difference, as it seems that everything is relative when it comes to finances. As noted in her profile in
Appendix A, when Martha Piper moved from McGill to Alberta in 1985,
she found it a "land of milk and honey" compared to Quebec and was
astounded to discover how financially beleaguered the Alberta administration felt at the time.

CHAPTER TWO

1 However, it should be recognized that some American universities manage
to get around these laws by holding their searches in neighbouring states
without such laws!

2 All quotes from the eleven presidents have been directly transcribed from
the interviews listed in Appendix A; they are not formally referenced
unless it is unclear who is speaking.

3 Indira Samarasekera, Mamdouh Choukri, George Iwama, Amit Chakra,
Feridun Hamdullahpur, and Alaa S. Abd-El-Aziz are respectively the
presidents of Alberta, York, Northern British Columbia, Western, Waterloo, and Prince Edward Island universities ("The New Face of Canadian
University Presidents," *University Affairs,* 21 November 2010).

4 Usher et al. 2010, 12.

5 Ibid., 41.

6 Algoma University, the nineteenth university in Ontario, is not included, as the survey was conducted before it was formally established as an independent university.

7 The comparable American evidence is that about 80 per cent of presidents come from outside the institution. Kerr and Gade 1986, 19.

8 Friedland 2002, 622.

9 Peter George, long-serving president of McMaster, could also be perceived as an internal candidate, although he came to the position after a stint as president of the Council of Ontario Universities, having been on leave from McMaster where he had held the position of dean of social sciences.

10 Muzzin and Tracz 1981, 335–51.

11 In my experience, it is almost a given that one's relief at leaving behind several daunting issues and/or difficult people in one job is very quickly overtaken by discovering the same number of difficult issues and people waiting in the new institution.

12 In the modern era, Ken Ozmon served Saint Mary's University as president for twenty-one years, while Neil Snider was president of Trinity Western for thirty-two years (long terms are much more common in faith-based institutions). Cyril James led McGill for twenty-two years in the mid-twentieth century, Robert Falconer was president of the University of Toronto for twenty-five years earlier in that century, and the Reverend George Monro Grant led Queen's from 1877 to 1902. The University of Alberta's first president was also its longest serving – Henry Marshall Tory was a twenty-year man. Cecil Charles Jones managed no fewer than thirty-four years at the helm of the UNB. John Forest holds the record at Dalhousie – twenty-six years. Roger Guindon served twenty years as recteur at the University of Ottawa after no fewer than twenty-seven predecessors had covered the previous 116 years. Sir William Peterson managed twenty-four years at McGill.

13 Birnbaum 1992, 73.

14 An examination of 106 presidencies in the forty-seven universities included in the survey suggests that about two-thirds of those who might have been interested in a renewal (i.e., who did not leave for another position, retire, or die) received a second term of office.

15 Unlike the American experience, where presidents are increasingly serving shorter terms of office, the average term has changed very little in recent years in Canada. Muzzin and Tracz's 1981 study, for example, found the average term of office to be about 8 years, not significantly different from

the 8.4 cited here. Muzzin and Tracz 1981, 335–51. A slightly more recent survey found an average US term of seven years, with a decline in the number of longer-term presidents. Kerr and Gade 1986, 30.

16 Government of Ontario, *Public Sector Salary Disclosure Act*, 1996.

17 Janice Tibbetts, Canwest News Service, "University Presidents' Pay Cracks $500,000," *Calgary Herald*, online edition, 4 April 2008, 1.

18 For example, according to the salary disclosures in Ontario for 2009 under the Public Sector Salary Disclosure Act 1996, the average rounded salary for thirty deputy ministers was about $234,000, while the comparable figure for the fifteen university presidents was $364,000, with four receiving well over $400,000; McMaster's Peter George topped the list at $524,000 (three universities were not included because of a transition in their presidencies during the year).

19 For example, the Ontario government froze salaries for two years for all MPPs and non-unionized public sector workers in its 2010 budget and went on to appeal to public sector executives and union leaders for similar voluntary actions (Karen Howlett, "Ontario to Appeal for Public Sector Wage Freezes," *Globe and Mail*, 19 July 2010, http://www.theglobeand-mail.com.

CHAPTER THREE

1 Schein 1999, 19.

2 Bergquist 1992, 3.

3 Duke 2002, 17.

4 Bergquist 1992, 18.

5 Ibid., 44.

6 Gouldner 1957, 281–306.

7 Bergquist 1992.

8 Bergquist and Pawlak 2008.

9 Ibid., 15.

10 Bergquist 1992, 210.

11 Shapiro 2006, 670.

12 Bergquist and Pawlak 2008, 43.

13 My actual title was "Directeur des Services Pédagogiques" (DSP), the term used throughout the CEGEP system. I have used the title of vice-president, academic, here to distinguish the role from the deans of faculties who reported to the DSP.

14 CEGEPs (Collèges d'enseignement général et professional) offered two-year pre-university academic programs and three-year professional programs.

15 Cohen and March 1986, 149.
16 Rosalie S. Abella, *Equality in Employment: A Royal Commission Report* (Ottawa: Royal Commission on Equality in Employment, 1984).
17 *Ontarians with Disabilities Act,* 2001, S.O. 2001, c. 32; *Ontarians with Disabilities Act,* S.O. 2005, c. 11, s. 42.
18 Bergquist 1992, 93.
19 Bergquist and Pawlak 2008, 73.
20 Bergquist 1992, 121.
21 This should not be misinterpreted as advocating the notorious cowardice of the celebrated Duke of Plaza-Toro from Gilbert and Sullivan's *The Gondoliers.*
22 Bergquist 1992, 101.
23 Bergquist and Pawlak 2008, 111.
24 Bergquist 1992, 153.
25 Ibid.
26 Ibid., 155.
27 Bergquist and Pawlak 2008, 147.
28 An early Australian book, to which I contributed a chapter, anticipated this development (Paul, in Kelly and Smith 1987, 139–55).
29 Latchem and Hanna 2001, 33.
30 Bergquist and Pawlak 2008, 185.
31 Ibid., 238–47.
32 Cohen and March 1986, 40.
33 Birnbaum 1988.
34 Ibid., 85.
35 Ibid., 102.
36 Ibid., 123.
37 Ibid., 127.
38 Ibid., 146.
39 Ibid., 168.
40 Cohen and March 1986.
41 Reflecting the huge range of post-secondary institutions in the United States, American writers tend to use the terms "college" and "university" interchangeably, whereas, to date at least, the distinction between the two institutions is much clearer in Canada.
42 Cohen and March 1986, xiv.
43 Ibid., xvii.
44 At the same time, it is far easier to hold leaders of such "simpler" institutions accountable for results because it is much more obvious whether or not they have achieved the specified goals.

45 Cohen and March 1986, 3.
46 Ibid.
47 Cornford 1908.
48 A. Jay and J. Lynn, *Yes Minister*, BBC television series, 1980–84.
49 Senge 2006.
50 Duke 2002, 55.
51 Ibid., 59.
52 Ibid., 33.
53 Crowley 1994.
54 Ibid., 126.
55 Ibid., 127.
56 Burns 1978, 3.
57 Ibid., 4.
58 Ibid.
59 Bass and Riggio 2006, 3.
60 Ibid., 5–7.
61 Crowley 1994, 129.
62 Ibid., 130.
63 Ibid., 132.
64 Crowley 1994, 143.
65 Katz 1977, 72.
66 Schein 1999, 29.
67 One of the considerations many candidates take into account is whom they would be following as president. It is, of course, easier to look better if your predecessor was weak, but it is probably ultimately more satisfying to follow someone who leaves a solid foundation to build upon.
68 Handy 1989, 113.
69 Ibid.
70 Fullan and Scott 2009, 41.

CHAPTER FOUR

1 Quoted in Alfred 2006, ix.
2 Bargh et al. 2000, 24.
3 Ikenberry, in Alfred 2006, x.
4 Ibid., xi.
5 Ibid.
6 Ibid., xiv.
7 Ibid.
8 Ibid.

9 Paul 1990, 179.
10 Ibid.
11 Paul 2003a.
12 This is the central theme of a recent book by Toma (2010) that emphasizes the implementation phase of strategic management.
13 Paul 2008.

CHAPTER FIVE

1 For example, in Alberta, faculty members are not allowed to strike and most salary negotiations are done by final offer selection.
2 Usher 2010, 34.

CHAPTER SIX

1 Clifton 2005, 306.
2 Frequent speculation to the contrary, there is no evidence of an oversupply of university graduates despite the rapid expansion of graduates in recent years. A 2010 study by Trent economist Toben Drewes shows that Ontario university graduates continue to far outpace those with lesser credentials in both access to jobs and earning power. T. Drewes, *Postsecondary Education and the Labour Market in Ontario* (Toronto: Higher Education Quality Council of Ontario, 2010).
3 See, for example, "Attitudes and Perceptions of Higher Education," a report prepared for AUCC by the Strategic Council (March 2007).
4 I did work for a president who only wanted the good news and never wanted to hear the bad. He was thus singularly ineffective in dealing with any of the institution's very real problems and challenges.
5 As a result of an earlier decision to eliminate grade 13, there were, in fact, two terminal high school graduating classes in 2003 (grades 12 and 13), resulting in double-enrolment pressures on the universities for that year in particular but also for the periods immediately preceding and succeeding the double-cohort classes.
6 This is the conclusion of an overview (in the *Chronicle of Higher Education,* 11 October 2009) of Neil Howe and William Strauss's discussion of students called "millennials" in their popular 2000 book *Millenials Rising: The Next Great Generation* (New York: Vintage); the *Chronicle* article suggests that there are all sorts of inconsistencies and contradictions in any such efforts to "label" a particular generation of students.
7 From this perspective, a recent initiative by the AUCC to host a workshop on undergraduate education in the spring of 2011 is welcome news. What

is particularly noteworthy is that participants, exclusively presidents and vice-presidents, academic, are strongly encouraged to bring a student as a third member of their institution's team. See Pierre Zundel and Patrick Deane, "It's Time to Transform Undergraduate Education," *University Affairs*, 11 January 2011, 20.

8 Several decades later, I was exploring the new facilities at the Institute of Education in London and there in front of me was a much older R.S. Peters standing at his desk, looking at a book. I wanted to say something to him but was inexplicably too shy and have regretted ever since missing this chance to tell a professor whom I had never met how much he had influenced my life and career. Ever since, I have always encouraged students to make sure that they not miss any opportunity to tell their best teachers and mentors what their impact has been.

9 Paul, "White Paper on Teaching and Learning," University of Windsor, 2001.

10 Paul, "To Greater Heights," Strategic Plan, 2004–09, University of Windsor, 2003.

11 Brindley and Paul 2004.

12 See, for example, Richard W. Stratton et al., "Faculty Behavior, Grades and Student Evaluations," *Research of Economic Education* 25, no. 1 (1994): 25.

13 Côté and Allahar 2007, 19–21.

14 Ibid., 212.

15 Ibid., chaps 2 and 3.

16 Ibid., 69.

17 See, for example, the vignette "A University President's Nightmare," written by Frank DeSanto and cited in Duderstadt et al. 2002, 3–6.

18 Miner 2010.

19 Ibid., 1.

20 Ibid., 17.

CHAPTER SEVEN

1 For an illuminating portrayal of the "old" and "new" Bishop's, see Donald Fisher, "Social Sciences at Bishop's University: The Professoriate and Changes in Academic Culture, 1950–1985," in Paul Stortz and E. Lisa Panayotidis, eds, *Historical Identities: The Professoriate in Canada* (Toronto: University of Toronto Press, 2006).

2 The acronym CREAD works well for three of the four languages in which it functions – French, Portuguese, and Spanish – but not in English. The organization was founded by francophones in Quebec in association with

Latin American institutions, with its French name being "Consortium des réseaux d'éducation à distance" (Consortium of Distance Education Networks).

3 University of Windsor website (http://www.uwindsor.ca), Common University Data Ontario (CUDO) Report, 2009.

4 University of Windsor website (http://www.uwindsor.ca), International Student Exchange.

5 Extrapolated from data in "Visible Minority Population by Census Metropolitan Areas," Statistics Canada 2006 Census; and 1991 to 2001 censuses, "Proportion of Foreign Born Population, by Census Metropolitan Area."

6 Ibid.

7 Jones 2009.

8 Ibid., 368–9.

CHAPTER EIGHT

1 See, for example, Strategic Council, *Attitudes and Perceptions of Higher Education*, a summary report to the Association of Universities and Colleges of Canada (March 2007).

2 Clark et al. 2009, 11.

3 Ibid., 10.

4 The "colleges" in the title refers to constituent parts of universities that also have AUCC membership. Almost all community colleges in Canada are members, not of AUCC, but of ACCC, the Association of Canadian Community Colleges.

5 The McGuinty government has responded directly by establishing caps on elementary school class sizes and has even issued a "class-size tracker" on its website (http://www.edu.gov.on.ca).

6 Clifton 2005, 306.

7 Dolence and Norris 1995, 86.

8 AUCC, "Funding the Institutional Costs of Research: An International Perspective," May 2009, http://www.aucc.ca.

9 Davenport 2002, 41.

10 Douglass 2010.

11 Ibid., 7.

12 David Johnston (chair), *A Time to Sow: Report from the Task Force on Learning Technologies* (Toronto: Council of Ontario Universities, March 2000).

13 Bates 2000.

14 Daniel 1996.

15 *Securing a Sustainable Future for Higher Education: An Independent Review of Higher Education Funding and Student Finance*, http://www. independent.gov.uk/browne-report.

16 For a thorough and compelling argument in favour of ICRP, see Guillemette 2003.

17 Ibid., 21.

18 This issue is explored further in a critical analysis of the Browne Report in Collini 2010.

19 A case in point is the massive investment in high-demand computer science programs in most provinces in the mid-1990s, an almost unprecedented intervention in a specific academic program area. When the "dot. com" bubble burst later in the decade, many universities were left with far too many professors and too much expensive equipment in an area suddenly in less demand.

20 Tony Bates, "Great Expectations for E-learning in 2010," 30 December 2009, http://www.tonybates.ca.

21 Duderstad et al. 2002, 267.

22 Duderstadt 2000, 236.

CHAPTER NINE

1 Quoted by James Mosley, in Toma 2010, vii.

2 A welcome exception is the recent book by J. Douglas Toma, *Building Organizational Capacity* (2010). The book proposes a strategic management approach designed to help universities take account of their unique organizational and cultural diversity. Well researched, it offers case studies of each of eight key components of strategic management in eight American universities. Its basic premise is that any strategy for change must take account of all eight factors to be successful.

3 I was always slightly amused by the inevitable greeting from someone in the community at one of the June convocations suggesting that I must be looking forward to my two-month summer vacation.

4 Birnbaum 1992, 89–104.

5 Bargh et al. 2000, 37.

6 This can be countered by meeting with people in their offices rather than in the president's domain. Not only does this increase the president's visibility on campus, but it also encourages better informal communications with faculty, staff, and students. Some of the most informative interchanges take place as a result of chance meetings in the halls or while walking across campus.

7 I have long been fascinated by Vilfredo Pareto's famous notion of the importance of the circulation of elites in any leadership group so that there is a predominance of neither lions nor foxes (although one is always tempted to introduce many more animals to the analysis). See Vilfredo Pareto, *The Mind and Society* (New York: Harcourt Brace, 1935.

8 These meetings need not always be formal. A wonderful support vehicle is the uniquely named PAPOOPSI (Presidents and Partners of Ontario Post-Secondary Institutions), which for some twenty years has held a weekend country inn retreat in February. Over great meals, much wine, an extensive list of sporting activities, outdoor and indoor, and much music, PAPOOPSI contributes to friendships, opportunities to express appreciation to the partners, and a better feeling of camaraderie across the Ontario system.

CHAPTER TEN

1 Emery, in Beach et al. 2005, 2.

2 "University Enrolment Continues to Climb," AUCC media release, 28 October 2010.

3 AUCC, "Trends in Higher Education, Financial Backgrounder," June 2008, http://www.aucc.ca.

4 Clark et al. 2009, 57.

5 For a useful outline of the evolution of COU, see Clark 2002.

6 Access to politicians and senior public servants is much easier in the smaller provinces. In Alberta, for instance, I could drop in on deputy or associate deputy ministers unannounced and would frequently see members of the provincial cabinet at various social functions.

7 Taking the wider definition of the Golden Horseshoe, which includes cities like Guelph and Waterloo, more than half of the COU member universities are located within easy driving distance of Queen's Park.

8 http://www.gooduniguide.com.au.

9 Denise Bradley (chair), *Review of Australian Higher Education* (Canberra: Government of Australia, December 2008).

10 "Denise Bradley Appointed to Set Up Tertiary Education Quality and Standards Agency," *Australian,* 9 July 2010.

11 On one visit to the Webster Foundation, I was amused when its president, Norman Webster, leafed quickly through our student brochure to note that, as in most Canadian university publications, almost all of the pictures seemed to have been taken in mid-summer when the fewest students were on campus. It was almost as if it never snowed in Canada!

12 Trachtenberg 2008, 9.

13 See, for example, Dick Dodds, *The First 120 Minutes: A Guide to Crisis Management in Education* (Toronto: Canadian Education Association, 1994).

14 I didn't really believe Marnie Spears, president of Ketchum, our consultants for our fundraising at Laurentian, when she told me that I would enjoy it. She was right and we were ultimately very successful.

CHAPTER ELEVEN

1 *CAUT Bulletin,* 57 (February 2010): 2.

2 See, for example, "Abrupt Exit for Concordia President; Judith Woodsworth," *Gazette* (Montreal), 23 December 2010, A3.

3 For an interesting discussion of the issues involved, see Patrick O'Neill, "Publishing the Unpalatable," in William Bruneau and James L. Turk, *Disciplining Dissent: The Curbing of Free Expression in Academia and the Media,* CAUT Series (Toronto: James Lorimer, 2004).

4 Quoted by Sheila Teitelbaum in "Jihad at 'Gaza U,'" *Jerusalem Report,* 21 October 2002.

5 Stephen Chase, "Ann Coulter's Speech in Ottawa Cancelled," *Globe and Mail,* 23 March 2010.

6 Until very recently, Laurentian was one of the very few Canadian universities without a chancellor, so the president presided over all convocation ceremonies.

7 Johns 1981, 163–70.

8 In Alberta, the senate is a community-based body not to be confused with the more academic senates in the other provinces.

9 Macleod 2008, 279.

10 Former Dalhousie president Howard C. Clark would take exception to this statement, claiming that the assumption that the senate should take account of the university's financial position in its deliberations weakened rather than strengthened its role in academic governance. Clark 2003, 104.

11 Birnbaum 1991.

12 Ibid., 10.

13 Mortimer and Sathre 2007, 30.

14 Hardy 1996.

15 Ibid., 199.

16 Mortimer and Sathre 2007, 73.

17 Hardy 1996, 199.

18 Mortimer and Sathre 2007, iii.

19 Ibid., 123.

CHAPTER TWELVE

1 It is more than slightly ironic that all the publicity around the challenges
   of getting into university at the time of the double cohort greatly raised
   the profile of the importance of going to university and likely contributed
   significantly to the increased participation rates (now over 25 per cent of
   the cohort).
2 Jones and Skolnik 2009, 6.
3 A comprehensive university is defined here as one that offers a broad
   range of both undergraduate and graduate, academic and professional
   programs to a significant student base of at least 12,000 students.
4 This discussion does not include Algoma University in Sault Ste Marie,
   which was converting from being a university college at the time of writing and is significantly smaller than Nipissing.
5 Clark et al. 2009, 56.
6 Steven Chase and Elizabeth Church, "Big Bets and Bidding Wars: Behind
   Canada's Play for Its 19 New Academic Stars," *Globe and Mail*, 19 May
   2010, A1.
7 Clark et al. 2009.
8 Jones and Skolnik 2009.
9 Ibid., 1.
10 Ibid., 28–33.
11 Consideration has been given to the idea of creating one or more "polytechnics" in the GTA by extending the mandates of local colleges. However,
   after examining the issue, Jones and Skolnik conclude that there is not a
   strong case for this. They suggest that the existing institutions can continue to deliver polytechnic education without necessarily being designated
   as polytechnics. Jones and Skolnik 2009, 27.
12 Edmund C. Bovey, *Ontario Universities: Options and Futures,* report of
   the Commission on the Future Development of the Universities of Ontario
   (Toronto: Ministry of Colleges and Universities, 1984).
13 The evidence is already in. Both Mount Royal and Grant MacEwan
   universities performed extremely well in the *Canadian University Report
   2011* (*Globe and Mail*, 24 October 2010), ranking at or very near the top
   in all categories of student ratings.
14 Jones and Skolnik, 5.
15 *Annual Report 2008*, Queen's University, Kingston, ON.
16 Ibid., 103.

17 Cited in Jones and Skolnik 2009, 21.

18 College-University Consortium Council, "The Ontario College-University Degree Completion Accord," 26 March 1999.

19 I remember being particularly motivated in this endeavour by the discovery, when I was president of Laurentian University, that we only gave half credits to Cambrian College students taking one of our first-year macroeconomics courses on their campus, even though the college had exactly the same curriculum, the same instructor, and the same marker as the identical course on our campus!

20 It is difficult to get world figures, but both distance education and online learning are booming worldwide. Tony Bates estimated nine million in distance education and four million online in 2003 (Bates 2005) with explosive growth in both developing and developed countries since. In the United States alone, the Sloane Consortium has reported that participation in online learning has increased by double-digit percentages for each of the past six years (up to 2009). For a complete report, see Allen and Seaman 2010.

21 Clark et al. 2009, 198–9.

22 As vice-president, Learning Services, for the fledgling Athabasca University during the entire decade of the 1980s, I was fortunate to be in on the relatively early days of a worldwide explosion in open and distance learning. Following the lead of the Open University of the United Kingdom (UKOU), Athabasca was established to extend accessibility to university to new groups of students through its tutor-assisted correspondence courses, open admissions, and flexible degree requirements. Print and telephone based at the outset, it has evolved with the rapid development of communications technologies into an online teaching institution – part of a worldwide trend towards the convergence of campus-based and distance learning institutions.

23 Jones and Skolnik 2009, 8.

24 Under the leadership of Maxim Jean-Louis, Contact North has issued a position paper, "Taking Online Learning in Ontario to the Next Level," that is available on its website (http://www.contactnorth.ca). It envisions building on existing institutions and networks to greatly enhance the accessibility and quality of distance delivery across the province.

25 Speech from the Throne, Government of Ontario, 8 March 2010.

26 Council of Ontario Universities, *The Ontario Online Institute: Achieving the Transformation*, August 2010.

27 CFS et al., "Opening Ontario for Whom? A Sectoral Vision for Integrating Online Learning into the Classroom" (December 2010).

28 Rae 2005, 33.
29 Skolnik 2000, 64.
30 Duderstadt 2003, 58.
31 Bergquist and Pawlak 2008.

CHAPTER THIRTEEN

1 Cohen and March 1986, 116.
2 Ibid.
3 As depicted in Stephen Leacock, *Nonsense Novels: Gertrude the Govern-ess* (1911).
4 This number does not include those who left for other appointments, reached the age of mandatory retirement, or died on the job.
5 Developmental psychologist Jane Loevinger. See, for example, J. Loevinger, *Measuring Ego Development* (San Francisco: Jossey-Bass, 1970).
6 Fullan and Scott 2009, 122.
7 Ponder and McCauley 2006, 213.
8 These, in turn, are similar to the conclusions drawn by Francis Lawrence in his compendium of the views of a dozen of his American presidential colleagues. Lawrence 2006, 443–9.
9 The concept is elaborated upon in my 1990 book *Open Learning and Open Management*.
10 As depicted in J. Carlin, *Playing the Enemy: Nelson Mandela and the Game That Made a Nation* (London: Penguin, 2008).

CHAPTER FOURTEEN

1 One of my first experiences at the executive heads table at the Council of Ontario Universities was participating in a *tour de table* whereby each president proposed what his or her institution's maximum intake of first-year students would be for the subsequent fall semester if the government failed to come through with full funding for student numbers above the quota. When everyone had put their respective institutional numbers on the table, the resulting total would have reduced the provincial intake from the previous year by some 3,000 students. The minister did not change the funding formula, a number of presidents caved in on their stand, and first-year enrolments actually went up that year!
2 Bates 2009.
3 Most Canadians view post-secondary education in hierarchical terms. There is some evidence, however, that Europeans place a higher value

on technical and vocational training than Canadians do, and thus don't assume that a university education is the best option for their children.

4 See http://www.ocw.mit.edu.

5 Press release, Athabasca University, 1 February 2011, http://www.athabascau.ca. Immediately after this announcement, three universities (Athabasca, the University of Southern Queensland in Australia, and Otago Polytechnic in New Zealand) announced the creation of an "OER University" to develop whole degree programs available via the Internet for free. See Rebecca Attwood, "'OER university' to cut cost of degree," *Times Higher Education*, 10 February 2011.

6 Paul Wells, "Our Universities Can Be Smarter," *Maclean's*, 28 June 2009.

7 Rob Annan, "G5 University Presidents Propose Academic Rethink," *Researcher Forum*, 29 July 2009, 1–4.

8 Emberley 1996, 277.

9 Shore 1992, 63.

10 Shapiro 2003.

11 Ibid.

12 Emberley 1996, 38.

13 Martha Piper, "Building a Civil Society: A New Role for the Human Sciences," Killam Annual Lecture, Halifax, 2002.

14 Ramsden 1998, 36.

15 I particularly enjoyed working closely with student leaders and have appreciated the number who stay in touch with me. I also worked with an MBA intern in my last year at Windsor – he virtually lived in my office and participated in almost all aspects of my job. I learned as much from the experience as he did.

16 Fullan and Scott 2009, 131.

Bibliography

Alfred, Richard L., et al. 2006. *Managing the Big Picture in Colleges and Universities: From Tactics to Strategy.* Westport, CT: Praeger

Allen, I., and J. Seaman. 2010. *Learning on Demand: Online Education in the United States.* Babson Park, MA: Babson College Survey Research Group

Anderson, Martin. 1992. *Impostors in the Temple: American Intellectuals Are Destroying Our Universities and Cheating Our Students of Their Future.* New York: Simon and Schuster

Badaracco, Joseph L., Jr. 2002. *Leading Quietly: An Unorthodox Guide to Doing the Right Thing.* Boston: Harvard Business School Press

Badaracco, Joseph L., Jr, and Richard R. Ellsworth. 1989. *Leadership and the Quest for Integrity.* Boston: Harvard Business School Press

Balderston, Frederick E. 1995. *Managing Today's University: Strategies for Viability, Change, and Excellence.* 2nd ed. San Francisco: Jossey-Bass

Bargh, Catherine, et al. 2000. *University Leadership and the Chief Executive.* Buckingham, UK: Society for Research in Higher Education and the Open University Press

Bass, Bernard M., and Ronald E. Riggio. 2006. *Transformational Leadership.* 2nd ed. Mahwah, NJ: Lawrence Erlbaum and Associates

Bates, A.W. (Tony). 2000. *Managing Technological Change: Strategies for College and University Leaders.* San Francisco: Jossey-Bass

Bates, Tony. 30 December 2009. "Great Expectations for E-Learning in 2010." http://www.tonybates.ca

Batten, Jack. 1992. *The Class of '75.* Toronto: Macmillan Canada

Beach, Charles M., et al. 2005. *Higher Education in Canada.* Montreal & Kingston: McGill-Queen's University Press

Benjamin, Ernst, et al. 1993. *Governance and Accountability: The Report of the Independent Study Group on University Governance.* Toronto: CAUT (January)

Bergquist, William H. 1992. *The Four Cultures of the Academy: Insights and Strategies for Improving Leadership in Collegiate Organizations.* San Francisco: Jossey-Bass, John Wiley & Sons

Bergquist, William H., and Kenneth, Pawlak. 2008. *Engaging the Six Cultures of the Academy.* Revised and expanded edition of *The Four Cultures of the Academy.* San Francisco: Jossey-Bass, John Wiley & Sons

Bernard, Clark L. 1998. *Reinventing the University: Managing and Financing Institutions of Higher Education.* New York: John Wiley & Sons

Birnbaum, Robert. 1980. *Creative Academic Bargaining: Managing Conflict in the Unionized College and University.* New York: Teachers College, Columbia

– 1988. *How Colleges Work: The Cybernetics of Academic Organization and Leadership.* San Francisco: Jossey-Bass

– , ed. 1991. *Faculty in Governance: The Role of Senates and Joint Committees in Academic Decision Making.* San Francisco: Jossey-Bass

– 1992. *How Academic Leadership Works: Understanding Success and Failure in the College Presidency.* San Francisco: Jossey-Bass

– 1998. *How Colleges Work: The Cybernetics of Academic Organization and Leadership.* San Francisco: Jossey-Bass

– 2000. *Management Fads in Higher Education: Where They Come From, What They Do, Why They Fail.* San Francisco: Jossey-Bass

Bogue, E. Grady. 1994. *Leadership by Design: Strengthening Integrity in Higher Education.* San Francisco: Jossey-Bass

Bornstein, Rita. 1996. "Assuming the Bully Pulpit." In *Leadership Transition: The New College President*, edited by Judith Block McLaughlin, 41–9. San Francisco: Jossey-Bass

Bowen, William G., and Harold Shapiro, eds. 1998. *Universities and Their Leadership.* Princeton, NJ: Princeton University Press

Brindley, Jane E., and Ross H. Paul. 2004. "The Role of Learner Support in Institutional Transformation." In *Learner Support in Open, Distance and Online Learning Environments*, edited by J. Brindley, C. Walti, and O. Zawacki-Richter, 39–50. Oldenburg: Bibliotheks-und Informationssystem der Universität Oldenburg

Bruce, Robert J. 2008. *Acting on Promise: Reflections of a University President.* Philadelphia: Polygot Press

Bruneau, William, and James L. Turk. 2004. *Disciplining Dissent: The Curbing of Free Expression in Academia and the Media.* CAUT Series. Toronto: James Lorimer

Burns, James McGregor. 1978. *Leadership.* New York: Harper and Row

Campbell, John R. 2000. *Dry Rot in the Ivory Tower.* Lanham, MD: University Press of America

Canadian Council on Learning. 2007. *Post-Secondary Education in Canada: Strategies for Success, Report on Learning in Canada, 2007.* Ottawa

Chace, William M. 2006. *100 Semesters.* Princeton: Princeton University Press

Chaffe, Ellen Earle, and William G. Tierney. 1988. *Collegiate Culture and Leadership Strategies.* New York: Macmillan

Clark, Howard C. 2003. *Growth and Governance of Canadian Universities: An Insider's View.* Vancouver: University of British Columbia Press

Clark, Ian. 2002. "Advocacy, Self-management, Advice to Government: The Evolution of the Council of Ontario Universities." In *The University: International Expectations*, edited by F. King Alexander and Kern Alexander. Montreal & Kingston: McGill-Queen's University Press

Clark, I.D., et al. 2009. *Academic Transformation: The Forces Reshaping Higher Education in Ontario.* Queen's Policy Studies Series. Montreal & Kingston: McGill-Queen's University Press

Clifton, Rodney A. 2005. "State and Service Institutions." In *Recent Social Trends in Canada, 1960–2000*, edited by Lance W. Roberts et al. Montreal & Kingston: McGill-Queen's University Press

Cohen, Michael D., and James G. March. 1986. *Leadership and Ambiguity: The American College President.* 2nd ed. Boston: Harvard Business School Press

Collini, Stephan. 2010. "Browne's Gamble." *London Review of Books* 32, no. 21 (4 November 2010): 23–5

Côté, James E., and Anton L. Allahar. 2007. *Ivory Tower Blues: A University System in Crisis.* Toronto: University of Toronto Press

Crowley, Joseph. 1994. *No Equal in the World: An Interpretation of the Academic Presidency.* Reno: University of Nevada Press

Daniel, John S. 1996. *Mega-Universities and Knowledge Media: Technology Strategies for Higher Education.* London: Kogan Page

Davenport, Paul. 2002. "Universities and the Knowledge Economy." In *Renovating the Ivory Tower: Canadian Universities and the Knowledge Economy*, edited by David Laidler, 39–59. Ottawa: C.D. Howe Institute

Doherty-Delorme, Denise, and Erika Shaker, eds. 2000. *Missing Pieces II: An Alternative Guide to Canadian Post-Secondary Education.* Toronto: Canadian Centre for Policy Alternatives

Dolence, M.G., and Norris, D.R. 1995. *Transforming Higher Education: A View for Learning in the 21st Century.* Ann Arbor, MI: Society for College and University Planning

Douglass, John Aubrey. 2010. *Higher Education Budgets and the Global Recession: Tracking Varied National Responses and Their*

Consequences. Research and Occasional Paper Series: CSHE.4.10. Berkeley: University of California – Berkeley, Centre for Studies in Higher Education.

Drucker, Peter F. 1999. *Management Challenges for the 21st Century*. New York: HarperCollins

Duderstadt, James J. 2000. *A University for the 21st Century*. Ann Arbor: University of Michigan Press

– 2007. *The View from the Helm: Leading the American University during an Era of Change*. Ann Arbor: University of Michigan Press

Duderstadt, James. J., et al. 2002. *Higher Education in the Digital Age*. Westport, CT: Praeger

Duderstadt, James J., and Farris W. Woman. 2003. *The Future of the Public University in America: Beyond the Crossroads*. Baltimore: Johns Hopkins University Press

Duke, Chris. 2002. *Managing the Learning University*. Buckingham, UK: Society for Research into Higher Education, Open University

Edersheim, Elizabeth Haas. 2007. *The Definitive Drucker*. New York: McGraw-Hill

Ehrenberg, Ronald G. Ehrenberg, ed. 1997. *The American University: National Treasure or Endangered Species?* Ithaca, NY: Cornell University Press

Emberley, Peter C. 1996. *Zero Tolerance: Hot Button Politics in Canada's Universities*. Toronto: Penguin

Emery, Herb. 2005. "Total and Private Returns to University Education in Canada: 1960 to 2000 and in Comparison to Other Postsecondary Training." In *Higher Education in Canada*, edited by Charles M. Beach et al., 77–112. John Deutsch Institute for the Study of Economic Policy, Queen's University. Montreal & Kingston: McGill-Queen's University Press

Finnie, Ross, et al., eds. 2008. *Who Goes? Who Stays? What Matters? Accessing and Persisting in Post-Secondary Education in Canada*. School of Policy Studies, Queen's University. Montreal & Kingston: McGill-Queen's University Press

Fisher, Donald, Kjell Rubenson, et al. 2006. *Canadian Federal Policy and Postsecondary Education*. Vancouver: Centre for Policy Studies in Higher Education and Training

Fisher, James L. 1994. *Power of the Presidency*. New York: American Council on Education/Macmillan

Fisher, James L., et al. 1988. *The Effective College President*. New York: American Council on Education/Macmillan

Flawn, Peter F. 1990. *A Primer for University Presidents: Managing the Modern University*. Austin: University of Texas Press

Friedland, Martin L. 2002. *The University of Toronto: A History*. Toronto: University of Toronto Press

– 2007. *My Life in Crime and Other Academic Adventures*. Toronto: University of Toronto Press

Fullan, Michael, and Geoff Scott. 2009. *Turnaround Leadership for Higher Education*. San Francisco: Jossey-Bass

Gouldner, Alvin W. 1957. "Cosmopolitans and Locals: Toward an Analysis of Latent Social Roles – I." *Administrative Science Quarterly* 2:281–306

Guillemette, Yvan. 2006. *The Case for Income-Contingent Repayment of Student Loans*. Toronto: C.D. Howe Institute

Handy, Charles. 1989. *The Age of Unreason*. London: Business Books

Hardy, Cynthia. 1996. *The Politics of Collegiality: Retrenchment Strategies in Canadian Universities*. Montreal & Kingston: McGill-Queen's University Press

Harman, Grant. 2005. "Implementing Comprehensive National Higher Educational Reforms: The Australian Reforms of Education Minister John Dawkins, 1987–90." In *Reform and Change in Higher Education: Analysing Policy Implementation*, edited by Ase Gornitza et al., 169–86. Consortium of Higher Education Research Conference. Dordrecht: Springer

Johns, Walter H. 1981. *History of the University of Alberta*. Edmonton: University of Alberta Press

Jones, G. 2009. "Internationalization and Higher Education Policy in Canada: Three Challenges." In *Canada's Universities Go Global*, edited by Roopa Trilokekar et al., 355–69. CAUT Series. Toronto: James Lorimer

Jones, G., and M. Skolnik. 2009. *Degrees of Opportunity: Broadening Student Access by Increasing Institutional Differentiation in Ontario*. Toronto: Higher Education Quality Council of Ontario

Kelly, Mavis, and Peter Smith. 1987. *Distance Education and the Mainstream*. New South Wales: Croom Helm

Keohane, Nannerl O. 2006. *Higher Ground: Ethics and Leadership in the Modern University*. Durham, NC: Duke University Press

Kerr, Clark, and Marian L. Gade. 1986. *The Many Lives of Academic Presidents: Time, Place and Character*. Washington, DC: Association of Governing Boards of Universities and Colleges

Laidler, David, ed. 2002. *Renovating the Ivory Tower: Canadian Universities and the Knowledge Economy*. Policy Study 27, C.D. Howe Institute. Ottawa: Renouf

Latchem, Colin, and Donald E. Hanna, eds. 2001. *Leadership for 21st Century Learning: Global Perspectives from Educational Innovators.* London: Kogan Page

Lawrence, Francis L. 2006. *Views from the Presidency: Leadership in Higher Education.* New Brunswick, NJ: Transaction Publishers

Lenington, Robert L. 1996. *Managing Higher Education as a Business.* Phoenix: American Council on Education and Oryx Press

Lewis, Michael. 1997. *Poisoning the Ivy: The Seven Deadly Sins and Other Vices of Higher Education in America.* Armonk, NY: M.E. Sharpe

McLaughlin, Judith Block. 1996. "Entering the Presidency." In *Leadership Transition: The New College President,* edited by Judith Block McLaughlin, 5–14. San Francisco: Jossey-Bass

Macleod, Rod. 2008. *All True Things: A History of the University of Alberta, 1908–2008.* Edmonton: University of Alberta Press

Magnuson, Roger. 1980. *A Brief History of Quebec Education: From New France to Parti Québécois.* Montreal: Harvest House

Martin, James, and James E. Samels and Associates. 2004. *Presidential Transition in Higher Education: Managing Leadership Change.* Baltimore: Johns Hopkins University Press

Mény, Yves. 2008. President, European University Institute, Florence, Italy. 5th Higher Education Policy Institute (HEPI) annual lecture, delivered at the Royal Society of London on 15 January

Miner, Rick. 2010. *People without Jobs, Jobs without People: Ontario's Labour Market Future.* Toronto: Miner Management Consultants. http://www.minerandminer.ca

Morrill, Richard L. 2007. *Strategic Leadership: Integrating Strategy and Leadership in Colleges and Universities.* Westport, CT: Praeger

Mortimer, Kenneth P., and Colleen O'Brien Sathre. 2007. *The Art and Politics of Academic Governance: Relations among Boards, Presidents and Faculty.* Westport, CT: Praeger

Muzzin, Linda J., and George S. Tracz. 1981. "Characteristics and Careers of Canadian University Presidents." In *Higher Education* 10, no. 3 (May): 335–51

Padilla, Arthur. 2005. *Portraits in Leadership: Six Extraordinary University Presidents.* Westport, CT: Praeger

Patenaude, Richard. 2000. "Administering the Modern University." In *Higher Education in Transition: The Challenges of the New Millennium,* edited by Joseph Losco and Brian L. Fife, 159–76. Westport, CT: Bergin and Garvey

Paul, Ross, 1990. H. *Open Learning and Open Management*. London:
  Kogan Page
– 1996. "Staff Development Needs for Universities: Mainstream and Distance Education." In *Distance Education and the Mainstream*, edited by
  Mavis Kelly and Peter Smith, 139–55. New South Wales: Croom Helm
– 2000. "Digital Technology and University Sovereignty – Compatibility
  or Collision Course?" In *Flexible Learning, the Workplace and HRD:
  Putting Theory to Practice*, edited by V. Jakupec and J. Garrick, 30–46.
  London: Routledge
– 2003a. "The Best of Both Worlds." Strategic Plan, 1999–2004, University of Windsor, Windsor, ON
– 2003b. "Institutional Leadership and the Management of Change." In
  Planning and Management in Distance Education, edited by S.K. Panda,
  75–86. London: Kogan Page
– 2008. "To Greater Heights." Strategic Plan, 2004–2009, University of
  Windsor, Windsor, ON
Paul, R.H., and J.E. Brindley. 2008. "New Technology, New Learners and
  New Challenges: Leading Our Universities in Times of Change." In
  International Handbook of Distance Education, edited by Terry Evans
  et al., 435–52. Bingley, UK: Emerald
Perlman, Baron, et al. 1988. *The Academic Intrapreneur: Strategy, Innova-
  tion, and Management in Higher Education*. New York: Praeger
Pocklington, Tom, and Allan Tupper. 1998. *No Place to Learn: Why
  Universities Aren't Working*. Vancouver: University of British Columbia
  Press, 2002
Ponder, Kathleen M., and Cynthia D. McCauley. 2006. "Leading the
  Unique Character of Academe: What It Takes." In *University Presidents
  as Moral Leaders*, edited by David G. Brown, 209–26. Westport, CT:
  Praeger
Rae, Bob. 2005. *Ontario: A Leader in Learning*. Report and Recom-
  mendations. Toronto: Ministry of Training, Colleges and Universities,
  Government of Ontario
Ramsden, Paul. 1998. *Learning to Lead in Higher Education*. London:
  Routledge
Riesman, David. 1996. "Afterword: Reflections on the College Presidency."
  In *Leadership Transition: The New College President*, edited by Judith
  Block McLaughlin, 85–7. San Francisco: Jossey-Bass
Schein, Edgar H. 1992. *Organizational Culture and Leadership*. 2nd ed.
  San Francisco: Jossey-Bass

– 1999. *The Corporate Culture Survival Guide.* San Francisco: Jossey-Bass

Senge, Peter. 2006. *Fifth Discipline: The Art and Practice of the Learning Organization.* New York: Doubleday

Shapiro, Harold T. 2003. "The Changing Role of University Presidents." Oral presentation in the Conversations with History Series. Host: Harry Kreisler, Institute of International Studies, University of California at Berkeley, 18 March

Shore, Paul. 1992. *The Myth of the University: Ideal and Reality in Higher Education.* Lanham, MD: University Press of America

Skolnik, Michael. 2000. "The Virtual University and the Professoriate." In *The University in Transformation: Global Perspectives on the Future of the University,* edited by Sohail Inayatullah and Jennifer Gidley, 55–68. Westport, CT: Bergin & Garvey

Smith, David, et al. 2000. "New Leaders at the Top? The Educational and Career Paths of UK University Vice-Chancellors, 1960–1996." *Higher Education Management* 11, no. 2 (January): 113–35

Smith, Peter. 2004. *The Quiet Crisis: How Higher Education Is Failing America.* Bolton, MA: Anker

Smith, Stuart L. 1991. *Report: Commission of Inquiry on Canadian University Education.* Ottawa: Association of Universities and Colleges of Canada

Tibbetts, Janice. "University Presidents' Salaries." *Calgary Herald,* 4 April 2008, 1

Tierney, William G. 2008. *The Impact of Culture on Organizational Decision Making: Theory and Practice in Higher Education.* Sterling: Stylus

Tighe, Thomas J. 2003. *Who's in Charge of America's Research Universities? A Blueprint for Reform.* Albany: State University of New York

Toma, J. Douglas. 2010. *Building Organizational Capacity: Strategic Management in Higher Education.* Baltimore: Johns Hopkins Press

Trachtenberg, Stephen Joel. 2008. *Big Man on Campus.* New York: Simon and Schuster

Usher, Alex, et al. 2010. *Courting Success in Senior Hiring at Canadian Universities.* Toronto: Higher Education Strategy Associates

Wente, Margaret. 2009. "Tuition Attrition? Reposition." *Globe and Mail,* 7 April, A11

Wiseman, Lawrence. 1991. "The University President: Academic Leadership in an Era of Fund Raising and Legislative Affairs." In *Managing Institutions of Higher Education into the 21st Century,* edited by Ronald R. Sims and Serbrenia J. Sims, 3–9. New York: Greenwood Press

Index